Thinking and Ma____g

Oxford Music Education Series

The *Oxford Music Education Series* was established with Janet Mills (1954–2007) as series editor to present concise, readable, and thought-provoking handbooks for all those involved in music education, including teachers, community musicians, researchers, policy-makers, and parents/carers. The series encompasses a wide range of topics and musical styles, and aims to provide 'food for thought' for all those looking to broaden their understanding and further develop their work. Written by acknowledged leaders of education who are passionate about their subject, the books present cutting-edge ideas and aim to stimulate good practice by showing the practical implications of research.

Recent titles in the Oxford Music Education Series

Janet Mills: *Music in the School* (2005)

Janet Mills: *Instrumental Teaching* (2007)

Adam Ockelford: *Music for Children and Young People with Complex Needs* (2008)

Thinking and Making

Selections from the writings of
John Paynter on music in education

Edited by
Janet Mills and John Paynter

MUSIC DEPARTMENT

OXFORD
UNIVERSITY PRESS

OXFORD

UNIVERSITY PRESS

Great Clarendon Street, Oxford OX2 6DP, England
198 Madison Avenue, New York, NY 10016, USA

Oxford University Press is a department of the University of Oxford.
It furthers the University's aim of excellence in research, scholarship,
and education by publishing worldwide in

Oxford New York
Auckland Cape Town Hong Kong Karachi
Kuala Lumpur Madrid Melbourne Mexico City
Nairobi New Delhi Shanghai Taipei Toronto

With offices in
Argentina Austria Brazil Chile Czech Republic France Greece
Guatemala Hungary Italy Japan Poland Portugal Singapore
South Korea Switzerland Thailand Turkey Ukraine Vietnam

Oxford is a registered trade mark of Oxford University
Press in the UK and in certain other countries

British Library Cataloguing-in-Publication Data

Data available

Library of Congress Cataloging-in-Publication Data

Paynter, John
  Thinking and making : selections from the writings of John Paynter /
edited by John Paynter and Janet Mills.
    p. cm.—(Oxford music education series)
  Includes index.
  ISBN 978-0-19-335591-0
1. Music—Instruction and study—Great Britain. I. Mills, Janet. II. Title.
  MT3. G3P39 2008
  780. 71—dc22
                                                              2008011604

10 9 8 7 6 5

Typeset by RefineCatch Limited, Bungay, Suffolk
Printed and bound by CPI Group (UK) Ltd, Croydon, CR0 4YY

Foreword

As one of John Paynter's earlier students at the University of York I read most of his writing on musical education as it appeared. Always I found the content affirming, thought-provoking, and intensely musical. In 2003, while researching my book, *Music in the School*, I read those publications again, this time in sequence. I was struck by the collective strength of the work: markedly more ambitious for students and teachers than is the national curriculum for music in England. Yet we know from schools we have visited or schools in which we work, that Paynter's philosophy of musical education reflects expectations that are reasonable. The danger is that, dispersed as it is among so many sources, the continuing relevance of his writing may be lost to younger teachers and policy-makers. Music teachers today have so much mandatory reading that the opportunities to search out books in libraries may be limited. I spoke with a number of music educators who have been influenced by John Paynter's work and they all agreed that an introductory book would be useful.

From journal articles in the late 1960s and the appearance of *Sound and Silence* in 1970, his thinking about musical education has shown a depth and an insight rarely matched today. Throughout the past fifty years and more he has developed these ideas through his teaching and in print: articles in academic and practitioner journals, conference papers, and curriculum materials published not only in English but also in German, Dutch, Spanish, Italian, Japanese, and all the Scandinavian languages. Some of this output has not appeared previously in English; hence the need for this book. Whilst on the one hand it celebrates an exceptional contribution to music in education, its principal role is to ensure that the work is not lost and that it may be consulted more readily by teachers and researchers in the future.

John Paynter has maintained his view that music should be an essential part of everyone's general education and that whatever is done in the name of music in schools should be *musical*; that is, concerned with the essence of music itself and not merely 'about' music. This philosophy is as relevant and pertinent for educationalists today as it was when first expounded.

John Paynter has been a prolific writer, and it has not been possible to include all the extracts that teachers and former teachers tell us have influenced them most. Nevertheless, we hope that readers who are introduced to Paynter's writing by this volume will be encouraged to read further and gain additional insights into the work of this most musical of educators.

Janet Mills, 2007

Publisher's note

John Paynter's philosophy of music in education is central to his argument and pervades much of the writing reprinted here. Although this has resulted in some re-statement of ideas, it was considered important to maintain the completeness of each article, allowing readers to 'dip into' the book rather than read from cover to cover.

The articles included in *Thinking and Making* have been selected from Paynter's work over four decades, making the collection valuable not only for its substance but also for its historical significance. With this in mind it was decided not to update the style of writing to reflect modern trends, such as the use of gender-neutral pronouns, nor to replace or omit references to recordings and scores that may now be accessible only in libraries.

About the author

John Paynter is a composer whose work in musical education, developed throughout more than forty years of teaching and research, has received wide international interest. In particular, he is known for his advocacy of composition as a basis for the school music curriculum. In the early 1950s, whilst teaching in primary and secondary schools, he began to explore ways of encouraging children to use their imagination musically. He developed techniques for both small-group and individual composing in the classroom and later, as Principal Lecturer in Music at a College of Education, he researched processes for appraising children's musical inventiveness.

In 1969 he was appointed to a Lectureship in the Department of Music at the University of York. Subsequently Senior Lecturer and then Professor, he became Head of Department in 1983 and remained in that post until his retirement in September 1994.

From 1973 to 1982 he directed the Project *Music in the Secondary School Curriculum* under the sponsorship of The Schools Council for Curriculum and Examinations. The Project worked with Local Education Authorities and schools throughout England and Wales, ultimately establishing regional music education centres as well as producing a report, a series of video programmes, and two documentary films of classroom composing activities. This work played a leading part in the formation of Music components in the National Curriculum and the General Certificate of Secondary Education; it also had influence upon school musical education in other countries.

John Paynter is an Emeritus Professor of the University of York. In the Queen's Birthday Honours 1985 he was appointed OBE; in 1985 he was honoured by the Guildhall School of Music, London; and in 1998 he received the PRS and Royal Philharmonic Society 'Leslie Boosey Award' for 'outstanding contribution to the furtherance of contemporary music'.

Acknowledgements

This book could not have come into being without the imagination, sensitivity, and determination of the Series Editor, Janet Mills. The idea was hers, developed in conversation with teachers in the course of her work as an Inspector of Schools and, subsequently, through the International Music Education Research seminars that she organized at the Royal College of Music. In spite of a long and debilitating illness, Janet worked bravely on this and other books she was preparing for publication until within a very short time of her death in December 2007. She will be remembered with gratitude and affection by all who had the privilege of knowing her.

My thanks are due, once again, to all the teachers, students, colleagues, editors, and publishers whose imagination and creativity gave substance to the writings from which extracts are reprinted in this volume; all were acknowledged in the original publications but here I have opportunity to reiterate my gratitude.

Finally, I should like to thank the staff of Oxford University Press Music Department, in particular David Blackwell, Kristen Thorner, and Robyn Carpenter, for all the help they have given in bringing this book to publication.

John Paynter

Contents

Copyright Acknowledgements

PART I

SOUND AND SILENCE (1970)

The ideas that characterize *Sound and Silence* evolved during the 1950s and 1960s in the course of teaching in primary and secondary schools and colleges of education. Later, the techniques were developed through collaboration with a wider group of schools and teachers in research based at the University of York. The article 'Learning from the Present' (1967) describes some early results. Among other things, this work challenged a widely-held view that most (if not all!) of the current 'new music' was unsuitable for the school curriculum because, unlike the established classics, it had no 'proven' values. However, with the development of what came to be known as 'creative experiment' —often using, as starting points, certain experimental strategies of the avant-garde—music teachers began to engage the enthusiasm and imagination of their pupils. Against this background, and in association with Peter Aston who had been working in similar ways with vocal resources, *Sound and Silence* was compiled in 1968 and published by Cambridge University Press in 1970. In his Foreword to the book Professor Wilfrid Mellers describes it as a 'primer',

because it asks fundamental questions and doesn't attempt to short-circuit the answers to them by an appeal to history. It's not concerned with what (say) Byrd's music was, or Bach's, or Mozart's, or Beethoven's: but with what music is inherently, here and now, both in its nature and its functions.

Teachers who have found *Sound and Silence* helpful often refer to the opening of the book with its account of six-year old Alan 'lost in the world of his imagination': it reminds us that children are born creative; we do not have to make them so. Thus, it establishes a philosophy, elaborated in later writings, at the heart of which is the conviction that 'schooling' should be characterized by education rather than instruction; the latter being concerned primarily with the transmission and acquisition of received ideas and skills whilst the former, by definition, should draw upon children's natural resources of wonder, imagination, and inventiveness. In *Sound and Silence* this precept is expressed through the 'Projects': first a principle, then its working out in creative activities to produce 'pieces' that are discussed by teacher and students. The Projects can be (indeed, should be!) adapted to the interests and enthusiasms of the group; and there is little room for standardized evaluation, marking, and grading because so much of what happens in the arts is not susceptible to that kind of thing. In particular, musical processes have an internal logic linking them with thought so that, to reach a true understanding of musical 'language', first-hand experience of the ways in which elements combine to produce form should be given priority over extra-musical information.

These principles are demonstrated in the two Projects reproduced here. In the first, we are reminded that silence is a positive aspect of music: a property to be exploited in composition. In the second, the emphasis is upon experimentation to discover and categorize particular ways of making sounds on one kind of musical instrument, the results being used to create pieces.

Music in a liberal education

Introduction from John Paynter and Peter Aston, *Sound and Silence* (Cambridge University Press, 1970), 1–7

Alan, aged six, moves stealthily across the classroom. He is the Wolf creeping out of the deep, dark forest. As he creeps he makes music: a pattern of mysterious taps and scraping sounds which tell us that the Wolf and the forest are sinister and fearful. No-one has instructed him: Alan chose the drum himself and decided for himself how the Wolf's music should go. As he creeps slowly across the room, he is lost in the world of his imagination, intensified by the music he is making.

A group of children in their early teens are on a camping holiday. They have just returned from an exhausting hike and are sitting with steaming mugs of cocoa around the glow of a camp fire. Someone is strumming a guitar. The others are singing. They know the song well because it's been sung at previous camp fires for as long as anyone can remember. As we listen we realise that not everyone is singing the tune. Now and again the music breaks into parts, the harmony enriching the melodic line. None of the children has heard of a dominant seventh or a perfect cadence and most of them cannot read music: yet they are responding to the harmonic implications of the melody by improvising other parts around it.

Two students at a college of education are playing music which they have painstakingly evolved for piano and drums: the lid of the piano is removed and Leslie gently strokes the strings inside with the flat of her hand. Catherine's drums reply, softly and sensitively. The music builds. It is coherent. They know now exactly where it should go. As they play, the piece becomes Theatre; their sensitivity to the sounds is reflected in their movements. Before this morning neither of them had ever thought of creating music. They chose to do this, decided on the sounds they wanted to explore, and have worked these sounds over and over until they have become the right sounds, the only possible sounds through which to say what has to be said. By this time tomorrow their piece will be refined and carefully notated in a system of their own inventing. They will have thoroughly explored their own music and met on the way with the music of Cowell and Stockhausen. They will not have been *taught* anything: can we say how much music they will have learned?

Why do we teach music anyway? How do we fit it into the pattern of education today? Certainly, school music now is a great deal more lively than it has ever been before, and the last few years have seen an enormous increase in the number of young players and singers taking part in school concerts and performing in youth orchestras and choirs. But while all this has been happening concepts of education have been changing, and it is not always easy to see where music fits in or what its rôle should be.

It might help us to find answers to these questions if we begin by looking at the essential differences between general and specialist forms of education. Apart from those of us who are concerned solely with certain clearly-defined skills such as the techniques of playing musical instruments, the work of most teachers in schools is essentially a contribution to the *general* education of children. Even if a teacher finds himself working in a school as 'the music specialist' or 'the science specialist' he must not let this cause him to forget his first duty: the education of the whole person. He makes a contribution to this 'total education' through the medium of his own subject. Moreover, he must not gear his work only to the abilities of the gifted few, but should find ways of using his specialist knowledge to serve the education of *all* the pupils in his classes.

Education does not begin with specialist boxes filled with facts to be memorized. It should be child-centred and start from the needs of the individual. As teachers we must try to see our subject, not as collections of highly-developed disciplines, but rather as areas of experience which embody some of the most fundamental human reactions to life. We can't teach history all by itself: it's concerned with people, their way of life, their reactions to their times and their relationship to us and our own times. Once we start looking at people we must consider not only how they live but *where* they live. Geography is inextricably linked with history and begins on our doorstep with a close look at our own immediate environment and what this means to us and those who have lived here before. Investigating our environment brings us face to face with the wonder and excitement of discovery. This is the mainspring of any work in the sciences and mathematics. When we look closely at nature and are filled with wonder by its intricacies, we are often moved and must find a way of expressing our feelings: it is from here that the arts spring, as do all aspects of language and the need to communicate ideas and emotions. The value of anything we learn in school lies in the extent to which it helps us respond to the world around us. Our 'special subject' cannot live if left in a box by itself, a set of disciplines and techniques unrelated to anything else. It is part of the wide field of human experience and needs to be understood in that context first.

Because all our knowledge comes from experience of living, its many areas are related and interdependent. If we begin by erecting barriers between them we shall be in danger of hiding from our pupils the essential relevance of our subjects. The liberal education we all wish for our children implies a breadth of understanding and experience that will be possible only when we make conscious efforts to remove the boundaries between 'subjects'. This applies to the more advanced work of the secondary school as much as it does to the work of the primary school. Areas of knowledge are often so closely related that they can be seen simply as various ways of saying the same thing; 'materials' through which we may communicate experience. Education should make us alive to what is happening around us and aware of our potential as human beings. Young people deserve a truly liberal education, alive with the excitement of discovery. This excitement is a first step: the details, disciplines and skills will follow. Without a sense of adventure true education is impossible.

What contribution can music make? It can give immense pleasure to the listener and to the performer. This side of it should certainly not be neglected. However, it is as a *creative* art that music is beginning to play an increasingly important rôle in education. Like all the arts, music springs from a profound response to life itself. It is language, and, as a vehicle for expression, it is available in some degree to everyone. If a child is to grow in awareness of himself and his world, he will need to be articulate. The very processes of becoming articulate deepen our perception. Perhaps we should place slightly more emphasis on creative music in schools than we have been doing. Music is a rich means of expression and we must not deny our children the chance to use it.

Society has always produced artists, poets, and musicians. They train our eyes and ears. Rarely do we look at things as closely or as intensely as artists do. They see the beauty in nature and their intuition and skills define it in terms we can understand. Sometimes this definition is in the form of an abstract elaboration of nature's patterns or an occurrence in human life. At other times it is more clearly a record of something seen in reality. But the artist does more than make a record: he projects feelings into his materials—paint, wood, stone, words, movement, sound or whatever—until the materials become like the reality of his imagination. Through his work we feel what he feels, we see with his eyes and hear with his ears. Henry Moore shows us new ways of looking at the human figure. Through his work we begin to appreciate forms we had never before noticed, though they were always there in nature. The recent interest in the music of India may owe something to the Beatles who were able to relate the sounds of Indian music to what they wanted to say through a song like *Within You Without You* on their 'Sergeant Pepper' disc. On another level Picasso, in his *Guernica,* painted during the Spanish Civil War, draws our attention to the suffering of ordinary people in time of war. The picture is at once a powerful comment and a terrible warning. Similarly the composer is able not only to make us aware of new qualities of sound but through his use of his material to say something to us about the great issues of existence. So Benjamin Britten, in his *War Requiem,* sees a relationship between the ancient text of the Requiem Mass and certain poems by Wilfred Owen—a relationship no-one had seen previously—and with his skill as a musician he presents this relationship to us in the setting of penetrating music. Nearly half a century earlier, Wilfred Owen had summed up his own task as a poet when he wrote, 'My subject is War, and the pity of War. The Poetry is in the pity. All that a poet can do is to warn'.

Artists of all kinds function as visionaries and commentators: their job is not simply to entertain us. We rely upon them to help us come to terms with life and its problems. The art that is *most* relevant to us is that of our own time. We need the professional artist but at the same time we must also cultivate the artist within ourselves, for each one of us has something of that child-like innocence which is the characteristic of the artistic mind, which draws fresh inspiration from familiar things and expresses feelings in words, action, visual symbols or music. We must not stifle this innocent eye or ear; our under-standing of the professional artists' work may depend considerably on our ability to participate, even a little, in their activities.

When, in school, we involve children in the creative use of language or the materials of visual art, we are encouraging them to think like poets and artists. The majority of subjects taught in school today begin with children's natural interests, and knowledge is acquired as much through feelings as from in-formation. In this context the arts in education take on a new importance. They are accepted as ways of saying what we feel. We all have the capacity to perceive, reflect and express. We all have the capacity to create.

The materials of music are as available for creative exploration as the mate-rials of any other art. However, this seems to be an area of activity where music has not kept pace with other school subjects. When the Plowden Committee reported on primary school education in England,* they said they had found the planning of music as a creative subject lagging behind work in language and the visual arts and crafts. One wonders why. What is it about music, or about us as music teachers, that makes us ignore the opportunities others have taken?

---

* *Children and their Primary Schools* (HMSO).

If any one aspect of education today is characteristic of the whole, it is probably the change of emphasis from children being instructed to children being placed in situations where they can learn for themselves. Teachers of English, drama and the visual arts have found the new ideas stimulating. They have used them as springboards for a great deal of exciting work. Music, on the other hand, has tended to go its own way and remains largely unaffected by recent moves in education. More often than not, school music has concentrated on the skills of performance. Even much so-called 'creative music' is really only an extension of directed ensemble performance. Of course these skills are important. Performance is an essential musical activity; but it is not the whole of music.

It is now some time since Marion Richardson and Herbert Read showed how art in education should start with what the *individual* has to say. They saw education taking place through art without in any way destroying the values of specialist art education. In school, necessary techniques can be developed through the self-directed exploration of materials. Similar attitudes can be found in creative drama, which has flourished under the inspiration of Peter Slade and others. Here again, real experience is taken as a starting point, and bodily movement, gesture, and language are the materials for experiment and expression. We have grown used to work of this kind over the past twenty years. More recently new attitudes to the creative use of written language have come into the schools, heralded by the work of Sybil Marshall, Margaret Langdon and David Holbrook, all of whom have encouraged children to write about things they feel deeply. As David Holbrook says in *Children's Writing* '... the process depends upon "whole experience" ... ', the writer is 'working on his inner world ... '. It's not surprising that when the Plowden Committee came to look at this aspect of education they found the amount and quality of children's writing 'perhaps the most dramatic of all revolutions in English teaching. Its essence is that much of it is personal ... and the writers are communicating something which has really engaged their minds and their imaginations'.

In art, drama, dance and creative writing children are using a variety of materials as language for the expression, not of second-hand experience, but of things that are close to them and real to them. What is more, the language they use is a living language; that is, it embodies in essence many of the techniques and attitudes of contemporary art and literature. On the walls of our primary school classrooms we can see paintings which reflect the experiments of painters like Jackson Pollock, Paul Klee and Ben Nicholson. Children who have experimented in this way would certainly be the better equipped to approach the work of contemporary artists. Giving examples of the creative writing of children in a variety of Secondary Schools, David Holbrook suggests literature the children would appreciate, having come to terms in words with similar experiences. His suggestions include work by Joyce, Lawrence, Hemingway, and Eliot. The boys and girls we teach rarely seem to find difficulty with the language of contemporary art. Young people today have an outlook which chimes in with the liberalism of the twentieth-century artist; they too are prepared to follow many paths and search in many directions. Fortunately there are teachers to help them in their search and to encourage them in their exploration. These teachers themselves draw considerable inspiration from the living art of the present while being aware of its roots in the past.

Music can be approached in the same way. The techniques used by composers in the twentieth century are comparable with the techniques used by their contemporaries in other arts. Here again we find the same diversity of style. A musician's imagination is stirred by many things: the technological achievements of science; post-Renaissance philosophies and traditions which make us what we are; a desire to reject the world as it is and begin again from primitive roots. The musical techniques of our time are relevant to our situation because they grow from it. They must, therefore, have a place in the work we plan for our classes in schools. Music is as much an aspect of language as any other means of creative expression; but if it is to matter, those who use it must be alive to the music of their own time as well as the music of the past.

Too often we are encouraged to regard music as a *leisure* activity, as though its only function is to entertain. This may have led us to emphasise *re*-creative rather than creative activities in school music; and although creative work in language, drama and the visual arts has quickly found general acceptance, creative work in *music* has often been challenged as being of doubtful value in itself, having little bearing on conventional musical education. The critics argue that to devote time to such work is to deny the more musical child the essential academic teaching he needs for GCE and other public examinations and for the acquisition of performing skills. However, the first step must be the understanding of the medium and its potential. We can only discover this through creative experiment.

Learning from the present

From *Music in Education,* 2/6, Nov./Dec. (Novello, 1967), 623–6

The basic resources of music are sounds and silences. These are 'materials' susceptible to productive exploration like any other materials. Music is an organization of these sounds and silences for expressive purposes. The purpose may be one outside music (for example, where music illuminates an idea already expressed in some other medium or concerns itself directly with comment upon some aspect of our existence), or the purpose may be in the materials themselves, and aim at revealing facets of sounds and their organization. As far as art education is concerned this is the obvious point at which to begin. Is music so very different? From time to time arguments are advanced to show how music is a special art with complicated techniques which must be acquired before any kind of creative work can be done. This, of course, is true if we confine ourselves to the well-trodden paths of music before 1900. It would also be true of art were teachers to restrict themselves to representational drawing as they once did. The liberalism which has released the professional artist today is a mainspring in work with children. A comparable liberalism has released the composer in this century; with our immensely widened view of what is possible musically we might begin to work with children from points not unlike those from which their art work starts.

We must provide sound-sources of great variety and these should be available for investigation by small groups of children or by individuals. Musical instruments of good quality are essential just as good quality materials are needed for other aspects of the curriculum. Too often we stint on items like this and hamstring a child's musical imagination before he even begins. Ideally we need space for this self-directed exploration and in our newer secondary schools at least, this should not be impossible. Good instruments will provide a wide range of expressive possibility. Once this has been experienced other sound-sources might be explored, for all sound is potentially music. Neither must we look upon the exploration of instruments in this way as a 'play' activity suitable only for the reception class of the infant school. Stravinsky's words, 'fingers are great inspirers' remind us of the composer's need for first-hand contact with the sounds he is going to use. All his life he may, to some extent, feel the need to go to his materials as a prelude to the act of composition. Time given to 'doodling' on an instrument is never wasted if the doodler is involved with the properties of the sound.

The creation of music supposes an intention. Experience of the instruments would obviously be an advantage, but on the other hand there is no reason why a certain amount of the more detailed investigation of the instruments should not take place as part of the creative experiment. We can provide percussion instruments, both pitched and unpitched, on which children can produce delightful sounds without first having to learn complicated techniques. There is great potential in a good stand-cymbal which may be played with soft or with hard sticks, producing different qualities of sound if struck at the rim or at the centre. A roll is not difficult. The cymbal can also be played with a cello bow, when it will produce a most exciting and spine-chilling sound. The various 'Orff' instruments will provide opportunities for exploration with sticks of different hardness.

In addition, stringed instruments can give us a much needed sustained tone and a new timbre. They do not present the problems of tone-production such as we must expect from woodwind (although recently Michael Vetter has shown that the recorder can produce an enormously wide range of sounds hitherto unused, many of them capable of control quite as easily as the more conventional repertoire of recorder sounds). Then there is the piano which may be played inside as well as on the keyboard, or 'prepared' to give unusual qualities of tone. Of course we must guard against giving the impression that this is the whole of music or that playing the piano is simply a matter of pressing on the keyboard with a length of wood $14\frac{3}{4}$ inches long as in Ives's *Second Sonata*. But it should not be outside the scope of our work to put these ideas before children and if possible to let them hear works by composers who have explored in these directions. If this can be done in the context of the children's own music they may be encouraged in their exploration. Ives's board of $14\frac{3}{4}$ inches does help to remove some of the mystique of music! John Cage likewise takes us back to fundamentals and blows away some of our pomposity. We may not wish to go the whole way with him but this should not prevent us from receiving refreshment from at least some of the exciting possibilities his music suggests. After all, Cage is not a youthful hothead and much of his work for piano is a development of attitudes first explored by Henry Cowell before the First World War. Perhaps by now we should be taking note of these attitudes: our colleagues in the visual arts have not denied the influence of Jackson Pollock or Barbara Hepworth and children's writing often betrays, in a round-about away, our own reading of Eliot and e. e. cummings.

It is one thing to know what sounds are available and even to have experienced them. It is another thing to use them to create music. The essence of this lies in selecting the sounds we need (and/or which we are able to control) and rejecting those which do not fit our purpose. Exactly the same basic decisions would apply to creative work with any materials. Educationally the need to make decisions about these matters is of value and here music can play as important a role as any other creative activity. Making the basic decisions about which instruments, and which sounds from these instruments, are to be used will be helped by some previously determined purpose. Musical expression broadly divides into the two categories mentioned above: music about something outside itself and music about sounds and silences. Which approach we choose will depend a lot on other creative work the children are doing or the particular enthusiasms of the teacher. Neither approach is more difficult than the other if related to familiar aspects of the curriculum. However, it is possible that children who have used music first as a 'support' for some other work (background to a drama or reading of a poem, music which 'tells a story' or music they have created for movement work) would come to the more abstract music 'about' sound with greater confidence in their abilities to create music at all. Children should have experience of both aspects and wherever possible their music should be tape-recorded and heard again, perhaps alongside music by a professional composer who has used sounds in a similar manner or with a similar purpose.

One of the more obvious ways of beginning is with music for drama. Spontaneous drama is well established in many schools and situations are often heightened by the addition of recorded music. Children are not unaware of the power of music as used in television plays, and once they have worked out an idea in dramatic terms it is a short step to discussing with them the moments which could be enhanced by music. Some preliminary exploration of the available resources will probably be necessary but once the most appropriate kinds of sounds are decided upon the organization of these sounds can go ahead. If we were working with a whole class it might be as well to 'commission' a small group to work out the music after the plans had been talked through with the entire class. Groups of about five are of a useful size for this work. Frequently drama work is organized as small group activity with each group working on its own dramatic situation. Instruments can be available for use by any group when needed, the teacher going to each group in turn and helping them, through brief discussion, to make their decisions and organize the music where it will be of most value. Children are capable of working at their own piece in spite of noise from other groups. In fact the degree of concentration is often surprising and one finds children gauging accurately the effect of a few tiny sounds on, say, indian bells while all around other groups are busy creating noisy music for more exciting episodes.

It is not difficult to see how this procedure can be used for music which grows out of creative writing. The reality of the initial experience is important. Part of our task is to encourage children to look at familiar environments with fresh eyes. Beginning with something in the immediate vicinity of the school (or even within the classroom) individual creative writing will follow from adventuresome discussion between teacher and class. Prose or poetry could take imaginative lines or could concentrate upon close but factual examination of some detail perhaps hitherto unobserved. From there we might proceed by taking one or two pieces of completed writing and discussing them further with a view to the writers 'presenting' them by reading aloud. A small group might be formed who would choose appropriate sounds and create music to heighten this reading. Discussion and improvisation will be the 'method'. Decisions must be made on a number of points: should the music actually accompany the reading? Should it precede the reading, setting the mood of the piece? Should it come after the reading, an extension into music of the writer's thoughts or a comment in sound upon what has been said in words? What kind of sounds should we use and how should the music proceed? Will it be melodic or do we concentrate on timbre and music of atmosphere? How should it end? The answers will only come by trial and error but this is valuable in itself: we should avoid giving the impression that there is only one acceptable way of creating music; in any case, the doing matters, perhaps, more than the finished piece, especially at primary school level which, Sybil Marshall reminds us, is 'not for finished work but for experiments'.

When their music is to be associated with the atmosphere of a piece of writing or drama children will frequently produce imaginative work of a high order quite uninhibited by our concepts of music. To begin with, however, we may find a tendency towards sound effects and the technique of line-by-line translation of a poem or event-by-event translation of drama. We must work to show children that, whereas sound effects can only imitate, music can help us to feel the words or action more deeply. The first technique of all creative work is selection and rejection to achieve wholeness. Too many different ideas will only break up the continuity of the music. One central theme must be found in, say, a poem a child has written, creating music about this theme and leaving the words themselves to deal with the details. It is not essential for the music to continue throughout and the value of music in illuminating selected action in a drama is obviously something which has to be experienced.

If we are really to broaden a child's view of what is possible musically and to do this by working, as in the visual arts, from the raw materials, the child acquiring techniques as we proceed, we shall not be in a position to say about his music, *that* is right or *that* is wrong. The only really valid means of judgement will be the one we wish him to acquire for himself by experience: *does this piece hang together? Is it consistent? Is there anything I have done in it which needs rejecting because it destroys the wholeness of the music?* Obviously, the intention will help to preserve the wholeness. Gradually the significance of organization itself will begin to emerge, and this may be the moment to turn towards our other broad category: music 'about' sounds and silences. Here some concentration upon pattern can provide the necessary starting point.

We might begin by looking at patterns in nature. We can select one object and record its design carefully on paper. This will give new insights into construction. Patterns which emerge can be taken as starting points for music or allowed to become trains of thought for further exploration in visual forms. Whereas music created for drama is often best worked at in small groups, this approach is territory for the individual. A child can investigate the implications of a pattern in visual materials and then, with the teacher guiding by discussion, begin to see possible transferences to the organization of sounds. It is vital to understand this as a starting point for musical organization and not as an interpretation in sound of the original object. In the end we shall have music—an organization of sounds and silences—and it will stand or fall as music and as nothing else. The only purpose of the previous visual exploration of a pattern is to give something on which to hang the organization of sound. Because it is visual it is easily understood and, being the result of an individual investigation, will not necessarily tie the child to any one way of organizing musical sound. He can see what he has done on paper and attempt to use sounds—whatever sounds he chooses, there need be no restriction—in a corresponding organization. The visual work can then be left behind, the finished music tape-recorded and heard for what it is—music. Any pattern could be used in this way. Number series provide many possibilities. Some numbers representing sounds, others silences; numbers suggesting groups of instruments which play together or play in order rather like a serial organization. Working from this basis can be a useful means of teaching children the value of silence in music, not as 'non-music' but as something positive, akin to the positive quality of white space as part of a pattern printed on paper.

Music based on patterns from nature or mathematics need not stop at the obvious level of *events* of sound or silence. Children may begin to explore patterns of tone-relation, creating tone-rows and scales as basic patterns on which to build pieces of music.

We should avoid making a system from ideas such as these. If music is to be meaningful as language it will need to work alongside other creative media and frequently to grow from these other activities. The examples given above are intended merely to start hares. Other lines of work can grow naturally out of special interests and develop music from the raw materials in just the way those same interests can develop into art or poetry from natural materials or every-day words. Vocal sounds present possibilities for music, particularly in connection with movement. There is, too, the whole field of specially constructed instruments, perhaps organized on a new scale or mode, or employing micro-tones. These in themselves can become the starting point, the basic material, for music. Again, there is the wealth of possibilities in magnetic tape and changed tape speeds. All these can be used to open children's ears and will be found to have their parallels of use in contemporary music. Moreover, there is much that can be done by the teacher who, although without conventional musical skills himself, may have worked successfully with children in language, the visual arts, drama, or movement. He will be able to see connections between the various activities and perhaps help children to follow an idea through in several media. Working in conjunction with the school's director of music such a teacher could make an extremely valuable contribution which could help to open the ears of the less musically gifted child, while at the same time widening the horizons for the child who has already made progress in the more conventional aspects of music education.

Music in education has still some way to go if it is to come into line with other aspects of the curriculum. If it can learn from the present as well as the past this may not take too long.

Silence

Project 6 from John Paynter and Peter Aston, *Sound and Silence* (Cambridge University Press, 1970), 61–2

Introduction

When we make music, we tend to give most of our attention to the *sounds* we are making. We may easily forget the importance of silences in a musical continuity. The dramatic effect of silence has long been appreciated by composers (for example, the general pause in the middle of the chorus 'Have lightnings and thunders ...' in Bach's *St Matthew Passion*). In the twentieth century silence has taken on a new importance as composers have broken away from the older formulae and looked for new ways of using the language of music.

In the music of composers such as Webern, silence is used to achieve a clear and uncluttered texture. It is also an essential element in atonal melody, producing drama at points of tension and giving the utmost sense of repose at moments of relaxation. In music of a very different kind, the American John Cage has made silence one of the raw materials of music. For him silence is the eternal background into which 'meteors of sound' explode at set points in time. The sounds have no relationship with each other beyond their coexistence in the eternal silence. Webern's music is tightly mind-controlled. Cage often uses chance operations to decide which sounds shall occur and when. Both composers make use of the positive quality of silence. In this sense silence is not non-music, any more than white spaces in a visual pattern or planned emptinesses between parts of a piece of sculpture are negative. Just as the painter and the sculptor exploit spatial properties, so the composer today exploits properties of time—which may or may not contain sounds.

Assignment

(i) Using percussion instruments (tuned as well as untuned) together with any other instruments used *percussively,* create a piece of music which makes extensive use of silence.

(ii) Using the same resources as in (i) make a piece of music 'about' silence (i.e. to convey the *feeling* of silence).

Record all this music on tape and discuss the essential differences between the two pieces.

(iii) Choose three instruments of contrasting pitch and timbre (high, middle-pitch and low—e.g. soprano glockenspiel, tenor recorder, cello). Let each player select four notes on his instrument (these might be the four open strings on the cello) and invent two or more rhythmic patterns using the four notes. The patterns should contrast with one another as much as possible. One might contain sustained notes; another short, hurried movement. One might move from note to note by step; another leap wide intervals. Try to make as much as you can from the limited materials. Experiment a great deal before making any final decisions about each figure. Clearly, the success of the final piece will depend a lot on the choice of notes and rhythmic patterns which make up the motifs on each instrument. When the players are satisfied with these short motifs and can play any of them at will, they can create a group composition using this material. The principal aim should be to get a *transparently clear texture*. Never have more than two instruments playing at one time and think carefully about how you use silences.

Exploring stringed instruments

Project 9 from John Paynter and Peter Aston, *Sound and Silence*
(Cambridge University Press, 1970), 77–82

Introduction

Quite a lot of musical compositions are inspired by their own medium.
The organ has 'produced' much of the music composed for it: usually by way
of the composer's own technique as an organist. Hermann Scherchen, writing
of Ravel's *Introduction and Allegro* for solo harp, clarinet, flute and string
quartet, says:

The fresh rhapsodic character of this work is derived from the surging, exuberant
timbre of the harp. The instrument's abundant richness in delicate sounds inspired the
structure and episodes of the piece ... The medium which inspired him provided an
incentive to create new modes of expression, and led Ravel's imagination to find an
ethereal shimmering texture never before realised in music.

Which came first, the music or the instrument? In his analysis of the harp
cadenza from the Ravel *Introduction and Allegro,* Scherchen says, 'All this is
derived—with exquisite imaginative mastery—*from the harp's natural sound'.*
Later he reminds us that Beethoven 'transformed the timpani from being
merely a means of rhythmic dynamism and textural accentuation into an
instrument of virtuosity and expressive power'.

Some are content to use the 'received wisdom' and look no further than what
others have been able to do with a musical instrument. Others push ahead,
extending the technical resources of an instrument and, having found these
new possibilities, giving us textures 'never before realised in music'. Paganini's
extension of violin technique led to virtuoso exploration of other instruments,
notably the piano. The outcome of this was an extension of the piano's range.
The exploration of the violin's potential as a sound-source continues today:
the Polish composer Krystof Penderecki has worked out a lengthy catalogue
of sounds, many of them so far unused, which can be produced by stringed
instruments. His 'catalogue' includes the highest sound of the instrument

without defining its pitch, sounds played between the bridge and the tailpiece, and sounds made by playing on the tailpiece. Penderecki has composed music employing many of these resources. By alternating and combining them with traditional violin sounds, arco and pizzicato, he is able to produce unusually colourful networks.

The work which follows now is designed for those who have studied the traditional techniques of stringed instruments as well as those whose knowledge will be no more than they can get by their own investigation of the instruments. If there are any of the former in the class, try to arrange for them to be distributed among the groups for some assignments and brought together as one group for others.

Assignments

(i) Bring to the lesson as many bowed stringed instruments as possible. Try to include all members of the string family. Experiment with the instruments and make written lists of sounds obtainable and techniques for producing them. Members of the group who have studied conventional techniques should include these techniques in their lists, even down to quite fundamental things such as 'bowing each string separately; bowing two strings together; stopping the strings with the fingers to get different notes'. When the lists are complete we can hear demonstrations of the sounds which have been found and can be controlled. Which are the best sounds? Is it really possible to answer that question? Which are the most interesting sounds? Why?

Make individual pieces of music using the sounds discovered. Work empirically from a single instrument. Those players who have studied the traditional techniques can be encouraged to use the more conventional sounds in alternation with those produced by less traditional ways of playing.

(ii) Make further pieces individually but limit each composer to *four* different sounds.

(iii) With the same sounds used in (ii), make group compositions employing various combinations of four instruments. Arrange some passages where everyone plays and alternate these with solo and duet passages. Remember the value of silences in music. Silence can be *positive*—like white space in a visual pattern. Silence in music is part of the composition; it is not non-music.

(iv) Make a group piece (three players) using only *bowed* effects.

(v) Make a group piece (groups as in (iv)) using only *plucked* effects.

(vi) Make a large-group piece—any number of players—using only sounds produced by sliding along the strings (bowed or plucked).

(vii) Make a large-group piece which employs only the lowest string of each instrument but uses a variety of bowed and pizzicato effects.

(viii) Make a piece for strings (group or individual) called *Music of Sleep.*

Examples

A 'sliding' piece by a Junior School violinist:

Having decided that the music would exploit the glissando idea, it was then worked out as a pattern piece, starting on the E string and working down with more or less the same pattern on each string, ending with the sustained open G. The music was not written down by the child. It evolved as an improvisation, the contents of which were remembered and held in mind firmly enough for the piece to be repeated without variation as often as might be required.

A piece for cello using the sounds made on the strings beyond the bridge:

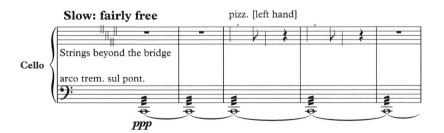

Follow-up work

Listen to the opening of Britten's opera, *A Midsummer Night's Dream*. Notice how he uses string glissandi to suggest the coming of sleep and the merging of reality into dream.

Compare the string effects of any quartet by Haydn with one of Beethoven's late string quartets, and again with the *String Quartet No. 3* of Béla Bartók.

Penderecki uses some interesting shifts of string sound and colour in his *Threnody: To the Victims of Hiroshima*. Examine also the string writing in the same composer's *St Luke Passion*.

The *String Quartet* (1950) by John Cage is an unusual and interesting work. The players are directed to play throughout without vibrato. The result is a curiously wistful effect. For a detailed account of this oddly beautiful work see Wilfrid Mellers's *Music in a New Found Land*, p. 181. A similar, though brief and fleeting, use of the non-vibrato effect can be heard towards the end of Bartók's *String Quartet No. 5*. The mounting excitement of the Finale is suddenly interrupted by this tiny fragment (the indication is 'allegretto con indifferenza') which has about it a pathetic and 'lost' quality.

Bartók's *Sonata for Unaccompanied Violin* also provides examples of a wide range of violin effects.

A rather unusual effect in orchestral music is that of playing on the four strings between the tailpiece and the bridge. There is an example of this in the symphonic poem *Amazonas* by Villa-Lobos (pocket score: Edition Max Eschig, p. 24, fig. 9). The violins, violas, cellos and basses are divided. Half play on the strings beyond the bridge, the music written thus with the instruction 'Dans les quatre cordes entre le tire-corde et le chevalet'. The remaining strings play harmonics to which are added harmonics on the viola d'amore and the bowed cythara. This shimmering string sound forms a suitably mysterious background for the clarinet solo as it weaves its way through the 'Enchanted Dance'.

PART II

FROM *HEAR AND NOW* TO *ALL KINDS OF MUSIC* (1972–9)

The mid 1960s saw the emergence of an emphatically avant-garde 'New Music'; as Paul Griffiths points out, the term itself became 'almost a slogan'.[1] Some music teachers were puzzled and, perhaps, alienated by these developments but publishers—especially those with long-standing interests in contemporary music—rose to the occasion. Universal Edition published George Self's *New Sounds in Class* (1967) whilst Oxford University Press brought out Brian Dennis's *Experimental Music in Schools* (1970) and Terence Dwyer's *Progressive Scores* (1971). It was in this context that *Hear and Now* (Universal Edition) appeared in 1972 as a guide to the new music's more prominent features and their potential as resources for musical education. The final chapter asks 'Where does it all lead?' and in conclusion quotes the composer Morton Feldman:

> When you are involved with a sound as sound ... new ideas suggest themselves, need defining, exploring, need a mind that knows it is entering a living world not a dead one. When you set out for a living world you don't know what to take with you because you don't know where you're going.

Accompanying the book was a disc containing recorded excerpts from works mentioned in the text, including a performance of *Autumn*. This is one of three short 'atmospheric' pieces for voices and *ad lib.* instrumentation designed for average classes of 10–12 year olds but also suitable for performance by older students or adults. Charles Byrne recalls his experience, in the 1970s, 'As a new teacher, freshly emerged [from College]':

> I revelled in the idea that young people could make music without recourse to standard notation, instead using their imagination to interpret the symbols and images selected by the composer. I can still remember a particularly evocative performance of Paynter's 'Autumn' by my junior choir.[2]

As with the other pieces in the group, *Autumn* exploits 'indeterminacy', allowing the performers a significant degree of freedom in their interpretation of the score.

---

[1] Paul Griffiths, *The Thames and Hudson Encyclopaedia of 20th-Century Music.* 1986, 127

[2] Charles Byrne, book review in the *British Journal of Music Education,* Vol. 23, No. 3, November 2006 Cambridge University Press

The Dance and the Drum, written jointly with Elizabeth Paynter, was published in 1974. Based upon folk tales from many parts of the world, the book provides material for twelve creative projects linking drama, dance, and music. 'The first sunrise' is typical of such myths and legends handed down by word of mouth across the centuries and having their origin in mankind's need to understand the world: why is the sky where it is? why do the seasons come and go? why do we grow old and die?

Doubtless it was from such fundamental questions that the arts developed—music, painting, poetry and drama helping our ancestors to come to terms with feelings they could not otherwise explain. Conversely, scientific discovery, important and essential as it is in today's world, may lead us to distrust our sensory reactions. 'The Role of Creativity in the School Music Curriculum' presents a case making the arts an essential element of everyone's general education.

All Kinds of Music is a classroom course for secondary schools.[3] Each book is accompanied by *Teacher's Notes* and recorded music examples. Colourful and attractive in design, the object of this course is to encourage school students to explore a variety of musical styles and to develop that experience through their own performing and creative activities. Thus,

The books and the recordings ... [are]... starting points—'springboards' from which pupils, individually or in small groups, can leap off in different directions ... [so that] ... Out of the ... ideas offered in these books there should grow other projects originating in the imagination of the pupils themselves ...[4]

The General Introduction to the series includes an explanation of 'The small-group "workshop"'—the teaching method that arose from the philosophy of *Sound and Silence* and was expanded in subsequent writings from which extracts are reproduced here.[5]

The four books of *All Kinds of Music* demonstrate various possibilities for notating music: from staff notation to diagrammatic, pictorial, and verbal forms, and from the precision of 'measured' notation to the interpretative freedom of 'indeterminate' scores such as Christopher Grant's *Reflections*. No prior knowledge of notation is needed to perform this piece: the score is self-explanatory and the first step is for the players to agree upon an interpretation of the symbols.

---

[3] Books 1–3 (*Voices, Moods and Messages* and *Sound Machines*), Oxford University Press, 1976; Book 4 (*Sound Patterns*), Oxford University Press, 1979.

[4] Book 1, *Teachers's Notes*, 1.

[5] See also *Sound Tracks,* four sets of work cards and Teacher's Notes, devised and written by John Paynter, designed and illustrated by Eve Matthews. Cambridge University Press, 1978.

Today's music is for everyone

From *Hear and Now: an introduction to modern music in schools*
(Universal Edition, 1972), 7–14

This is a book about modern music in schools

What is this new music about?
Like all other music it's about ways of building with sounds
different kinds of sounds

single sounds
sounds in twos and threes
many different sounds together

patterns and directions of sounds
high sounds
low sounds
long sounds
short sounds

textures and colours of sounds
rough sounds
smooth sounds
bright sounds
dull sounds

In fact, anything you care to do with sounds.

Above all
Music is about feeling
it is about being sensitive to sounds
about saying things through sounds
about listening to sounds you've never heard before

Go right back to beginnings. Try to forget all the assumptions we make about music; about rhythm and melody. At its most fundamental

Music is about getting excited by sounds.

There's not such a big gulf between the music of today and the music of the past. In fact there's no gulf at all. All that has happened is that

Resources have increased.

There are now more sounds to be used for making music and more ways of using them.

Find some sounds and try making music.

The trouble with books about music in education is that people tend to think they are always aimed at music specialists. This one isn't (at least, not primarily so). There are any number of musical things that can be done by people who've not had conventional musical training and, happily, more teachers (especially those who teach English, art, dance and drama) are now making use of music in their work and so supplementing what the often hard-pressed music specialist is able to do. Educationally, music is a powerful and important area and these days lots of exciting things are happening. New possibilities are being opened up: music linked with other subjects; teachers evolving projects in which pupils create their own music—frequently in association with drama or the visual arts; the word 'music' itself beginning to take on a new and broader meaning as influences from the world of the contemporary composer are felt in the classroom. The opportunities seem infinite. There's so much to be done, not only by the specialist music teachers but by teachers of general subjects and teachers of English and art as well.

In fact, just because there are so many possibilities and so much experimental work is starting up, it may seem a bit confusing to those who have not yet begun to explore these things for themselves. This book will be looking at the musical and educational principles behind the new approaches, but primarily we hope it will encourage teachers to experiment and explore, introducing music-making into the classroom in a variety of new forms.

We make a lot of assumptions about music. We may need to get rid of some of these before we begin. For example, music isn't crotchets and quavers. It's not dots on paper: it is *sounds*. The sounds come first and there are many ways of creating music without ever writing it down. The mysteries of musical notation have been one of the things that have put people off. Not that musical notation is difficult. It's just that those who couldn't read it have tended to confuse these symbols with the real thing. We used to regard music as very much a 'specialist' subject, partly because it involved an apparently complicated written language and partly because a great deal of emphasis was placed on performance: choirs and bands, orchestras and recorder groups. Taken together these two things were quite enough to make those who had no musical training feel it was an activity completely closed to them. But important as it is that we should encourage children to play and sing (and to do that extensively you *will* need specialized training) there are, nevertheless, lots of other aspects of music-making that can be tackled by the non-specialist teacher.

Many of these will be related to what is happening in modern music. Twentieth-century musicians have widened the resources of music so it stands to reason that they have made more musical things possible. These are not all complicated: many of them are very simple and offer opportunities to people who would not have dreamt that it was possible for them to make music.

We can see this process at work in all those areas of education that have adopted creative ways of learning. They've all drawn heavily on the methods of contemporary artists. They all begin at the same fundamental points: imagination, the individual and what he can do with the materials he's got. So we have 'creative-writing', 'creative-drama', 'creative-dance'—and we couldn't imagine Art as an *un*-creative subject. So why not 'creative music'? Could we not find some absolutely basic area of music-making where everyone could take part?

This doesn't mean that 'creative work' is something for the 'un-musical' while the real stuff is left to those who can handle the crotchets and quavers and play the piano. But it does recognise that music, like any other art, has basically very simple raw materials (sounds) and that these materials can be explored and moulded, shaped into musical ideas without great knowledge of what other people have done before. In other words, you don't need first to acquire advanced techniques: you can—indeed you must—just begin. You must start using sounds, finding out by experience what they can do for you. Of course, the more you know about handling the materials the more you'll be able to do with them. And it will be important at some stage to see what other composers have done with their resources.

But we often forget that artists of every kind (even the most highly advanced professionals) have to start by experimenting with ideas and materials. They don't work by 'rules': they work by imagination and experiment, shaping their materials to fit the ideas they've imagined. In terms of education this kind of activity is of the greatest importance. Along with similar opportunities in creative-writing and the visual arts, drama and dance, music-making—in the most fundamental sense of actually *creating* music—can offer a child plenty of scope for self-realization. It will increase his sensitivity to the world around and educate that part of his intelligence that is concerned with *feeling*.

In the past music hasn't always distinguished itself as a very popular school subject. Yet there's no doubt that the young people we teach want music. Most of them are involved with music, often in quite a number of different ways. Apart from the music of the discothèques and the folk groups, increasing numbers of young players and singers are joining youth orchestras, bands and choirs. Most of these activities happen *outside the classroom*. That's inevitable because most of them call for an atmosphere or an organization that could hardly be reproduced in the classroom for the usual half-an-hour once-a-week music lesson. It's so easy for the music teacher to get depressed over the half-hour lesson, to wonder what on earth he can do that's of any value, and so dismiss it and concentrate on other more obviously profitable things, such as the school orchestra. But, of course, it's not just that half-an-hour once a week. We're really concerned with something that's basic to all education. We're concerned with the relevance of what we do; with involving these youngsters in a totally related process. This is why the music lesson should overflow into other areas, and the other areas—English, art, mathematics or whatever—overflow into music. The music specialist is out on a limb. We need to bring his work into the orbit of the whole educational scheme and to supplement the work of 'the music lesson' with activities that build bridges across from other subject areas. When we put art or drama or music on to a school timetable we're not necessarily hoping to turn out painters or actors or performers on musical instruments. We're doing something educationally fundamental: we're educating the feelings. We ought to remember that this needs as much attention as the techniques and skills. In a way sensitivity *is* a technique that needs to be developed in us all. And it should properly come first because without it other skills will be empty and of little value.

But sensitivity isn't something that can be pushed into a child; it is rather something to be drawn out. We can try to create in our lessons a workshop atmosphere where projects in musical exploration can carry on more or less under their own impetus from one timetabled period to the next. Projects can be set up which span several subjects and may involve a number of teachers working as a team alongside their pupils. We might even begin to think of new timetable arrangements. For example, more could possibly be achieved in the arts subjects if a teacher worked with a class on a project lasting two whole days and, when the project was completed, did not meet with that group again for several weeks. Working on a piece of music, either creatively or interpretatively, we need extended time so that the players or composers can become deeply involved and give themselves more whole-heartedly to the job in hand. Moreover, the sense of achievement that is gained by seeing a task through in this way is worth a great deal in terms of the insight it brings with it. This is hardly ever achieved in a series of half-hour once-a-week lessons. On the other hand, we should have to remember that some subjects are best served by shorter periods; 'little and often'. But it shouldn't be beyond our wits to make timetables that would cater for both these situations. Already attempts are being made in some schools and although for many people that kind of organization may be a thing of the future, the important thing now is to keep an open mind and to admit of possibilities other than those with which we are most familiar—in other words, to rid ourselves of some of the assumptions.

That applies to the content of lessons too. Whatever the timetable situation we can begin to encourage experiment with sounds. The teacher's first task is to open his pupils' ears. Composers today are exploring new sound-making techniques, discovering new ranges of expressive possibility. We shall find that our pupils cover some of the same ground in their experiments. If we look at the kind of freedom of exploration that has entered the visual arts and literature in education we shall not be surprised to find the same thing happening in music. There's every reason why it should: this is something that is happening in the world of the professional artist and that in turn is a reflection of a spirit of discovery that is part of our twentieth-century society—and, of course, it pervades our thinking about education as a whole.

So it will be useful, as our pupils experiment with sounds, to let them hear music by composers of this century who have explored similar territory. And it will help even more if we can also organize classroom performances of new music. That won't be as difficult as it may seem. Quite often modern composers find that the kind of sounds they want can't be written down in traditional notation, so they have to invent new notational signs which are really 'drawings' of how the sounds should go. These notations are more or less self-explanatory with the advantage that they help us to get started on the performance of quite complicated music very quickly and without previous musical instruction. Not that there's anything especially difficult about traditional notation. Every child in school should learn to read it. But it takes time to master it and there's little doubt that it has in the past formed something of a barrier for some pupils (and some teachers!). Semiquavers and semibreves somehow seem to suggest that there's a mystique about music; an esoteric knowledge that can only be mastered by a few 'musical' people. The new notations of much contemporary music help us to get round this difficulty. The barrier disappears and we all start at the same point. Now *everyone* can read music. There's a quantity of music in this genre available for young players. It will form useful links with the players' own experimental music and with most of the music that composers of our own time are writing. And if the enjoyment and insight that performing this music gives is not enough in itself, then there are many ways in which it will be possible for the music teacher to demonstrate the links with more traditional music. For, in spite of a widely held belief, the music of today is not a radical break with tradition but a steady and natural growth from it. Education, over the past one hundred years, has broadened everybody's outlook (and presumably all of us who teach in schools are in favour of its doing just that). One result of this educational process has been the broadened outlook of the arts. It would be a bit unfair if we who in part have made this possible should now want to restrict the scope of the artist. Education and art must keep pace with one another and that is not to be achieved by putting the reins on either. The French-American composer, Edgard Varèse, remarking on the popular view that a composer is always ahead of his time, pointed out that the composer is in fact an *observer* of his time and it is his audience who is usually about fifty years behind him. We should certainly feel that something was wrong if the work of the schools was thought to be even twenty years behind developments in society. As educators we know that we must keep abreast of events and discoveries. This will include whatever is happening in the world of the arts. We shall make it our business to see that our pupils are able to 'read' what artists, poets and musicians have to say to us all today. Logically, the music of our own time should be as relevant to us as any will be. Certainly there is an immediacy about so much twentieth-century music that young people seem to respond to it more readily than they do to older music. Performance of simple music in the idioms of today can be a useful 'bridge' by which pupils who might resist some of the traditional material of the music lesson may be encouraged to take a deeper interest in music altogether.

The arts are more than entertainment and decoration. They are a vital force by which we are made aware of truths. By understanding the work of artists we increase our own sensitivity. Possibly, then, the most suitable point at which to begin would be with the work of living artists, poets and composers. Unfortunately this is often the very point at which communication seems to break down for many people. Somehow we have come to believe that 'modern art' ('modern music', 'modern poetry') is difficult. Although we may apparently experience no difficulty with music from the past (even though it springs from a society and environment very different from our own), we nevertheless find the music of our own time confusing. Part of the problem undoubtedly stems from the *variety* of musical expression in the twentieth century. It's difficult to catch on to one thing that we can recognize as a continuing thread. It appears to lack stability, whereas we think we see stability in the art and music of past ages. Perhaps the truth is that we're much more used to the sound of, say, Beethoven's music. He doesn't take us by surprise. He may not disturb us very much—but then he may not thrill us to the same extent that he was able to thrill his first hearers who recognised that he was saying some pretty positive things to them about their own time (as well as the things he said about eternity). As mighty—and timeless—as the *Eroica* Symphony is, we have got used to it. Maybe we feel that that's how it should be: art should be understood after the event and should not disturb. But for a great many people—especially young people—that way of looking at things seems more than a little unreal. If we are to express real things through the arts, the results may sometimes be disturbing. This doesn't mean that painting, poetry and music must always be about social issues and problems. 'Disturbing' doesn't mean that music has to be 'frightening'. What it does mean is that for art really to communicate (as opposed to being a kind of escapist entertainment which we view from a distance) we need to feel the excitement of discovery and a freshness of expression and ideas. Art can be very exciting, moving and full of feeling when it is concerned *with itself*—that is, concerned with showing us something we'd never noticed about its materials: paint, stone, wood, words, sounds, movement. And it was like this for Beethoven. He 'said' things in his music about the world in which he lived—about its social order, about the natural world which was so close to him, and about the sounds he could discover and imagine. He said these things intensely and people were often disturbed. Now we live in different times and artists are speaking in a language suitable to our own society with its extended horizons and all its diversity of thought and expression. It just wouldn't work if they tried to use the kind of language Beethoven or Wordsworth used, vital and exciting—and revolutionary—as those two great men were. Their art was for their age: the art of our age is for us. If we're going to understand what's happening in music today we must at least start by coming to terms with its diversity. We must not expect twentieth-century musical language to sound like the musical language of one hundred or more years ago. We wouldn't expect a poet today to use words as Milton or Shakespeare did. So much has changed in our ways of life and that affects how people speak and write. It is so with music also. Some of the problems of understanding will be eased if we make experiments with sounds ourselves. That's where it all starts. We shall begin to see how it is possible to broaden the meaning of the word 'music'. Many different ways of organizing the sounds and making them 'go on', of fashioning them into a unified piece of music, will be found. We shall find our sense of adventure increasing and we shall see how the business of organizing sounds into meaningful patterns can relate to our present situation and to all kinds of things that happen around us and about which we get excited. Making music is something everyone can do. And you may be surprised at what you discover in the process. In the next chapter we shall be looking at some of the things composers have been doing during the past seventy years—at the sounds and ideas that have excited them. This may give you ideas for experimental projects.

Autumn

Music for Young Players (Universal Edition, 1972)

Directions for performance

This is a sound-picture for an average class of 10–12 year olds; although players of any age could play it, the voices should preferably be high-pitched, and the instruments must never overwhelm them.

Aim at creating an overall impression of the sadness of autumn—leaves falling and piling up, raindrops steadily dropping and the feeling of summer fading away. Let the top line gradually build up this atmosphere, using any instruments or sounds which give the right effect: the ones named on the score are only suggestions. These players should improvise freely but very softly, with only the slight variations in colour as indicated, until they reach 7, when each player chooses one note and repeats it in a steady pulse, gradually slowing down and becoming even softer from 8 to the end. The metallophone or chime bars must stand out from this background—rather like fir-trees when all the other trees are bare.

At 5, the voices come in, all together on the first note and then each singer continuing the rest of the phrase at his own speed so that each arrives separately on the last syllable and holds that note until all the singers have arrived there, the sound piling up gradually as each new voice joins. Then move on to the next phrase, with all the voices starting together again and then the individual singers proceeding at their own pace, until the next assembly point. Sing very slowly and quietly all the time holding each note for as long as possible (perhaps until your breath runs out?): when you reach the final syllable of the piece, hold it until the sound dies completely away.

Throughout the piece listen to the continually-changing sound colours as they very slowly and softly appear. The conductor should give a signal on each number using his discretion (and his ears) in judging the time between each but never allowing less than 6 seconds.

Autumn

for Voices and Instruments.

Music by JOHN PAYNTER

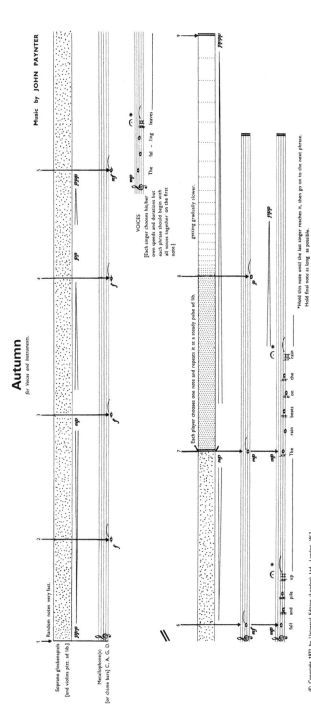

The role of creativity in the school music curriculum

From Michael Burnett (ed.), *Music Education Review: A Handbook for Music Teachers,* Vol. 1 (Chappell, 1977), 3–7

'Creativity' is a word that has caused quite enough trouble. It would seem all too easy for misunderstandings to arise at the merest mention of this topic. Yet we continue to use the word—presumably because there is no other that will suit our needs. The large number of activities to which the label 'creative' is applied in junior and secondary schools is sufficient in itself to emphasize the need for a definition of terms, and before we embark on discussion of the role of creativity in classroom music-making, we might profitably look at the implications of some other labels, such as 'education' itself. 'The school music curriculum' covers a range of *educational* possibilities. 'Music education'; 'musi*cal* education'; 'music *in* education'. Precisely which of these are we discussing? If we are to consider creativity in the school music curriculum, it is important that we understand why music should be part of the curriculum at all. What, then, is the role of *music* in the curriculum?

Music and the other arts in general education

Education implies 'a leading out'; a process of growth from what is already present; a development of existing potential. It suggests a divergent progress, since the 'leading out' could take us in almost any direction—sometimes along unforeseen and unexpected paths, depending upon the interests and motivation of the person being educated. But we also use the word education to cover those essentially *convergent* procedures, skill-training. By association, the term musi*cal* education describes a course of training in which the student practises and perfects certain established techniques, and where a high degree of expertise may be attained without necessarily having to aim at the development of such deeply personal qualities as imagination or inventiveness. Obviously, there will be some elements of training in any educational method, but in the establishment of a system of universal education—that is to say, classroom education as we know it in our schools—we may have fallen into the trap of assuming that all aspects of the curriculum should operate on one and the same pattern. The convergent procedures of training are most likely to come to mind first. They have an immediate attraction in that the teacher can define the skills which are to be learned, and when the period of training is completed it is relatively easy to devise tests which will show whether or not the pupils have acquired what was prescribed. The divergent process, on the other hand, is much more of a problem; and difficult to assess satisfactorily. Yet it is an essential part of a complete education, and it is here that the arts have an especially important function.

Jean Piaget suggests that education should enable us to do new things—not simply to repeat what other generations have done. It should develop the explorer—the discoverer—in each one of us. The arts jointly cater for that need. The problem is how to introduce such enterprise into the curriculum. If the basis—in music, for example—is to be a *training* in established skills it would be unrealistic to suppose that a normal mixed-ability classroom group would get far beyond elementary stages. That is to say, if we gear the content of the work to a limited range of 'received skills' it is probable that only a minority of pupils would be able to make these techniques their own—to a degree that would enable them to make independent musical use of what they had learned. The temptation might then be to ignore the majority interests in favour of encouraging the few who are able to respond—either through innate ability or through skill already acquired outside the classroom lesson.* But if the arts have general importance in education, and if opportunities are to be offered to all, it is up to us to find a suitable mode for the arts in the curriculum so that benefit may indeed be given to the majority and not simply the gifted few. As far as music in schools is concerned, it would seem necessary to accept a distinction between music*al* education and music *in* education. The former term could describe adequately the training essential for anyone who is to follow a musical career. But 'music *in* education' suggests something much broader—the *use* of music in the general school curriculum in such a way that it can make a significant contribution to the education of all pupils. More surely than in any other area of the curriculum, the arts should be able to offer opportunities for everyone to participate in his/her own way without the necessity for keeping pace, characteristic of a programme of training.

---

* That this has happened would seem to be supported by the evidence of pupils' own statements in documents such as *Enquiry 1: Young School Leavers*, HMSO, 1968.

In this context artistic activities which offer the greatest scope for the majority of pupils to develop their innate sensitivity, inventiveness and imagination might have strong claim for a place of importance in the curriculum. It has been said that:

The lack of art–activity in our schools causes not only the weakening of art–activity in our culture but also an inadequate relationship with reality; the weakening of the perception of the world which is needed in all human activity. That is why the situation today is not only catastrophic to art culture but to society in general. The products of art-less schools are people who can only mimic the patterns of activity impressed on them from outside.

[R. Wilenius, *Education as Creative Activity*, 1974.]

Outside the creative arts there are very few opportunities in the curriculum for pupils to take decisions which are genuinely personal decisions. The performing aspects of music, drama and dance may provide refreshment through re-creation of 'realized forms' (the works of artists and musicians 'captured' in some form of notation), but freedom to devise and develop our own ideas in the medium of sound, words, gestures and bodily movement is educationally important because it presents us with the possibility of *organizing our experience.* This is what creative artists do. They 'work' their materials—sound, paint, clay, space, movement, or whatever—gradually bringing the medium under control; and because the control springs from within the individual, so the ultimate organization of the chosen elements bears the mark of the artist's personality—which is the product of his experience. Artistic enterprise is indeed a way of 'saying' something personal, but it is also a means by which we may discover ourselves and crystallize that discovery in what is made—a piece of music, a painting, a poem or a dance. Susanne Langer has shown that the arts are essential to us—and always will be—because they yield insight into the 'unspeakable' realities of life:

The emotive content of a work is apt to be something much deeper than any intellectual experience, more essential, pre-rational, and vital, something of the life-rhythms we share with all growing, hungering, moving and fearing creatures: the ultimate realities themselves, the central facts of our brief, sentient existence.[1]

Although, to a great extent, we have accepted in education the arts as necessary areas of imaginative activity, we may not have been prepared so wholeheartedly to acknowledge the curriculum implications of these very special experiences, the quintessence of which is that they go beyond word-bound thought.

---

[1] Susanne K. Langer, *Philosophy in a New Key*, 1942.

Perhaps our inability to accept the arts on their own terms and to find a role for them in the school curriculum based on such an acceptance is due to our respect for words and rational argument. Schools tend to emphasize verbalization, and the tradition has a long history. As Marshall McLuhan pointed out, it all began with Gutenberg! Printed resources have been vital tools for scholarship for many hundreds of years, but if we are not careful they may easily overshadow other apparatus for learning. Print has produced in most of us a reverence for verbal reasoning and a paramount respect for words as vehicles of expression. Understandably, we have come to believe that all education starts here: with literacy (and numeracy); with the heritage of the written (printed) word and with numbers—symbols of logical thought which we have come to regard as superior to *intuitive* cognition. Non-verbal means of 'coming to know' must assume an inferior position. This emphasis upon the printed word has helped to strengthen the belief that education should largely be concerned with the transmission of a received culture: the wisdom of past generations, tried and tested by time; a touchstone against which to measure our own thinking. There is, of course, a great deal of good sense in this point of view. It would be foolish indeed to turn our backs upon the heritage of past wisdom, and while, in our fast-moving modern world, we must educate people to cope with change, we must at the same time keep in touch with our roots by carrying our culture with us. The difficulty for the educator is to avoid reducing the heritage to a mass of lifeless information. This is no new problem. In 1931 the Hadow Committee urged teachers to think of the curriculum 'in terms of activity and experience rather than of knowledge to be acquired and facts to be stored ... it should not be loaded with inert ideas and crude blocks of fact which are devoid of significance ... It must be vivid, realistic, a stream in motion not a stagnant pool.' [Board of Education, 1931] In our attempts to streamline the learning processes—in order to ensure success in the transmission of heritage ideas—it has become essential to emphasize training. 'Basic skills' have to be defined and codified. Literacy and numeracy are treated, in the main, like craft skills with the teacher as the master craftsman and the pupils as apprentices. No doubt this is the right way to produce a literate and numerate society, but it is a mistake to apply the logic behind these processes to everything else in the curriculum.

As new subject areas have been added, there has been a tendency to make them fit the established pattern based on the 'master craftsman/apprentice' model. What happens in education must then be either 'useful' (in the vocational sense) or 'improving' (in the moral or cultural sense). There is little room for other interpretations. In such a scheme the only place for the arts is either on the 'craft' side (providing us with 'leisure' pursuits to entertain or to offer some relaxation from the 'reality' of existence) *or* on the 'cultural' side, acquainting us with the realized forms—most commonly the masterworks of post-Renaissance Europe. If the former, then the arts are likely to be relegated to a humble position in the school curriculum—or indeed out of it altogether—becoming purely recreational activities, less important than the real stuff of learning—the academic curriculum. If the latter, we may feel obliged to give the arts 'academic' standing by bringing them into line with the essentially information-based areas of the curriculum, so that it becomes more important to 'know about' the arts than to have 'experience of' them.

This attitude to the arts in education has created for music in schools a situation in which information (theory of music, lives of composers) has come to be regarded by some as basic to musical understanding and of greater importance than experience of sounds themselves—the raw materials of music.

But music is not an 'information' subject. And for all its intellectual content, it is ultimately one of those non-verbal, intuitive areas of experience which help to characterize our individuality and which open doors on a totally different kind of 'knowing', not dependent upon received information. In such experiences lie the clues to individual self-realization and fulfilment, and it is this that the arts offer; something not covered by any other aspect of the school curriculum. For if, in schools, we were to be concerned entirely with imparting information, our sights trained only upon the vocational usefulness of what was taught, we should find that, once the institutionalised 'feeding in' had ceased, those who had received education would be left with sadly undeveloped—and, therefore, effectively limited—resources of imagination and sensitivity within themselves. Yet these are the very resources we need to stimulate and sustain our perception of the world around us. To be literate, numerate and knowledgeable is essential; but it is not enough. We need the 'skill' of imagination as well. More than forty years ago the American educator James L. Mursell[2] warned of the hazards that would confront us if we educated 'in reverse order'. There would be no point in giving people the techniques of expression unless we made an effort to see that they had something to express. Uniquely, the *creative* arts in education provide opportunities for all our pupils to discover what they want to say and to express it through a personal exploration of materials. And in that intangible world of the imagination, sound is an especially valuable resource.

---

[2] J. L. Mursell, *Human Values in Music Education*, 1934.

An interdisciplinary approach to music

Introduction from John Paynter and Elizabeth Paynter, *The Dance and the Drum* (Universal Edition, 1974), 9–11

This book provides material for a series of classroom projects in music-theatre. The aim is to draw on the imaginative and creative abilities of every member of a class or group right from the start. A lot has already been written about creative music-making and improvisation in dance and drama. The projects that follow offer some suggestions for an integration of these activities so that an idea may be explored by the pupils on several different levels simultaneously.

Teachers are now making efforts to rid education of the problems of specialization. We recognize that while each subject must continue to have its own techniques and procedures, there is, nevertheless, common ground between all branches of knowledge and experience. It is part of the teacher's job to help his pupils grasp these connections so that the essential wholeness of knowledge is apparent. 'Education is active; it involves a reaching out of the mind'; it is concerned with our awareness of the meaning of experiences and our ability to be articulate about them.

The arts in education have a big part to play in the expression of ideas. Creative music-theatre offers opportunities for a number of related arts experiences. It also draws on the wide variety of imaginative talent to be found in any group of children. Everyone can contribute. Even so, this is something more than just a device to 'start us off' on imaginative work in music and the other arts. Music-theatre is an art form in itself. In fact, it is possibly the oldest 'art-form' of all, and its revival today—with the frequent inclusion of some kind of audience participation—has particular significance when it is seen side-by-side with those developments in modern education that aim to release the creative artistic potential in all the children we teach—not merely the 'artistic' or 'musical' ones.

What is music-theatre? It is, quite simply, the total integration of all those elements of human expression which we call art. That is: words, movement, music, and the two- and three-dimensional visual arts. They have a lot in common. Once they were inseparable. Even now, in very primitive communities, there is no word for what we would call music—as an art form by itself. Musical 'gestures', divorced from the gestures of word and action, are unknown, indeed are inconceivable. As the arts of mankind have developed, the elements have tended to separate and techniques have grown more complex. Obviously this has meant enormously increased opportunities for expression in certain directions, but it is also evident that a great deal may have been lost on the way.

The arts arise out of man's need to understand himself and his environment. Their principal function is to yield insight. They help us to 'understand' things that cannot be comprehended by any other means—ideas apprehended intuitively and, therefore, not to be 'explained' by concise and reasoned argument from scientific experiment. The arts are about *feeling* and man's emotional response to the intangible information he receives through his senses.

Long ago men made up stories to explain how things had come to be as they are. How everything began; why the sky is where it is; why the seasons come and go; why we grow old and why we die, and what happens to us after death. The story-makers' sources of 'information' were their own intuitions. There was nothing scientific or reasonable (in the modern sense) about their explanations. Neither was there anything of modern science in their ways of expressing these ideas. Because the answers to the problems were *felt*, so they were expressed intuitively in the most natural outlets of expression—vocal sounds and bodily movement and gesture; that is, in poetry, dance and music. With the addition of extensions to the voice and body in the form of simple musical instruments, masks and costumes, these forms of expression grew into rituals that represented a whole community's 'understanding' of the mysterious and sometimes hostile world around them. This kind of expression was only possible through a collaborative effort; insofar as it was 'art', the art belonged to everyone.

That may seem a very long way removed from our own modern society but it is in fact only just below the surface and is perhaps more surely part of our lives than we realize. You can still see primitive rituals of music, words and movement enacted any day of the week in the playgrounds and streets of Liverpool, London, New York, or Sydney: indeed anywhere children play together. But this isn't just a hangover from the past, neither is it a form of expression confined to children's games. Rituals and ceremonial of all kinds are still an important thing in most people's lives. Whether it's a wedding or the opening of Parliament, a military tattoo, a visit to a fairground, or the start of the Cup Final: music, word and action integrate to say something to us through our feelings. It is the coming together of the different elements that creates the powerful emotional effect. Music-theatre today is an attempt to recapture the 'totality' of this kind of artistic experience, and its revival has arisen partly out of a need to bring the performing arts again into the orbit of everyday experience.

The European Renaissance gave us individual artists of genius. Men of letters, music, painting, and sculpture followed their separate paths. The process was a valuable one and it produced peaks of achievement that would have been unthinkable by any other way of working: the plays of Shakespeare, the music of Bach, the sculpture of Michelangelo, the painting of Rembrandt. We would not want to be without the masterpieces of European art that have come down to us, representatives of the highest points of our civilization. All the same, we have to admit that the very processes which produced them also ensured that the arts became the province of a minority group. Often it seems that the greater the artistic achievement of an individual painter, composer, or poet, the further he has drawn away from the mass of ordinary people. Yet what he has to say is of importance to ordinary people: it is, after all, about the life we all share. But the artist must do what he has to do, and he must do it *his* way. So, if for no other reason than that it will help us to understand a little more about his way, we should perhaps try to redevelop that creative participation that was once assumed to be part of everybody's way of life. In schools we now encourage children to take part in the activities of artists: to write poetry, to create their own music, to express themselves in the visual arts and in drama and dance. We do so not only because this kind of self-fulfillment through artistic expression is valuable in itself but also because, however humble the results of such creative experiment may be, it brings young people closer to the work of the professional artist.

There is also much to be gained by reuniting the elements so that music, art and drama blend to form new and even more telling forms. This is the art of ritual play that is immediately meaningful to everyone because it springs from natural forms of expression that are common to us all. At root the arts are nothing more than developed *games*. It isn't coincidence that we speak of 'playing' on a musical instrument or of going to the theatre to see a 'play'. Someone once said that children's games become art when they are directed towards an audience. Playing those kinds of imaginative games and taking part in symbolic rituals are not things we leave behind us when we grow up. We continually express things in rituals, often without thinking about them (such as the rituals of greeting and saying goodbye) because these symbolic gestures have such a depth of meaning. Music-theatre draws upon this natural language of symbolism and heightens it and intensifies it so that its meanings are driven home. This is an art that has remained as a great tradition in the East much more than it has in the West. The Japanese Noh plays are a real integration of music, word, and action. With their ancient costumes and evocative masks the performers mime, dance, and sing to almost continuous instrumental accompaniment stories that have been handed down from the distant past. But, ancient as these ritual plays are, they still have meaning for a modern audience. Their message is usually a simple one.

For the purposes of this book we have chosen twelve of the old stories: myths and legends that, like the stories of the Noh plays, embody simple and timeless truths. Whatever the details, there is always the underlying feeling that at the heart of the story is a message that applies to us now every bit as much as it did to people thousands of years ago. In all probability many of these stories were once part of ritual performances involving music and action as well as words. They are, therefore, ideal material for use in schools as a basis for creative music-theatre projects. But we wouldn't wish it to stop there. Additional material could be gathered from similar sources and from children's own creative writing. Poetic language is older than the language of prose and, as the questions (and answers) of two twentieth-century ten-year-olds will show, the themes children choose are frequently those universal gropings after truth that have been part of life on this planet since men and women first started to look around them and wonder:

> What's inside the moon?
>   There's hot water inside.
> What's the sky made of?
>   It was made out of white snow.
> If you cut the sun open what would you see?
>   Terrible looking enemies.
> When you write you look at your words. Have you thought
>   of cutting open a letter to see what's inside?
>   No. But if a person was crazy the answer would be yes.
> What's inside colours?
>   There's pink stars.
> Where is the end of the universe?
>   In back of the swimming pools.
> How old is adventure?
>   It is 60,000 years old.
> What colour is older, black or white?
>   Black because you can outline me.

The first sunrise

From John Paynter and Elizabeth Paynter, *The Dance and the Drum* (Universal Edition, 1974), 27–8

When the world was made the sky was so close to the earth that no light could get in. Everyone had to crawl around in the darkness collecting things to eat with their bare hands. Living was difficult and uncomfortable. There was no space where the birds could fly. Then the magpies, who were the cleverest of the birds, had an idea. Working together they could, perhaps, raise the sky a little and so make room.

They collected long sticks. Then slowly and all together, using the sticks, they began to push the sky upwards away from the earth. Resting, first on low boulders and then on higher ones, they lifted the sky until there was room for everyone to stand upright.

With all their strength they tried to get the sky even higher. Struggling to do so they split the sky open, and through the broken cloud came a first few rays of light. The gap widened, revealing the sun. The magpies burst into glorious song as the broken pieces of sky floated away in clouds. Daybreak and the first dawn chorus began.

Assignments

Music

(i) *Music of Darkness.* Experiment first to find 'dark' sounds. Try to depict a world where living is hard and comforts are few. Barren, empty and desolate.

(ii) Make music suggesting cramped space and discomfort. 'Limited' sounds that do not move—or cannot move very much. *Restricted* music.

(iii) Rehearse and perform *Sound Patterns 3* by Bernard Rands (Universal Edition). The composer calls this a 'project for voices': it explores music made with the simplest of materials—spoken words. Make more music about speech sounds.

(iv) Make a song of determination: people rising against injustice or people resolved to find a solution to a problem. Listen to some of the 'protest' songs of Bob Dylan.

(v) *Pushing Music.* Thrusting upwards with great strength.

(vi) *Sun Music.* Bright sounds; high and intense. Listen to the opening of Roberto Gerhard's Symphony No. 3, Record No. ASD 2427 and *Sun-Song* from Wilfrid Mellers' *Life Cycle* (Philips 6589 001).

(vii) Make a piece of music called *Birds Flying.* Watch the movements of different kinds of birds. Choose three and use the rhythmic features of the different movements as a basis for contrasting sections of the music.[1]

(viii) With a cassette tape-recorder collect examples of birdsong. Listen carefully to these and try to imitate them on musical instruments. Make a piece of music that uses various snatches of birdsong to build up sound patterns. Vary the texture so that sometimes there is a single line of melody and at other times several strands together. (Rehearse and perform *Music for Sleep* by Harrison Birtwistle (Novello). Listen to the 'Dawn Chorus' Epôde in *Chronochromie* by Messiaen).

Dance, drama, and visual art

(i) People crawling about in darkness. Life on an inhospitable planet. Elemental. Nothing but work and death.

(ii) Read about the working conditions of poor people in the 19th century. Make a play about work in the mines.

(iii) A committee meeting.

(iv) Use the sounds of words to suggest movements. Dark, slow words. Fast, light words. Record Bernard Rands' *Sound Patterns 3* and use it as music for movement.

(v) Movement: pushing upwards. Weight bearing down—you force it up. Work this out as a movement pattern on its own and then in association with the *Pushing Music.*

(vi) Darkness gives way to light. Awakening. Joy. (Read the poem *Everyone Sang* by Siegfried Sassoon).

(vii) Flight.

---

[1] See pp. 195–200 for further discussion and example.

The Story

Characters:

People and animals—crawling about in darkness. Oppressed.

Birds—unable to fly but trying to do so nevertheless.

Magpies—creatures of superior intelligence. A group apart.

Episodes, situations and places:

 (i) The world in darkness and with the sky very low. Uncomfortable.

 (ii) The birds try to fly in the very limited space.

(iii) The magpies confer and make their decision. They experiment with sticks.

 (iv) The magpies push the sky upwards. They enlist help from the others.

 (v) All the inhabitants of the earth unite for a supreme effort to push the sky even higher.

 (vi) The sky splits open. Light streams through. The sun itself is revealed.

(vii) Daybreak and dawn chorus. Awakening of the whole earth.

The small-group 'workshop'

From *All Kinds of Music: 4 Sound Patterns,* (Oxford University Press, 1979), 4–7

Increasingly, 'standard' class-teaching patterns are giving way to other methods and organizations more suited to the particular needs of a subject. Different areas require different kinds of arrangements and even within a subject one aspect may call for treatment quite different from another. The distinction between education and training is a real one. We may succeed reasonably well in *training* a large number of people simultaneously in some simple skill or technique; but the process of 'leading out', which characterizes true education and implies recognition of the qualities of originality which the pupil himself brings to the situation, is not easily realized by *instructing* whole-class groups. Of course, this is not to say that the educational process does not or should not include training, nor does it imply that there will never be occasions when it is right and profitable to teach the whole class together. It all depends on what is being done. Some things are more easily accomplished with large groups (some, indeed, with very large groups—say, sixty or more). Other projects are better suited to a 'workshop' type of approach where pupils work, largely under their own impetus, in groups of about five or six. In general the projects suggested in *All Kinds of Music* are designed for working in this way. Occasionally it may be desirable to increase the numbers. On the other hand, some topics will probably produce several related but different ideas which can be worked on by individuals. The basic organization remains, nevertheless, the small-group arrangement.

There are several ways of initiating this. The teacher may start the lesson with a few words addressed to the whole class—a brief summary, perhaps, of the kind of thing the small groups will be exploring, or a statement or demonstration which in itself is a challenge to experiment. After this the class quickly divides into groups and the groups set to work.

Alternatively, in the first lesson the class can be divided into small groups right at the start and directed to materials on which they will base their work (e.g. the appropriate book, or topic in the book, recordings, instruments, 'found object' sound-sources, etc.) and allowed to go straight to work without any preliminary comment addressed to the whole class.

If possible, provide a separate work space for each group. This may be difficult in the majority of schools where music is taught in once-a-week half-hour periods in one classroom—though even in such situations ways have been found of surmounting the problems. Corridors and stock rooms, entrance vestibules and the like can sometimes be used. If the school hall is available the class can be divided up to work at points around the hall—generally a satisfactory arrangement because pupils find that, in a reasonably large space, they are able to concentrate on their own tasks and cut out sounds coming from other groups, provided that the general sound level is not excessively high. Of course, such working conditions are far from being ideal and it is easy enough to build up arguments for not attempting work of this kind without the proper facilities. But it is also arguable that if we all wait for ideal conditions most of us will probably never get started at all. Better, perhaps, to do what we can with what we've got, however much that may limit us or fall short of our ideals.

Whatever method you adopt, the teacher's role is a vital one, and the techniques of handling a 'workshop' are crucial to its success. They cannot be left to chance. Plan in advance the kind of guidance you will most likely be called upon to give, on the reasonable expectation of the kind of work your pupils will produce in response to the material. At the same time, allow for the unexpected and be ready to encourage unusual and imaginative work when it appears. Be ready too with appropriate follow-up examples (e.g. recorded music) to back up a line of experiment or inventiveness as it arises. Devise extra 'support material' to help individuals or groups extend ideas or ways of working which are especially productive.

Having set the groups to work, move quickly from one to another, if possible making contact with all groups within the first few minutes of working. It is important, during the first part of any session, that no one group is left for too long without a visit (which should encourage, and help to focus more closely on the task in hand). Don't *explain* too much, but do ask the right kind of questions. These may be of the simplest nature, e.g. to a group creating an original piece or working on a song arrangement: 'What ideas have you got for the beginning? Let me hear them, please.' Then: 'How is it going to end?' Or: 'That's a good idea for the end; now, how do you get from your starting ideas to there? In what ways can you develop those first sounds?' And so on. Simple as they are, these are essentially the same basic questions that every composer or arranger must ask about each new work.

After about ten minutes, stop all groups and bring them together for a 'stock taking'. This may be (in the early stages especially) a mainly verbal reporting back (e.g. 'I want someone in each group to tell me how the group is getting on; what ideas you've got and so on.'). But encourage *performance* of work in progress, however rudimentary and unfinished the ideas may be. Comment and give support. Draw everyone's attention to the good things and to ways in which certain ideas may be developed—but don't let it develop into a litany, or interest may quickly be lost. Perhaps you will not hear from all the groups every time but certainly all should share in the process. Keep up the atmosphere of endeavour. When a sufficient number of ideas have been discussed, send the groups away to continue work while you proceed as before, visiting each in turn and helping with a few challenging observations or well-chosen questions.

Reasonably frequent 'stock taking', all together, can help to promote a purposeful working atmosphere and it is good for everyone to share experiences of things which are going well *and* things which, for one reason or another, are proving difficult to develop. Precisely how often you should interrupt the groups' progress for a 'plenary' session will depend on the nature of the assignment. Each occasion will have to be judged separately.

During the first weeks it may be necessary to begin every lesson period with a few words to the whole class before dividing into small groups. Gradually, however, it should be possible to establish the 'workshop' style and, with projects which are not brought to a conclusion neatly each week but develop ideas that must be carried over—groups reaching the completion stages at different times—the need for an opening statement from the teacher may disappear. Ideally, groups and individuals should be able to pursue projects at their own pace, working through—as materials and imagination dictate—on ideas suggested by books, recordings, or the stimulus of creative impulse. Then the teacher can 'service' the workshop processes by encouragement, advice, and above all by asking pertinent questions.

For this is how music works. Whether it is a creative problem for the composer or a *re*-creative challenge for the performer, the ideas behind the music pose questions which must be answered in terms of aesthetically satisfactory *sound*-structures. Music education should not be concerned only with technical instruction, nor with simply feeding pupils ready-made answers to well-established lines of inquiry. It should help them to set up and answer problems of their own devising in the organizing of experience—which is what all artistic enterprise is about.

Performing from indeterminate notation

From *All Kinds of Music: 4 Sound Patterns* (Oxford University Press, 1979), 57

Perform this short piece. The notation is *indeterminate*—that is to say, the details are not precise. The composer indicates the kind of sounds the instruments are to play and roughly when they shall play (in relation to each other) but the performers must make the final decisions themselves. Every performance will be different. This is something like a game of cards. You know the rules of the game and, therefore, you know, in a very general fashion, the kind of things that are likely to happen. But you can't tell exactly how the events will work out until you actually play the game. Sometimes we refer to music of this kind as 'Open Form'. The composer gives us the 'rules' but we must make our own decisions in working things out. We may even have to decide first what the signs on the score mean for us.

All that matters is that the sign you draw should show as clearly as possible all the things we need to know:

Is it a high sound or a low sound?
Is it a long sound or a short sound?

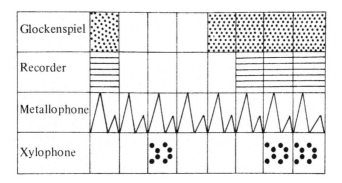

Is it a loud sound or a soft sound?
Does it start loudly and get softer?
Does it start softly and get louder?
Does it start low and get higher?
Does it start high and get lower?
Does it stay the same for a long time?
How long?

And so on. Ask yourself *exactly what happens in the music.*
Then invent a sign which will get the sound.

Talking point: if it's good to look at will it also produce something interesting to listen to?

Try to play this piece called *Reflections.* The conductor makes a downbeat at the beginning of each bar only. Entries not at the beginning of a bar are left to your own discretion.

The piece may begin and end at any bar, although group B always begins and ends approximately half a bar after group A, in other words it 'reflects' group A.

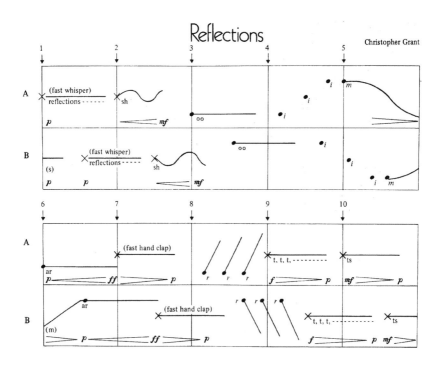

PART III

THE SCHOOLS COUNCIL SECONDARY MUSIC PROJECT (1973–82)

Early in the 1970s The Schools Council for Curriculum and Examinations ('possibly the most important post-war curriculum development body in England and Wales until its demise in 1984'[1]) allocated funding for a study of secondary school music teaching. The outcome was a nationwide project that, throughout a decade, worked with Local Education Authorities and more than 250 schools across England and Wales.

From the start it was a matter of principle that the Project's 'method' should be derived from ideas put forward by head teachers and teachers and that participating schools should be self-selecting. They could choose to operate either as Pilot Schools (helping to determine the course of the Project by demonstrating and recording work in progress and by initiating new activities) or as Trial Schools (willing to test, review, and report on methods and materials introduced by the Pilot Schools or in discussion with members of the Project Team). The final action (following the formal conclusion of the Project) was to establish regional Music Education Centres to take the work forward in whatever ways seemed appropriate at local level. At the same time the strategies, conclusions, and recommendations of the Project were explained in the book, *Music in the Secondary School Curriculum*.[2] In his Foreword, Professor Harry Rée, Chairman of the Consultative Committee from 1973 to 1980, wrote,

The Project has involved hundreds of teachers ... They have met together over the years, discussed processes, made music, and contributed schemes, often ... in their spare-time and unpaid. And they have produced a powerful instrument which introduces a new note, and promises a welcome 'crescendo' in the teaching of music in schools throughout the country.

The book begins by setting out principles 'evolved ... through discussion with teachers, Heads, Music Advisers and others'; for example, that 'All musical

---

[1] Gordon Cox, *Living Music in Schools 1923–1999*. Ashgate, 2002, 3.

[2] John Paynter, *Music in the Secondary School Curriculum*. Cambridge University Press, 1982.

activity ... requires creative thought; the exercise of imagination influenced by personal choice and preference' and that 'Music-making is more important than musical information ... Our first task is to involve young people with music itself.' Reviewing the Project twenty years after its completion, Stephanie Pitts suggested that 'perhaps the most significant legacy' was

its recognition that educational change originates in the classroom, and that ideas need to be shared and discussed between teachers if effective practice is to develop.[3]

In retrospect it would appear also that the Project influenced, first, the writing of both Secondary and Primary sections of the HMI document *Music from 5 to 16*[4] and, second, the structure of the GCSE—in that the Education Reform Act (1988) established Music as one of ten obligatory subjects for all students in state schools, the schedule for GCSE emphasizing the importance of performing and composing.[5]

The first two chapters of *Music in the Secondary School Curriculum* are included here because they set out the reasons why, in 1972/3, it was thought necessary to establish this development project. In Chapter 1 the review of the history of musical activity/knowledge as an element of 'schooling' reveals long-standing uncertainty and disagreement about an appropriate content for the music curriculum (e.g. [p.70] 'the unfortunate Mr Arthur ... [who] ... thought that he had been teaching 'singing', only to find that what he had done was not considered "real" singing'). Notwithstanding the encouraging evidence of successes and the great amount of good that had been done by dedicated teachers over the centuries, it would appear that 'the place of music in general education has never been completely thought through.' Therefore, The Schools Council Secondary Music Project would attempt to establish a rationale for music in the school curriculum, not by imposition but by inviting teachers, head teachers, Local Education Authority Advisers, Education Officers, and others with an interest in the matter to collaborate in a long-term exploration of the possibilities—starting from the questions, 'Why do we have music in the curriculum at all? What, precisely, is music *for* in schools?'.

---

[3] Stephanie Pitts, *A Century of Change in Music Education*. Ashgate, 2000, p. 112.

[4] DES, 1985.

[5] Cox, op. cit.

How did we get here?

From *Music in the Secondary School Curriculum: trends and developments in class music teaching* (Cambridge University Press, 1982), 1–19

A long-standing controversy

Throughout the spring and summer of 1872 James Arthur, headmaster of a small church school hidden among the back streets of a northern industrial town, made an effort to bring some musical pleasure into the lives of his pupils. Probably very little of the spring or the summer managed to penetrate the city smoke or find its way into the classrooms through the windows set high in the walls, but Mr Arthur tried to make up for this by teaching his pupils songs about far away places and colourful characters. Week by week he recorded in his log book the songs taught and the progress made:

Taught the singing class 'Over mountain.'
Taught a round, 'The Bell.'
Taught new tune, 'The Skaters' to the Singing Class.
Taught the singing class 'The Swiss Toy Girl.'
The Singing Class learned 'The Hero.'

Sometimes circumstances were against him:

This week has been very wet ... gave no singing lessons because I had a cold.

But as soon as was possible he did what he could:

I taught them the first part of 'Lightly Row!'

And then, with renewed confidence:

I taught them the whole of 'Lightly Row' this week.

In November the School Board inspector paid a visit and noted in the log that 'The school is in fair order.' However, somewhat surprisingly he added that, as a condition for an unreduced grant the following year, *'Singing should be taught!'*.

What could he have meant? Had not Mr Arthur conscientiously taught singing for the past seven months? But an earlier, heartfelt entry may provide a clue to this apparently perverse recommendation—not without significance in the days of 'payment by results'. In June, James Arthur had written:

I am trying to make them learn the modulator, but it's dreadfully uphill work.

After the November visitation he tried again with this 'uphill work' but the entries seem somehow less enthusiastic than his earlier list of songs:

The Singing Class improves very slowly with the modulator,

he wrote in late November. And by January 1873 he was really quite depressed:

I have been endeavouring to make the singing class master the Modulator rather than [he wrote 'teach them' but then crossed it out] acquire new tunes. So many of them are young that it is rather hard.

All of which suggests a difference of opinion between the headmaster and the inspector. We may easily identify with both points of view; with the teacher for concentrating upon the immediacy and the delight of simple music-making, and with the inspector in his desire to see something of more permanent value learned. But reading between the lines of this more than one hundred-year-old school record we can see the elements of a dilemma which, in one form or another, has been a feature of music education for a very long time—and which to some extent is with us still. The history of music in schools is the continuing story of an apparent dichotomy between practice and theory; between the 'fun' of making music *now* and the hard grind of acquiring techniques which will (or should) make it possible to have much more musical enjoyment *later on*. Even today one may occasionally come across a school timetable which allocates for a class, say, two periods of music each week, labelling one period 'Singing' and the other 'Music'!

The implication that there is something slightly frivolous about the activity of music-*making* while the study of musical theory is academically respectable, is an echo of a controversy going back to the Middle Ages and having its origins many centuries earlier.

During the Roman Empire, academic study of music was purely a matter of philosophical speculation coupled with the theory of harmony, rhythm and metrics as a branch of mathematics, unrelated to practical musicianship. Meanwhile, there was both glorification for the virtuoso performer and, at the other extreme, the use of music as a crude background accompaniment to gladiatorial combat. With the growth and spread of Christianity, instrumental music in particular was anathematized—doubtless because of its association with the less pleasant aspects of Roman culture—and for a time even the academic theory of music was felt to be unworthy of study.

In the sixth century, when Boethius and Cassiodorus transmitted the ancient harmonic theory to the Latin West, the spirit of the earlier restrictions prevailed. Medieval thought divided music into three levels with *Musica instrumentalis* ('sounding music', both vocal and instrumental) at the lowest point and *Music mundana* (the 'music of the spheres') at the highest—the music of heaven itself. Musicians too were placed in categories, with the practical music-makers—the cantores—in a relatively lowly position. For it was not considered enough merely to know *how*; it was also important—indeed more important, in cosmic terms—to know *why*. Medieval philosophy regarded the numerical relationships of the harmonic series as a mirror of God's eternal order, and although the Boethian approach recognized the need for the practical as well as the speculative in music, it was the theory of 'number made audible' which lay behind all academic study of music, and which made the *musicus* ('he to whom belongs the ability to judge') more valued than the *cantor*. The curriculum of medieval universities was based upon the Seven Liberal Arts in two divisions: the *Trivium,* which consisted of Grammar, Dialectic and Rhetoric, and the *Quadrivium* of Geometry, Arithmetic, Astronomy and Music. Although 'Music' may have included some knowledge of plainsong (and, of course, as a means of transmitting the corpus of the chant, singing was taught in the monastic schools), in the main 'Music' meant a theoretical knowledge of acoustics.

The division between theory and practice persisted, so that later in the Middle Ages we find a number of practical treatises emerging in parallel with those of a speculative nature modelled on Boethius. The practical 'manuals' were directed principally at singers and at the correct performance of liturgical music. In one of the most famous of these books, Guido d'Arezzo points out: '... I have simplified my treatment for the sake of the young, in this not following Boethius, whose treatise is useful to philosophers but not to singers' (from Guido of Arezzo, *Epistola de ignoto cantu,* quoted (in translation) in Oliver Strunk, *Source Readings in Music History,* Faber, 1952, p. 125).

Throughout the sixteenth and seventeenth centuries in Europe the Church, both Catholic and Protestant, continued to provide musical training for its singers, and in secular life it was increasingly anticipated that educated people should have musical skills. The rise in status of music-*making* had some influence in schools and in sixteenth-century Britain there were educators, such as Sir Thomas Elyot and Richard Mulcaster, who were prepared to argue a place for music in the curriculum—though largely as a relaxation from more serious studies. Yet there were still plenty of people, then and later, who continued to see music as a wholly frivolous occupation and certainly not an area for serious study; an attitude which was not without influence during the eighteenth and nineteenth centuries and was effective in persuading many that music deserved no more recognition than as a 'polite accomplishment' for the upper classes. For example, the philosopher John Locke (1693) states: 'a good Hand upon some Instruments, is by many People mightily valued. But it wastes so much of a young Man's time, to gain but a moderate Skill in it; and engages often in such odd Company, that many think it much better spared' (from *Some Thoughts Concerning Education*, Fifth edition, 1705 ¶ 197). And Obadiah Walker (1699) agreed with Locke that music took too much time to learn and 'little to lose it'.

Nevertheless, in England the establishment of universal education during the middle years of the nineteenth century awakened a new interest in music's educative potential. The poet Matthew Arnold was a Board of Education inspector, and in his 1863 report he recommended music as a means by which teachers could 'get entrance to the minds of children more easily than they might through literature'. Much of the impetus for music in schools from this time on into the early decades of the twentieth century was derived from educators such as Jean-Jacques Rousseau, Pestalozzi, and Froebel—all of whom advocated the use of music as a means to an end in a child's general education.

Although extensively involved with music, and active as an amateur composer, Rousseau had no formal training in musical techniques. Perhaps because of this he was able to bring a fresh and uninhibited mind to bear on questions of music and its role in education. Certainly, through his writings on these subjects, he exerted great and lasting influence. In many ways his theories were well in advance of his time and for the most part were developed from a 'back to nature' premise ('Retournons à la nature'). In his famous 'Treatise of Education', *Emilius* (Edinburgh, 1763 (first English edition), Vol. 1, p. 222. *et seq.*), he outlines a scheme for instructing his pupil (Émile) which stressed the need for substantial experience of singing and composition (the latter presumably by way of improvisation) prior to instruction in music reading:

... you should endeavour to render his voice clear, equal, easy, and sonorous; and his ear susceptible to measure and harmony: but nothing more. Imitative and theatrical music is above his capacity. I would not have him even make use of words in singing; or if it were required, I would endeavour to compose songs on purpose for him which should be adapted to his years, interesting and equally simple with his ideas.

It will be easily imagined, that, as I am not very pressing to teach him to write, I shall not be more so to make him learn music. No, we shall not require him to pay a very earnest attention to any thing, nor be in too much haste to exercise his judgement on signs.

At this point Rousseau admits to some doubts because in singing 'we make use of the ideas of others' and 'to express the ideas of others, it is necessary we should first be able to read them'. Nevertheless, recognizing that music depends first and foremost upon what we can hear, he writes:

... in the first place, instead of reading, we may hear them, [the ideas of others] and a tune is more faithfully conveyed to us by the ear than by the eye. Add to this, that to understand music, it is not sufficient to be able to play or sing; we must learn to compose at the same time, or we shall never be masters of this science. Exercise your little musician at first in regular, harmonious periods; join them afterwards together by a very simple modulation, and at length mark their different relations by correct punctuation, which is done by a good choice of stop or cadence. Above all things avoid any thing fantastic and whimsical, nor ever affect the pathetic in your expression; but choose a melody always easy and simple, always naturally arising from the chords essential to the tune, and indicating the bass in such a manner as that he may easily perceive and follow it: for, to form the voice and the ear, it is to be observed, he should never sing to any instrument but the harpsichord.

Later the need for theory to supplement practice troubles Rousseau again and he describes a sol-fa method 'for the better distinction of the notes'. Interestingly Rousseau's is a moveable-doh system—as we should use today—and he spends some time criticizing the French for having 'strangely perplexed these distinctions' with the fixed-doh principle! But in the end Rousseau is adamant that, whatever method is adopted, the pupil should not become so weighed down by the technicalities that he loses sight of the simple joys of music-making:

... you may teach him music in whatever manner you please, provided you only let him consider it as an amusement.

Both Pestalozzi (1746–1827) and Froebel (1782–1852) believed in a similarly simple approach that valued music primarily for what it could contribute to the general education of children rather than for its potential to make 'some sort of artist out of every pupil'. And they were convinced that singing—for Pestalozzi in particular, the singing of national songs—could have beneficial and harmonizing effects upon character.

The pleasures and benefits of vocal music also found a place in popular (adult) education during the nineteenth century. Choral singing caught the public imagination, inspired in the first instance by the sight-singing movement of John Pyke Hullah (1812–84). Even here music education could not avoid controversy! Hullah held classes for large numbers of people in a specially-built hall in London where (ignorant no doubt of Rousseau's strong words on the subject!) he taught the French fixed-doh system—and had great success. Many people who would never have thought they could acquire the skill, mastered the elements of sight-reading and grew to enjoy singing. But the Hullah method had severe limitations and was eventually displaced—not without a struggle—by the moveable-doh 'Tonic Solfa' developed by John Curwen and Sarah Glover. As so often happens in such controversies, the musical pros and cons were to some extent overshadowed by other matters. The more conservative musicians favoured Hullah, who was an inspector of music in teacher training colleges and seems to have used that position to wield influence.

Furthermore, the Curwen supporters were despised for their connection with non-conformist religion and the Board Schools, and were accused of lacking musical taste. In the end the Curwen system—intervallic and basically the method promoted by Guido d'Arezzo 800 years previously—was seen to be superior and more easily adaptable to music with complex key changes. Yet in spite of the argument and ill-feeling it generated, this was a genuine breakthrough in music education for the majority. It enabled vast numbers of people, who by social position would normally have been barred from access to musical training, to become proficient sight-readers. The dissemination of this skill in effect brought into being a new class of musical people and stimulated the enormous rise in the popularity of choral singing which was so characteristic of the late nineteenth century and early twentieth century.

Developing the curriculum

Understandably, those whose task it was to develop the *school* curriculum seized upon tonic-solfa as a means of extending the scope of music in education. The modulator became an essential piece of equipment for class music teaching, and the hope was that if sight-singing could be taught to *all* children as effectively as it had been taught to many adults there would be a clear line of continuation from schools into the ever more numerous choral societies, inculcating through music a love and understanding of 'higher things'. It was a convincing argument though, as we have seen, children generally lacked the motivation of those who attended the adult classes. For the adults, learning to sight-sing opened doors a world away from the drudgery of the daily routine, and produced a widespread enthusiasm similar to that which has characterized the brass band movement. For children in school, however, the modulator was just another 'subject'; symbols and formulae to be learned—possibly with difficulty and often, no doubt, out of fear rather than pleasure.

The universities went their own way, basing their music degrees in the main upon musicological study and 'academic' composition (orchestration, species counterpoint and fugue). Independently the Colleges of Music developed their own style of instruction, which for the most part concentrated upon performance. Although there was serious professional composition teaching in these institutions, most students, during the last years of the nineteenth century and throughout the first part of the twentieth century, went through a somewhat unreal study of written techniques—what came to be known as 'paper work'; harmony and counterpoint according to 'rules', the product bearing very little relationship to genuine music in any recognizable style. Interestingly, Ebenezer Prout (1835–1909), Professor of Composition at the Royal Academy of Music and later Professor in Dublin, a prolific writer of books on musical theory, whose name has so often (and quite wrongly) been associated with the 'dry as dust' approach, had a refreshingly enlightened view of these techniques. In his *Double Counterpoint and Canon* (§ 311), written in 1891, he makes a scathing comment about those who teach counterpoint as though it were a series of mathematical equations. Once more we seem to hear an echo of Rousseau when Prout writes: 'Music is meant for the ear, not for the eye; however ingenious these puzzles may be, they are not music.'

In time the influence of the universities was felt in the school curriculum through the matriculation examination and, later, the General School Certificate. These examinations were used to test a candidate's potential for higher education. Applied to music they never attracted large numbers of candidates, a situation which changed hardly at all when GSC and HSC gave way to O and A levels at the beginning of the 1950s; and it remains much the same today. The areas examined have normally concentrated on topics in music history (generally European and within a time span of about 300 years—from 1600–1900 or thereabouts), together with elementary training in harmony and counterpoint on established ('traditional') models. The conservatoires' influence came mainly through the more wide-ranging development of graded instrumental examinations administered by The Associated Board of the Royal Schools of Music (with a corresponding series controlled by Trinity College of Music). These examinations have encouraged countless youngsters to persevere with piano playing and have stimulated many thousands more to take up orchestral instruments—an important factor in the growth of school orchestras and county youth orchestras, as we can see when we observe the dramatic rise in the standard of instrumental playing among young people since the end of the Second World War. Exciting and valuable as these developments have been, their influence upon music in the general curriculum of schools, both primary and secondary, has been two-edged. On the one hand there is little doubt that higher academic standards for music in public examinations coupled with an increase in performing standards have added to music's status in secondary education. But these same features have, by their very nature, tended to exclude large numbers of young people who do not have conventional musical talents and have no intention of pursuing music as a career. At the same time, the areas of music represented by the examinations have become major influences in teachers' designs for music in the secondary curriculum as a whole, which in turn has to some extent conditioned musical activity in the primary schools. The understandable demands from university music departments that undergraduates should be proficient in basic musical techniques and have a reasonable general knowledge of music history on entry to higher education has strengthened the predictive nature of 'O' and 'A' level, but this has then become the tail that wags the dog, with the result that the place of music in general education has never been completely thought through. Even where attempts have been made to expand the scope of music in the curriculum, the influence of skills and accomplishments ultimately the province of the minority has generally prevailed, so that the ideals of majority participation have had to give way to the interests of the few.

Oddly, music seems to have suffered more than most curriculum subjects from the problems of ensuring adequate preparation for the specialists while not losing sight of an obligation to others. This is certainly not for want of trying. If we return to the early years of the present century we can see the diverse background of music education in the nineteenth century and earlier forming the starting point for a whole range of strategies, methods and systems for the expansion of music in schools.

Early twentieth century

A programme of work devised in the 1920s by Margaret Donington, music mistress at the Mary Datchelor School, Camberwell was specifically designed to expand music in the school. The scheme, which was worked out in great detail for an age-range of 4–18 and covered basic musical concepts, notation, music history, vocal and instrumental performance, and creative work, received widespread recognition for its attention to the needs of the majority. Appearing first as a series of articles it was subsequently published in book form (*Music throughout the Secondary School/A Practical Scheme*, OUP, 1932). At the head of her introductory chapter Margaret Donington places a quotation from [Edward?] Dickinson: 'The teacher's business ... is to help prepare the eager, joyous, personal acceptance of music as a living reality.' And she ends her book with the following:

Conclusion

The aim of the whole scheme is to treat Music as an ordinary class subject such as History. Every girl takes it as a matter of course whether she is gifted or not. The classes are *not* graded ... There is no attempt at specialising in any direction whatsoever—the aim is rather to place within the reach of each child the opportunity of understanding and appreciating every side of the Art of Music.

The scheme drew unqualified support from the headmistress, Dorothy Brock, who in her Foreword to the book writes enthusiastically about the development of music in the school curriculum 'in the last twenty years':

From being an accomplishment for a young lady, a soft option for the dull girl, or an expensive extra for the technically gifted, it is slowly but surely winning recognition as a part of the education of a normal girl (and in some quarters also of a normal boy).

Margaret Donington's work is then commended because:

... nothing here described requires for its accomplishment a lavish expenditure of money, or impossibly ideal conditions, or extravagant timetable allowance ...

That has an unfortunately familiar ring to it! But it is clear what is meant and, to be fair, the paragraph continues—with sound educational reasoning:

This is Music as a form subject, taught in class to every girl, not a course of specialised instruction for a selected few.

By 1931 and the publication of the Hadow Report (Board of Education, 1931), music had certainly become a topic for serious educational discussion:

The educative value of music has been often overlooked in the past. It has been sometimes mistakenly regarded as a soft relaxation ... If taught on sound lines it should react upon the whole work of a school. In no subject is concentration more necessary; in no subject is there so much scope for the disciplined and corporate expression of the emotions ... (p. 188)

High priority was given to the arts. They were linked with physical culture in the belief that 'the simultaneous development of physical and mental powers in harmonious interplay' produces 'poise and balance ... qualities ... intimately connected with intelligence and character,' and, it was stressed, 'Dancing, singing, music, the drama, are the means of cultivating them.'

Frequently the pages of the Report read like an inspired statement of belief:

... the curriculum should not be loaded with inert ideas and crude blocks of fact ... It must be vivid, realistic, a stream in motion, not a stagnant pool ...

a plan that has the arts at its centre:

Of music we need say nothing here except to indicate that we count it among the indispensable elements of the primary school curriculum. The subject enjoys a long established place in primary education, and its teaching in the schools shows a response to the present revival of the art as a constituent of the cultural life of the nation.

Neither does it stop at such general support; there is a substantial section of detailed proposals, together with comment on and evaluation of methods in vogue at the time. For example, the following in which we have italicized the key points:

The importance of good music teaching in the early stages cannot be too strongly urged. The facts of daily life do not form a corrective to poor teaching in music, as in some other branches of the curriculum, and unskilled teaching in the early stages may quite easily blunt the musical sense *that nearly all children possess* ...

The artist is strong in the child and it is to this side of the child's nature that the teacher should appeal...

Of recent years many experiments have been made in the teaching of the more theoretical part of music to young children. Many artificial aids in the form of pictorial representations of the stave have been found to be of doubtful value ...

The subject of musical appreciation has lately occupied the attention of teachers, perhaps to the detriment of other branches of music teaching. At first undue emphasis was laid upon the importance of programme music or music with a story, or music that 'painted a picture'. Other and more important aspects were overlooked. The best results obtained when the children *have accomplished the music with movement* ...

... if the child in the early stages learns a considerable number of songs of a simple character he has more chance of developing the musical sense. These songs should be carefully chosen. A song is not necessarily good, or even appropriate for children because it is childish. Good clear melody and good poetry are essentials ... The importance of inculcating a sound melodic taste cannot be over-estimated. For this purpose *the use of national and folk songs is strongly recommended*. The melodic directness of the songs makes an instant appeal to the child, and forms an *instinctive and never failing criterion in after life*. (pp. 186–8)

The Hadow Committee drew much of its own inspiration from the writings of educationists such as John Dewey, whose own credo, 'Learning is active; it involves a reaching out of the mind,' may well have informed the Report's emphasis upon 'doing'—as opposed to the passive reception of facts. Thus music is frequently linked with dancing and with Eurhythmics. The watchword is 'participation'; providing something that everyone can do. And running through the entire Report is the recognition of our obligation to average children; the majority of children.

The twenties and thirties saw a great deal of enthusiastic experimentation with music teaching methods, most of it directed towards the younger child but almost all of it in some way concerned with extending the scope of music in education. In its detailed comments, the Hadow Report reflects this mosaic of different approaches. There was, for example, the percussion band which had much to recommend it, even with quite small children: a whole class could participate, it would draw upon and develop a child's natural rhythmic sense, it could be used to teach the elements of notation and ensemble playing, and—because the principal melodic and harmonic material was played by the teacher on the piano—it could be a way of ensuring that children heard, and perhaps remembered, some of the greatest melodies in the classical repertoire.*

As with the percussion band, so with folk songs and national songs; they could be seen as worthwhile experience in themselves but (and, in the view of some teachers, possibly more important) they could lead to the acquisition of musical knowledge. They were in effect 'a method' for teaching music:

Such songs may form the basis of the early teaching of what is known as 'musical appreciation'. Elementary ideas of form, melodic outline, rhythmic balance, and climax can be learned from them. Every child should be steeped in the strong British idiom and musical flavour of these songs. Nothing can form a sounder foundation for a musical education. (p. 187)

The development of the gramophone and broadcasting gave impetus to the 'Music Appreciation' movement, which by the late 1920s had spawned an extensive literature but was also at the centre of an 'all-or-nothing' controversy, something of which may be glimpsed in the following extract from a chapter 'On Listening to Music' from John E. Borland's *Musical Foundations/A Record of Musical Work in Schools and Training Colleges, and a Comprehensive Guide for Teachers of School Music* (OUP, 1927):

The last fifteen years have witnessed a veritable revolution in the teaching of music, and one important part of this revolution has consisted in the establishment of the subject known as 'The Appreciation of Music' in a large proportion of schools of all types ... There has been a danger that teachers may neglect the thorough ear-training in favour of the 'appreciation' lessons because the latter appears to offer more immediate enjoyment both for teacher and for pupil. One supervisor of music in America calmly announced a few years ago that he was going to turn sight-singing out of the schools in his district and to teach the children to 'love music'. One wonders if such rubbish could be talked about any other subject. Imagine English children being taught to 'love' Shakespeare without learning to spell and read English. (p. 491)

The writings of Dr Thomas Yorke Trotter—notably *The Making of Musicians* (1922) and *Music and Mind* (1924)—had considerable influence at this time. His 'system for the practical education of children in the elements of music' had much in common with the methods of Émile Jaques-Dalcroze. Both made extensive use of improvisation and the child's natural feeling for rhythm, balance and phrase-length, and both were, in a sense, the direct descendants of Rousseau's dictum: 'The sound first, and then the sign'. Subsequently Yorke

---

* The present writer can remember quite clearly taking part (on triangle!) in a classroom percussion band in the infant department of a London primary school in the mid-1930s. One piece in particular comes to mind; Schubert's famous *Marche Militaire* which the teacher played on the piano while the band added its rhythmic accompaniment. The Schubert tune remained strongly in the memory, to be identified many years later.

Trotter's ideas were taken up by Gladys Puttick, who in her own work with children and in her training of teachers made an important impact upon music in schools in the 1940s and 1950s.

Meanwhile instrumental playing in class, from having been primarily rhythmic (i.e. the percussion band) took a new direction with the introduction of recorder playing. A similar development, though on a less extensive scale, was the making and playing of bamboo pipes; an idea which had begun in America in the twenties and was fostered in some British schools throughout the thirties, largely through the energies of Margaret James, the founder of the Pipers' Guild.

Music in schools also received encouragement and stimulus from composers. Ralph Vaughan Williams, who in association with Cecil Sharp had done so much to promote the singing of folk songs in schools, also took an interest in the Pipers' Guild and composed for bamboo pipes. While abroad, two major schemes of work were brought to fruition; the *Schulwerk* of Carl Orff (again linking music and movement) and the 'choral concept' devised by the Hungarian composer Zoltán Kodály. Orff and Kodály have had influence on music education in Britain and America, both directly—through the translation of their work—and indirectly by way of other schemes which imitate and adapt the originals. Notable has been the widespread adoption of the 'Orff' classroom instruments, independently of the musical materials in the six books of the *Schulwerk*. Indeed, many of the teachers who use the instruments and employ the basic elements of Orff's ideas have not studied the approach in any detail.

Although a large proportion of the ideas and methods developed between 1920 and 1955 were designed mainly for primary schools, almost all of them had some influence upon general music teaching in secondary schools. The establishment of [secondary] modern schools after the 1944 Education Act presented teachers in the secondary sector with the challenge of working without the incentive of public examinations. In such circumstances the arts and crafts could have a new and vital role to play. With a background of many years of experiment and exploration in music education methods, including a substantial literature and any number of successful published schemes of work, it might have been expected that by the late 1950s we should see music in the very forefront of curriculum development. In fact, the opposite was the case. Although there was quite a lot of very creditable music activity in schools, there was also a certain amount of confusion. Music had not flourished *within the curriculum* as it might have done, and it was clearly not reaching a very large number of pupils. The severely subject-orientated curriculum of the grammar schools, together with the demands of GCE, generally worked against music, and the introduction of GCE to the secondary modern schools soon produced a similar situation there. 'General' music classes tended to feature less and less, so that by 1963 the Newsom Report noted that more than half the schools in the survey had no provision for any kind of music, and that 'music is the subject most frequently dropped from the curriculum in boys' and mixed schools ... the only subject in the practical group for which one period a week is common' (DES 1963. See particularly paragraphs 412–20.) Newsom commented too on the shortage of *suitably* qualified teachers for music:

... not all music teachers who are highly qualified themselves are able to bridge the gap between the popular enthusiasms and the much more varied and demanding forms of music to which they rightly feel the school should be introducing the pupils. It takes a particular skill to use that initial interest, and without rejecting what the young people have spontaneously chosen, to sharpen perceptions and extend capacities for enjoyment over a wider field. (para. 416)

The Report also revealed the disadvantages under which many secondary music teachers were working (criticism which may be applicable even now):

... music is frequently the worst equipped and accommodated subject in the curriculum ... Of all the 'practical' subjects, it had the least satisfactory provision. Equipment is often similarly inadequate ... the teacher has to begin with virtually nothing and build up very slowly through the years, with his equipment supplied by small grudging instalments, often of poor quality. (paras 418 and 419)

Paradoxically, this was a period of growth for selective extracurricular music activities:

there are the individual schools, or whole areas where music flourishes, extending beyond the classroom to choirs, orchestras, brass bands, concerts ... (para. 413)

But as a curriculum subject, even in the primary schools, music had not kept pace. The Plowden Report (DES, 1967) acknowledged much worthwhile progress, yet at the same time found 'the present position' unsatisfactory; something that would have 'to be tackled systematically and resolutely'. (para. 689)

The climate of opinion was 'favourable to musical education' but equipment and timetabling were still major problems; the teaching of notation was not sufficiently related to active music making—'... it must be functional, not theoretical'—and, significantly, 'The planning of music as a creative subject lags behind work in language and the visual arts and crafts'. (para. 692 (c) and (d))

This last criticism is particularly surprising, for, as we have seen, 'creative work' was a crucial part of class music training for Donington and others forty or fifty years before Plowden, and rhythmic and melodic improvisation were central in the schemes of Dalcroze, Yorke Trotter, and Orff. What had gone wrong?

Ironically the answer may lie with the emphasis given to musical *activity*. It is true that we learn by doing, and music can have no meaning apart from its sounds. Moreover, to aim to involve all young people, of whatever age, aptitude and ability, in the direct experience of making music is surely laudable. But like every other art form, music alters with the passing of time and with changes in social outlook. Methods and lesson content appropriate in the 1920s become outdated and need at least a moderate amount of adaptation for children in the 1960s, 70s, 80s and beyond. The Plowden Report hinted at this and made some suggestions for new techniques (para. 692 (c) and (d)). What it did not sufficiently stress was the need for teachers to have a clear view of music's overall function within a programme of education *before* they started to work out specific methods and strategies. Understandably, the tendency has always been for us to skip the philosophy and go straight to the 'meat'; the 'things to do'. With hindsight, and fifty years on, we may now see that the Hadow Report provided all the stimulus needed for us to interpret and reinterpret its observations. The essential recommendations lay not so much in the detailed discussion of subject methods but in the underlying principles of its visionary general chapters. Had these been held firmly in the forefront of every music teacher's mind it is possible that the lagging behind which Plowden noted might not have occurred. Moreover, had the educational rationale for music in the primary school been clearly understood and strongly maintained, the position of music in the *secondary* curriculum could now be much more secure than it is.

1960 and beyond

There have, of course, been many heartening developments in primary school music in the years since Plowden. The range of activities is wide, as is so admirably indicated in the 1975–7 survey of primary schools (DES, 1978). Even so, in that document it is still the 'things to do' which receive most attention, and one may look in vain for clear indications that all these exciting and enjoyable activities are indeed the diversification of an *Urlinie* of educational principle which is understood by everyone and which will be capable of *re*-interpretation and *re*-development as the years go by. But for the time being, at any rate, the inspectors' view of primary school music is a sunny one and full of hope.

Much less encouraging is the corresponding survey of the secondary sector (DES, 1979). If the picture drawn by the Inspectorate is a characteristic one (and we must assume that it is), then examples of the diminishing role of music in general education are not hard to find:

... the price usually paid for the introduction of a second language into the second and/or third years is the loss or severe reduction of contact with the creative/aesthetic area of the curriculum (art, music and the crafts) for the able pupils concerned. (p. 19, 3.12)

In the timetabling of options music quickly becomes the exclusive province of those who receive help and stimulus outside school (e.g. those having instrumental lessons):

... music ... tended to be chosen by well-motivated pupils, *producing groups of less diversity.* (p. 27, 9.1)

Whatever the reason, groups of fewer than 12 pupils occurred most often in additional second languages *and in music*, in all types of school ... (p. 33, 11.2)

This is also a subject where pupils with particular aptitude are likely to be given special attention, perhaps at the expense of continuing general classes for the majority. For example, *Aspects of secondary education*[*] notes that:

Talent of a particular kind was most frequently mentioned with regard to sports and athletics. *Next came music.* (Appendix 4, 2)

with regard to the identification of pupils with particular talents ... examinations of the Associated Board or Royal Academy of Music were mentioned ... (Appendix 4, 3)

But only about 8 per cent of the schools visited included non-examination music in the fourth year. Where the survey does specify types of musical activity it is the 'out of class provision' of 'choral and instrumental music' with which 'The formal curricular programme was ... supplemented'. (*Aspects*, p. 258, 5.6) It is to be hoped that, at least in the school described there, the choral and instrumental activities produced useful and exciting feed-back into the class lessons. Unfortunately, details are not given. In many schools there is often no connection between 'in class' and 'out of class' music. Indeed, in the secondary sector, unless we take very determined steps to prevent it, the law of diminishing returns works with a vengeance as far as music is concerned. The more we exploit the opportunities for extracurricular ensembles and encourage the talented pupils to increase their skills, the less spin-off there may be within the curriculum as a whole. As we have seen, other pressures may force teachers to give extra attention to the musically talented and so slant the programme towards the 'out of class' activities anyway. Where this happens it is not uncommon to find that, far from causing others to want to join in,

---

[*] DES, 1979

musical activities assume an exclusive appearance, with a correspondingly weakening effect upon general class music.

Obviously, it is easy enough to fall into the trap of thinking that, because we commonly refer to choirs, orchestras and bands as 'extracurricular', they are not part of the curriculum at all: they are indeed part of the school curriculum, and an important one. But at the same time, we cannot ignore the fact that they cater for a minority, and if we allow our efforts on behalf of that smaller group to impair what we are able to do for other pupils, we should at least recognize this as an educational decision, even if it is not one with which we feel completely happy. There are, for example, areas of the country where the youth orchestra figures so large in the Authority's view of 'school' music that individual teachers can be forgiven for thinking that their prime duty seems to be to ensure the continuing supply of suitable recruits for the orchestra. This should not be taken as a criticism of 'extracurricular' music, nor of youth orchestras (about which we shall have more to say later on), but it is an indication of the continuing state of indecision about the place of music in the curriculum and there is no doubt that some teachers are puzzled by it. For example, in one Authority with approximately 75,000 pupils in its secondary schools and a justifiably renowned youth orchestra, the Project met teachers who felt that insufficient attention was given to the needs of class music teaching. It seemed to them that a decision had been taken to give priority to the orchestra, and that the LEA regarded that group of 100 players as the main justification for music in education. So, in a sense, it might be argued that 'school' music was geared to 1 in every 750 pupils. The point is that, whether or not this was actually so, there was the impression of a bias in that direction.

One of the strongest indicators of a tendency to emphasize selective 'out of class' music-making at the expense of 'in class' work with the whole ability range is the *Aspects* survey itself. In the whole of this 307-page document (approximately 60,000 words and more than 60 statistical tables) there are only 10 very minor references to music, and in the main these point to specialism in music rather than to the development of a broader 'general curriculum' approach.

GCE, CSE, and 16+

Currently the discussion is again focused upon examinations, in particular the proposals for a single examination at 16+. Inevitably this has aroused much controversy, and music teachers have not been slow to express their feelings on the subject. Certainly, 16+ raises questions which, if they are not satisfactorily answered, will only aggravate the indecision about music's education role.

Examinations evaluate educational processes; they also *create* educational processes. The implications of any form of assessment are inescapable, for whatever system we adopt it must influence curriculum design and content and teaching method. Examinations *compare*. They compare students with 'norms', students with other students, students present with students past. Comparisons are odious—and that is the root of our problem!

Matriculation was needed for university entrance so, by arrangement, the General Certificate of Education—intended primarily as a summation of 'general schooling'—was allowed to carry with it 'matriculation exemption' if the candidate achieved the necessary number of passes at one attempt. This was then seen to create an unfortunate comparison between those who achieved matriculation exemption and those who 'only' got a School Certificate. The change to GCE modified this and made it possible to collect individual subjects. Even so, there was still the vast majority of pupils, those who attended secondary modern schools, who had no opportunity to take any kind of public examination from school. Some LEAs devised their own 'school leaving certificate' to encourage the secondary modern pupils, but this only emphasised the differences between secondary modern and grammar. So GCE was introduced to the modern schools. Immediately this created another unfortunate comparison. Many of the secondary modern pupils were achieving no more than one or two GCE 'O' levels, whereas their grammar school contemporaries were generally taking nine or ten subjects and, on the whole, realizing higher grades. Even the development of comprehensive schools did little to remove the stigma of the 'less able' when it came to GCE. So the Certificate of Secondary Education was devised; an examination in which everyone gets a certificate.

The implications are now very clear; GCE is the predictive examination, the direct descendant of Matriculation, while CSE is a summative examination, intended to give candidates a sense of achievement at the close of their school career. (Admittedly the position can be complicated by the attention which employers may or may not pay to these qualifications.) But there is also the unavoidable comparison. Out of renewed efforts to improve the entire assessment process, and if possible to avoid the implication of comparison between school students of different abilities, the idea of a single examination has been born. But how do we devise an examination for everyone that will be a useful prognosis of some students' potential for more advanced work and, simultaneously, act as a meaningful record of achievement for students of quite different ability who are unlikely to want to go further? Apart from the obvious problem of the very wide range of ability which must be *suitably* tested, there are far-reaching implications for curriculum content.

Music presents a particularly pertinent example of this problem. It is regrettably one of those subjects about which it has sometimes been said we have 'made important what is examinable instead of making examinable what is important'. That is, perhaps, a trifle glib, since certain types of skill are essential for those who intend to pursue conventional musical studies even if those skills are not in themselves of the essence of musical experience. Nevertheless, as far as music's place in general education is concerned, trends in recent years have been towards a much broader view of music. Where development along these lines has taken place, it is now clear that the range of work produced can be very wide indeed. Were we to dodge the issue of assessment with such work and continue to limit 'examinable' music to those things which are most conveniently tested (i.e. more or less 'the mixture as before'), we should perpetuate yet another unfortunate comparison between 'real' (= examinable) music and everything else. If that happened we could find ourselves in just the same position as the unfortunate Mr Arthur whose story was told at the start of this chapter. He thought he had been teaching 'singing', only to find that what he had done was not considered 'real' singing.

Yet there is much to be hopeful about. The DES and Schools Council have published their declarations of good intent for the future of the curriculum and for the 16+ examination, (DES/Welsh Office, 1981 and Schools Council, 1981) and although it is to be regretted that neither paper does much more than pay lip-service to the place of the arts, the principle is clear enough. Coupled with what we have learned over the past ten years from our attempts to 'refresh' class music teaching and to find new approaches suited to the changed and changing attitudes of young people, the DES and Schools Council ideals could provide just the sort of stimulus we need to make sense of music in schools. The Project *Music in the Secondary School Curriculum* observed a great variety of music-making with many hopeful signs for the future. Some of this work is described in the chapters which follow. There are topics which have been at the centre of vigorous debate among music teachers; a debate which continues, sometimes resulting in unfortunate misunderstandings, sometimes producing bitterness and polarized arguments. The tendency to concentrate upon 'things to do' is still strong, but there is also a much greater awareness of the need to seek out and discuss sound educational reasons to guide decisions about the music curriculum. The establishment of regional centres for music curriculum development has assisted this process and could do much to bridge the gaps between differing viewpoints as well as drawing the primary and secondary sectors closer together. And if we can distance ourselves, for a short time, from the 'What-do-I-do-next-Monday-morning?' problem, we may also take heart from the evidence of the past. For in spite of all the arguments about what aspects of music are appropriate, virtually every scheme for general education, from Plato to the latest DES pamphlet, has included music somewhere. If that is what people want, then that is a really hopeful sign.

Music in school and society

From *Music in the Secondary School Curriculum: trends and developments in class music teaching* (Cambridge University Press, 1982), 20–30

The many sounds of music

Music in school has to serve many different purposes—just as it does in society at large. It offers relaxation and entertainment; it supports and integrates with other experiences (art, dance, theatre, film); it can give us a sense of achievement through the mastery of skills and provide a satisfying group identity (through membership of a choir, an orchestra, a rock band or whatever). Music enlightens and inspires; it can give pleasure or it can disturb. Whether we play or sing, invent or listen, music may excite and move us in many ways and for many different reasons. All these experiences can in some sense be said to be educative.

School also serves a variety of purposes, not all of them 'academic' in the conventional sense but all in some way potentially educative. There could be a number of answers to the question 'What is school for?' but whatever basis we adopt, the aims are surely the same for *all* children; to help them make the best use of their particular talents in school and later in adult life.

Although we would probably all acknowledge the educative nature of the total school experience, we may also have a notion of a centrally educational curriculum which we regard as the real core of schooling. What goes into (or is left out of) the curriculum is significant. As we have seen, the definition and development of the secondary sector curriculum has been fairly haphazard. Although there seems not to have been much doubt about the basics, literacy and numeracy, in areas beyond those basic skills, curriculum content is largely the result of opinion and historical accident. Moreover, as far as these other areas are concerned, we have been influenced largely by the procedures adopted for those already agreed 'basics'. Rarely have we questioned this or asked ourselves whether the system which has grown up is always appropriate for subjects which involve different ways of 'coming to know'. There would appear to have been an unwritten assumption that all subjects worthy of a place in the curriculum should be seen to operate and to be studied in the same way, and that the prime task is one of imparting information, inculcating clearly defined skills, and testing to see if the imparting and inculcation has been successful.

Perhaps more than anything else, these assumptions have been responsible for the uncertainty that surrounds the arts in education. Music especially is in a difficult position. By its nature it is intangible, abstract and mysterious. Whereas most people would feel they could understand painting or sculpture (particularly if it is reasonably representational), precisely what is involved in 'understanding' music is for many a mystery in itself. With the apparent complexities of notation on the one hand and exacting instrumental skills on the other, it is small wonder that the general conclusion has been that 'music is what musicians do'—and what non-musicians may listen to. As such it has no obviously useful role in general education. This has been aggravated by the long-standing belief that the most valuable aspects of education are those that express ideas in words or numbers. Obviously books are and always have been important tools in education, but to some extent we have been blinded by discursive prose, by verbal reasoning, rational explanation, and the power of facts and proof. In consequence we have educationally downgraded imagination and feeling, poetry and the non-verbal means of expression—music, painting, dance, and dramatic gesture. These things offer experiences which are essentially different from the world of facts, theory, explanation, measurement and proof, but they are no less important. Our attitudes to the arts in education would appear to flow from this difference in character. The arts are considered to be of lesser importance simply because they are not based upon the same kind of 'evidence' as, for example, history, geography, mathematics and the sciences.

Yet a very large number of people have a *use* for music. It is all around us and in one way or another most of us 'receive' some music almost every day; through radio or television, in the supermarket, in the cinema, in cafés and restaurants, in discos, in church—even in railway stations and in the streets. Some people, with the help of transistor radios and cassette tape-recorders, literally carry their music with them! The extent to which we are attentive to the music or even aware of it in these differing circumstances will vary, of course. Nevertheless, most people would probably acknowledge a use for music more readily than they would recognize the usefulness of painting, sculpture, dance, drama, and poetry. Music, even though it may be no more than a background, does appear to have some significance in our lives. Clearly, then, it should also have a place in school education. But what place?

Should it be the traditional 'academic' study of music as it was developed in the past by the scholars and theorists of the older universities and the conservatoires? In school that would surely have limited application. Those techniques were designed primarily for students who are already 'far gone' in music. Even if we extend that approach to include various vocal and instrumental activities, unless we are prepared to break through the whole theoretical basis of music and admit many aspects of music-making which did not find a place in the traditional university/music college courses, the appeal will still be a limited one, leaving out a vast amount of the music most of us meet day by day. Yet school is a microcosm of society, and if education is to meet the needs of those for whom it is designed it cannot afford to pretend that some things do not exist. If music has something to offer to all pupils ought we not to recognize music as it is—with all its variety of style and purpose—and not take arbitrary decisions about what we can admit into the classroom and what we must, for 'academic' reasons, reject?

The demands on the music teacher

If we decide that we cannot accept in school and in the general curriculum music 'as it is', may this not raise some questions about our role as *school-teachers*? For example, can we justify limiting the application of music, in the main, to those pupils who are already motivated (such as those who are having private instrumental lessons) and for whom 'music' can safely be encompassed within O and A level syllabuses and the lists of instrumental 'Grade' examinations? Is this how we see music in education—apart, possibly, from some general class lessons in the lower school principally of a 'cultural' nature; singing and listening to standard repertoire works on the gramophone? As an experience of music this has obvious limitations and tends to ignore the interests and potential of a large number of pupils simply because it recognizes only a small area of music activity. Would we be prepared to argue that music in school *must* be limited? That it is a highly specialized field; and that we can only afford time to address ourselves to a very clearly-defined area of musical experience and expertise, regrettably having to ignore those huge areas of music-making which do not have the definition and confirmed 'standing' of the traditional courses of study? Even when we add the participation in bands, orchestras and choirs, a music programme which is geared to the conventionally 'musical' minority (on average not more than 10% of secondary school students) is hard to justify in general curriculum terms. Eyebrows would certainly be raised were we to suggest that for roughly 90 per cent of school students mathematics was more or less irrelevant. But if music doesn't seem to matter like mathematics, perhaps we should accept some of the blame ourselves. For if our curriculum planning has suggested to pupils and colleagues alike that only a limited range of established music is 'suitable' for school, it is hardly surprising that some (perhaps the majority) will not find our musical choice immediately relevant.

For many people 'school music' means 'special occasion music'. The model is in the tradition of the independent public schools where music has often been an 'extra' academically, coming into prominence only once a year as part of the public display of Speech Day or Founder's Day. This is still the most widely accepted image of music even in comprehensive schools. Indeed, quite a few head teachers have been known to defend use of music on the grounds of its 'public relations' value. The appointment of a music teacher carries with it the expectation of a high standard of termly/annual concerts, the occasional Gilbert and Sullivan (or some suitable equivalent: *Oliver* or *West Side Story*), the school band playing at morning assembly, and so on. You do not need a dedicated class music teacher for that kind of work; you *do* need a gifted and skilful musician who can produce publically acceptable music from amateur players and singers. If it is a question of priorities, the general educational values of music (that could be applied in the classroom for the benefit of the majority) may have to give place to demands of a specialized and musically restricted extracurricular programme.

True, it doesn't have to be either/or: it *is* possible to do both things. But it is extremely hard work for the music teacher, and if the unspoken assumption seems to be that the priority is working with the select choral and instrumental groups who will blame us if, almost without considering it, we place the emphasis there? For apart from anything else, it has to be admitted that in the majority of cases our training as music teachers will have disposed us towards the organization and direction of choirs and orchestras, and we should not be musicians worthy of the name if we did not enjoy those activities. Then again, our training will probably have concentrated on standard repertoire works and established music techniques. Very few training courses seem to encourage much in the way of adventurous exploration or experiment, or even a passing acquaintance with music of our own time. The tendency is to stay within the safety of the traditional and the well known. Moreover, those same courses often strongly suggest priorities in such a way as to make choices for us and so 'enclose' our tastes. As a result it may become difficult for the music teacher to remain open-minded or to be enthusiastic about unfamiliar music. His dilemma is that he must be a skilful and perceptive musician, aware that some kinds of music will mean more to him than others, yet at the same time avoiding the inhibiting effects of those preferences.

Listening to music

Furthermore, we are also, to some extent, handicapped by popular misconceptions about our art. Much of the uncertainty about music's place in education probably stems from characteristics of music itself. Although music is constructed with logic, precision and often with incredible ingenuity, to the average person it is not generally clear what it *does*, beyond producing a (possibly) pleasurable effect. The common assumption is that music is an experience we should allow to flow over us, taking charge of our emotions ('... charms to soothe a savage breast', and so on). This may to some extent explain why it is relatively easy to get an audience for a standard repertoire symphony concert but extremely difficult to fill a concert hall if the programme contains new music. It isn't that the audiences necessarily find the familiar works more exciting or musically interesting, but rather that these works are precisely those that most easily permit the 'flow-over' idea to operate. New music, on the other hand, speaks with an unfamiliar voice and therefore forces itself upon our attention. If we are at all uncertain about *how* to listen to music that can be a depressingly uncomfortable experience—whereas it should be a delightful adventure, exciting and invigorating.

Regrettably, instead of helping uninitiated listeners to deal with the *sounds*, the 'specialists' have tried to translate the experience into words. So, audiences are provided with elaborate and scholarly programme notes which seek to explain retrograde canons and '*sui generis* serial procedures'; the kind of thing of which Bernard Levin once wrote, 'The trouble with this stuff is that the people who can understand it don't need it, and those who need it can't understand it'. Such description helps very little, even though we may persuade ourselves that it does. We do not listen to music analytically. Some recent experiments have suggested that the part of the brain which 'processes' musical experience has been developed primarily to deal with *whole* sensations; with the integration of many inputs and overall patterns of relationships rather than the linear, analytic thinking which is needed for speech and language functions, for reading and writing words and for decoding symbols.[1] Although music is a logical process, with the exception of monody its logic is used to combine a number of different parts, patterns and connections which the brain must perceive simultaneously. We have only our ears to help us. Information may possibly, in some roundabout way, motivate us to listen more attentively, but it will not of itself aid us in our perception of music. There is nothing

---

[1] David Galin, 'The Two Modes of Consciousness, and The Two Halves of the Brain', *Symposium on Consciousness*, (Viking Press, 1976), 28–9.

that can be said that will equal the direct experience of the sound. The gateway to musical understanding is to work with sounds; to try things out for ourselves. We have to learn to receive music on its own terms. To be told about music is no substitute.

Unfortunately the damage has been done. Many music teachers, blinded perhaps by the tradition of programme notes, continue to follow the 'soundless' path of old-style musicology. Thus the 'O' level bar-by-bar description (falsely called 'analysis') persists as a norm in music teaching, and, incidentally, does much to support the layman's belief that music is not self-sufficient: to be understood it must be explained or linked with some more tangible and familiar form such as a visual or literary image. Intentionally or not, this view acquired prominence in the Music Appreciation movement with its attendant efforts to find a cultural and 'improving' role for music in schools. But although the aim of this information style of music teaching is a laudable one—to produce more informed and intelligent listeners—it has often had the opposite of the desired effect. Children, aware in an uncomplicated way that the sound of music is something they can get excited about in all its complex simultaneity if they open their ears to it, and sometimes allow their bodies to move to it, are inclined to reject the complicated explanations, the wordy descriptions, discourses and dictated notes, which are so far removed from the first-hand reality of the sound which they *know* and enjoy. Their rejection of what is offered in the music lesson may be interpreted by the teacher as lack of interest or simply philistinism. Unconsciously he gears his lessons to those most likely to respond—the pupils who are receiving instrumental tuition. Before long we are back with the old problem; for the majority the lesson content is irrelevant and 'unreal', confirming their suspicions that music, as it is presented in school, is not for them. Boredom sets in, and music as a 'subject' loses credibility.

Whilst we shall, naturally, want pupils to hear as much music as possible, paradoxically it is the excessive use of recorded music which so often seems to generate a feeling of 'unreality'. We should look closely at the common assumption that music can be passively absorbed from recordings if it is sufficiently explained. Obviously, to the teacher it makes good sense to play records of the music he is introducing to the class. But *he knows the music already,* and when he listens to the recording he automatically makes the necessary 'transfer' which compensates for the missing 'live' elements: the subtle interaction of performers and listeners in the same room recreating the music *together.* For a concert performance is (or should be) a creative act in which the listener plays a part. Listening is an adventure of the imagination in a world of sounds and to anyone who has not been involved with such first-hand participation, to approach music first by way of recorded performances can present difficulties. A recording has about the same amount of value as a photograph of a painting: it is a useful tool for further study if we have already had the direct experience, but without previous and substantial encounter with the reality of music in performance—either as listeners or as singers/instrumentalists—a recording conveys only a small part of the whole. Those of us who cannot remember what life was like without practical musical involvement may find this difficult to accept. It is easy to see why, given that other barriers have been overcome by our explanations and pupils are reasonably motivated to listen, we should think it logical that they should be excited by the music on record as much as if they heard it live. But understanding music is a subtle combination of feelings and circumstances. Teenagers are aware of these things no less than adult concert-goers. A disco, for all its atmosphere, does not attract the same kind of enthusiastic support given to live performance, for example at open-air rock concerts and pop festivals. No matter how good a recording is technically, as an experience of music it is limited. The position becomes even more confused with the increase in music produced 'for the disc' and intended primarily to be heard through loudspeakers. This is the case with a great deal of 'top ten' pop music, and is more obviously so with electroacoustic music produced directly on to tape for which the only 'performer' needed is the engineer who presses the 'play' button of the tape recorder. The difficulty which even some regular concert-goers have in listening to electronic music in concert halls is possibly due to the disturbing absence of the rhythm and movement that is normally visible in the actions of performers. A listener who has had experience as a performer will probably find it easy enough to compensate and immerse himself in the sounds; one who has not may well find the 'music from loudspeakers' experience unsatisfactory.

For although music is fundamentally an aural sensation, in its origins it must surely have been a corporeal art, inseparable from bodily movement and gesture. Public performance before an audience is a relatively modern invention, but at least we *see* the musicians' movements and we feel with them the rhythmic direction of the sound patterns and textures. It is simply unrealistic to assume that, by explaining structure and background history, we can ensure an interaction between recorded music and a cross-section of young people sitting in a classroom having had little or no previous experience of live musical performance.

Music in and out of class

In summary, then, it would appear that, in trying to determine strategies for music in school, we face some fairly daunting problems. Music has significance for almost everybody, but there is evidence that its functions are only imperfectly understood. The popular misconceptions and the historical accidents have been compounded and transmitted through higher academic training to school courses which then seem to have little or nothing to offer the majority of pupils, and even for serious students of music frequently appear to concentrate on the wrong things. The aims of the music teacher may sometimes conflict with the aims of the head teacher. And what passes for music in schools often seems to be out of touch with music as we find it in a multiplicity of circumstances outside school.

Yet since, in one form or another, the experience of music matters to so many people, it is clear that it ought to have a role in education. How then can we capitalize upon the *reality* of musical experience and avoid those methods which have alienated so many young people and left music in a curriculum backwater?

One of the biggest obstacles to progress has been the conventional, limited and relatively fixed image of 'The Musician'. For many of us that image has become a goal in itself and we have seen our task in schools primarily in terms of producing more Musicians (with capital Ms!); an outlook appropriate enough for a specialist music college, perhaps, but unsatisfactory for normal schooling where the curriculum must be constructed with all pupils in mind.

Obviously music can be an 'out of class' selective activity for those who enjoy playing and singing together in choirs, orchestras, brass bands, rock bands, recorder groups, steel bands, or whatever. It can also be a formal subject of study for those who are going to want to take it further into Higher Education and the music profession. We must not neglect those with musical talent: they need our encouragement and we must provide opportunities for them to develop their skills. But they can also contribute in general music lessons if we devise activities in which their special skills can be used alongside the non-specialist work of other pupils, and for the talented pupils this experience could add something of musical worth normally absent from the standard 'O' and 'A' level courses. The core of our work should be in the general class activities offered throughout the school, because music is not exclusively for the classically trained musician, nor even for any one kind of musician! Everyone can respond to it and in some way be involved with it. Music stimulates the imagination; it engages the intellect. And it does this through *sounds*, not through words about sounds.

This is all part of the much needed broader approach; one that sees music as 'an education' and our task 'to educate *through* music'. Our goal should be musical understanding (in the broadest sense) because musical experience, when it is properly understood, is concerned with 'wholeness' and provides an essential complement to the sequential, linear and analytic aspects of schooling. Many writers have identified this need for a balanced education but none has expressed it more succinctly than Robert Witkin in his concept of 'the intelligence of feeling' [*Intelligence of Feeling*], 1974. If we fail to educate the feeling side of understanding, we educate only half the person. Music has a vital role to play here in the complete education of all school pupils, and music teachers are the only people who can provide what is necessary.

Our task is to find a way of working which will accommodate the widest diversity of talent and musical awareness, and which will also allow for changes of direction. For if we concentrate too strongly on one manifestation of music or musical technique, or upon certain kinds of instrumental talent while ignoring all others, we may easily fail to recognize the presence of musical perception in those outside our prescribed area. This may be a considerable challenge for some who teach music in schools. But if we are to see a broader and more successful application of music in education it must be possible for all the pupils to feel that what they experience in a 'music room' is part of the universal *reality* of music.

Any musical styles may find a place in our work. But 'reality' goes much deeper than the outer shell of style and fashion. Classroom work should be based upon music-*making* (performing, improvising, composing) and, in the forefront of all activities, the development of aural sensitivity and awareness. Keeping our ears open to sounds—all sounds, any sounds—is the most basic and therefore the most 'real' of musical skills. From there we can develop activities which are inventive, interpretative, and perceptual in whatever styles, forms and structures are appropriate for the pupils we teach. In this way the gap between music in school and music outside school may be narrowed so that the understanding derived from either sphere will react with the other.

Links across the curriculum

In the chapters which follow we shall examine in greater detail the practical application of these proposals, but before we do, perhaps we should remind ourselves that the problems we face are not confined to music. There has long been widespread misunderstanding about the role of all the arts in education, but progress is being made [see Malcolm Ross, *The Creative Arts*, 1978] with potentially exciting developments such as the establishment of creative arts 'faculties' in some secondary schools.

Unfortunately music has lagged behind and even stood aside from many of these developments. Our colleagues in the visual arts and in dance and drama focused their *educational* sights long ago and struck the right mark. Far from resting on achievements, they have continued to extend their classroom techniques individually and in association. We have a lot to learn from them. Although each art form has its own integrity, there are substantial regions of common ground; good reason for us to try to work together—not necessarily always in integrated or combined arts projects, but certainly in efforts to foster more positive attitudes to the arts in the curriculum.

No-one will take us seriously in these things unless we ourselves treat them as serious matters. That means going a lot further than merely a desire to pass on a limited range of musical skills. It is first and foremost a question of our attitudes to education and to the value—in educational terms—of what we do. Concepts of schooling tell us something about people's aspirations for the kind of world they want to live in. This is where we shall find the most telling clues to our responsibilities in the inevitably new world of tomorrow.

Looking to the future

Technological development of an order that would have been unthinkable seventy years ago has released masses of new information in every branch of knowledge. It has also made possible the extensive information storage, retrieval, and communications systems which underpin yet more scientific and technological advance. Education as a whole must change to meet new social needs, and individual subjects in the curriculum must face problems of content. There is now so much to know! It is difficult to tell where we should begin, what we should include, and what we should leave out. One thing, however, seems certain: we can no longer rely solely on *received* values and inherited wisdom. Such things are important, of course, and must still find a place in the school curriculum, but education must also enable people to develop their own wisdom to deal with totally new problems. It should equip them to take decisions and to use imagination so that they can cope with the rapid change which is characteristic of our time. Education must try in every way possible to provide opportunities for young people to interpret information as well as simply to receive it. For in a society which relies heavily upon technology and automation, the sparks of insight which mark human individuality may easily be extinguished.

There are complications and problems ahead, and all educators should be prepared to face them. Technological developments may produce for some less job satisfaction, and for many as we know already in the more traditional areas of work, widespread unemployment—experiences that can be deadening to the spirit and damaging to self-respect. But, serious as these difficulties are, we should be losing sight of education's function if we allowed them to force out of the curriculum anything that was not obviously going to lead directly to employment. Indeed, as many people have foreseen, it is probable that before long we may have to take a different view altogether and reorientate the curriculum towards a life of greatly extended 'leisure time' instead of the present bias towards a life of 'work' for everyone. One very obvious possibility is to modify our ideas about the meaning of 'work' and 'leisure'.

Education cannot hope to find an answer for every social problem, and it would be a pity if we made that an excuse for ignoring the humanizing influence of certain areas of the curriculum. Whatever the social, financial, and industrial problems we have to face, educators should give high priority to safeguarding independence of thought and those vital opportunities for the development of sensitivity and imagination which go hand in hand with the expression of ideas and feelings. To acknowledge the importance of the individual is not to advocate an anarchic society in which everyone 'does his own thing'. It is simply to recognize our responsibility in helping people to maintain self-respect through self-realization.

Artistic experience offers something special here; something which is not precisely equalled by any other area of the school curriculum. It is not without significance that we speak of 'the creative arts', for although the artist does not have a monopoly of creativity it *is* the principal characteristic of what he does. Because the creative element is so strong in artistic activity it is this, more than anything else, that justifies a place in the curriculum for the visual arts, for dance, for drama, literature, poetry—and for music.

PART IV

INTEREST FROM OVERSEAS

Between the mid 1950s and the early 1970s a new liberalism became evident in the school curriculum, notably in the primary sector, where there was now greater emphasis upon expressive activity in art, dance, drama, and creative writing. This owed much to the pioneering work of Herbert Read and Marion Richardson in the visual arts, Peter Slade in drama, Lisa Ullman in dance, and (later) David Holbrook and Sybil Marshall;[1] and as it developed it began to attract the attention of teachers and administrators in other countries.

Among the first visitors were College Principals and others involved with teacher-education in Scandinavian countries. Initially they were interested in the organization of schooling in Britain, in particular the devolution of responsibility to Local Education Authorities. In so many countries—for geographical reasons—the administration of the school system could not be other than remote and, to a large extent, impersonal. However, in Britain at that time, local responsibility and small catchment areas made it possible for Education Officers and Advisers to give support easily to head teachers and class teachers. It was this, as much as anything, that had helped to promote innovative methods that were clearly *educational*—'leading out' from students' ideas, interests, and sensibilities—and this too caught the imagination of the visitors from overseas.

Links were soon established between like-minded institutions in Britain, Norway, Denmark, and Sweden, and publishers in those countries began to produce translations of English books and articles, subsequently commissioning new writing; a process that continued fruitfully for many years. 'The Pursuit of Reality in Music Education' was written in 1981 for the journal of Landslaget Musikk i Skolen (the Norwegian National Association for Music in Schools). An extract is reprinted here: the first occasion on which this text has appeared in English.

By the 1990s the development of musical education in this country had attracted considerable attention around the world. The article 'Keeping music musical: a British perspective' was written in response to an invitation from

---

[1] See Peter Abbs (ed.), *Living Powers*. Lewes, Sussex, The Falmer Press, 1987, 105 et seq.

The Australian Society for Music Education and published in 1994 as a contribution to 'A Symposium in honour of Emeritus Professor Sir Frank Callaway', Professor of Music at the University of Western Australia. Similarly—and in this instance reflecting interest shown by sociologists and musicologists in the idea of 'creative music-making' as an element of general education for all school students—the article 'The Composer as Educator: Things that Matter' was written at the invitation of the editors of a *Festschrift* published in 1993 to mark the 85th birthday of Georg Knepler, the distinguished Austrian musician who, between 1959 and 1970, was Professor of Musicology at the Humboldt University in Berlin.

The pursuit of reality
in music education

From S. Stolpe and E. Nesheim (eds), *Musikk og Skole: Festskrift for Landslaget Musikk i Skolen* (H. Aschenhoug & Co. (W. Nygaard), 1981); rev. John Paynter 2007

I too will something make
And joy in the making.

Robert Bridges, 'I love all beauteous things', 1890

What educates is significant experience.

James Mursell, *Human Values in Music Education* (1934)

Identifying the Problem

Recently, in an interview on British television, the American novelist Toni Morrison spoke of ways in which her writing had been influenced by memories of her childhood and the community in which she had grown up. In particular she recalled the presence and the power of music—'singing in the home and on the streets'—and she contrasted that childhood experience with the African American music of today: 'Now it is the music of the record industry, slick and all about ratings, giving the impression that those involved are sometimes merely playing at it'; but *then* 'it was not "playing", it was not frivolous, it was a way of *being* in the world when they did that'.

The intensity of Toni Morrison's memories of that vital music-making brought to mind another contrast: that between the current status of music education in our schools and the reality of music in our society. All too often classroom 'music lessons' appear to offer little of musical substance. This is not for want of ability or effort on the part of teachers; rather, it stems from the unhelpful expectations of the school curriculum. Thus, we have music lessons consisting only of talk about music. Why? Is it not possible for us to make music in the classroom an experience; 'a way of *being* in the world'?

Of course, there is a degree of unreality in the way any school subject is presented. In normal, day-to-day living we have interdependence of expertise and understanding; we do not departmentalize ideas and skills, labelling them History, Mathematics, Music, or whatever. School, on the other hand, gives each area an unnatural distinction. Music may be included as 'aesthetic education' or 'leisure activity', but either way, for many school students, music in the classroom is likely to be an unsatisfactory encounter; over-academic on the one hand, superficial on the other.

Yet one of the more obvious characteristics of music is that it functions on many different levels. It provides entertainment; it supports and integrates with other arts in dance, theatre, film, and television—usually with considerable expressive importance. For some it offers the satisfaction of achievement through the mastery of vocal and instrumental skills, and for others a sense of identity as they make music together in choirs, orchestras, chamber music groups, and bands. Music may inspire us and excite us in a variety of ways and for many different reasons, and its range of expression is as varied as humanity itself. Surely, the very breadth of musical possibility is itself an education? The nub of the matter is, of course, that *music has to be experienced*; and for each of us that experience is unique. But, as James Mursell pointed out, it is 'significant experience' that educates, not passively received information. We are mistaken if we believe that information alone will lead us to musical understanding.

Part of the problem is that our notion of 'school' has remained more or less unchanged for a long time. Some well-established features may be no longer appropriate and yet they remain whilst potentially useful new ideas are ignored simply because they do not fit in with the conventional view of school work. Perhaps we should begin again by asking ourselves 'what is school *for*?' There could be many answers to that question but should we not all agree that, primarily, schools are for students, and what happens there should happen for all and not merely some of the students? And is it not our responsibility to nurture whatever talents each student may possess so that all can make good use of their aptitudes now, in school, and subsequently in adult life? In this way every school could strive to become a microcosm of our best aims for society, recognizing the variety and worth of individual abilities and drawing upon them for the benefit of the community as a whole. How often do we give the impression that it is only the teacher's knowledge or expertise that matters? Of course, teachers have a duty to teach, and undoubtedly their wisdom and experience is of value; but students also have experiences and ideas that can be shared and developed, and a school system that neglects or damages that awareness misses the point of education. Indeed it would be anti-educational because, instead of 'leading out' to new ideas and possibilities, it would leave students more or less where they were. Piaget believed that the first aim of education should be to produce people 'capable of doing *new* things, not simply repeating what other generations have done ... [people] who are creative and inventive; who are discoverers'. Similarly, Herbert Read observed that. 'Appreciation is not acquired by passive contemplation: we only appreciate beauty on the basis of our own creative aspirations, abortive though these be'. [Herbert Read, *Education Through Art*, 1958.]

Yet, whilst we acknowledge the value of the total school experience, academic and social, schooling has to be something more than simply 'experiencing'. To make the most of our cultural heritage we need a range of intellectual skills, including that of knowing how to find and use information. For most people, no doubt, it is this aspect that truly represents 'school'. However, it can create a hierarchy of school subjects. Notwithstanding our belief that education should extend and broaden awareness, subjects that form a 'core' curriculum will almost certainly be considered more important than others; and, by inference, the teachers of those subjects will be deemed to have a more important role in education than others.

A curriculum hierarchy can affect the way we teach. If Music appears to occupy a lowly place in the overall scheme and there is a feeling that, educationally, music does not 'matter', a teacher could be forgiven for concentrating upon 'extracurricular' work with choirs, bands, and other ensembles involving an enthusiastic minority.[1] Unfortunately, such a decision might further diminish the subject in the minds of students and music education would have even less chance of raising its status within the curriculum. As a preserve of a minority it would, in effect, remain outside the scheme of general education.

Then again, if there is an assumption that all elements of a curriculum should be evaluated on the same criteria this may foster competitiveness in the striving for academic targets, suggesting, perhaps, a relationship between the inferred importance of a school subject and the extent of writing and fact memorization involved. In such cases, teachers of 'low-status' subjects may feel they have to increase the amount of time pupils spend in writing notes and essays. Certainly, the quest for academic approval can run away with itself, occasionally in ways that may even appear comical—as is evident in the results of a survey conducted by HM Inspectors of Schools.[2] The investigation

---

[1] DES, *Aspects of Secondary education in England*, 1979.

[2] It is interesting that we have come to accept the idea that school choirs and orchestras are 'extra' (i.e. 'outside') the school curriculum. 'Out of time table' would be a more helpful way of describing this work.

recorded the number of words written by one secondary school student during just one term of his fourth year in the school:

English 6,000 words
History (essays and notes) 10,000 words
French 6,000 words
Geography 2,300 words
Physics 3,500 words
Music 10,000 words of copied notes

The inspectors observe that 'It is an example which could too easily be replicated'. We should note too that, although this student's output of written words in music was equalled only in one other area, history, his writing there included essays—presumably, drawing upon at least of some of his own thinking—whereas his written work in music was entirely second-hand copied information!

Musical understanding

So much thought and experiment has been directed towards curriculum development that it is surprising to find a strong and continuing emphasis upon received knowledge, memorized and subsequently tested. The teaching methods appropriate to linear thinking—essential, of course, in certain areas of the curriculum—have dominated and influenced the whole, and we seem reluctant to admit that there could be other ways of 'coming to know' and other ways of perceiving meanings and relationships, such as those that call for holistic rather than analytic thinking and support a different kind of understanding; one derived not from instruction and inculcated facts but from individual response to what is perceived. Delacroix drew an interesting distinction between himself, as a painter, and one who writes words: 'The writer has to *say* almost everything to express himself; in painting there seems to be a mysterious bridge between the image and the beholder'. In other words, the visual arts, like music, do not require step-by-step logical explanation. Images and sound patterns speak to us directly and require no additional information. Were that not so, then clearly the efforts of artists and composers in formulating and refining structures would be a waste of time. The very presence— the *reality*—of the painting or the music is enough. Neither other people's opinions nor technical information can do much to help us understand that reality. Rather, we must ourselves develop sensitivity to the medium, preferably by working directly with those materials.

The widespread uncertainty about the arts in education is due, surely, to the primacy of verbal explanation, note taking, and essay writing in almost every area of the school curriculum. Music, as a curriculum subject, has suffered from this uncertainty. Of course, it has inbuilt difficulties; you cannot see it or touch it, and it does not relate directly to objects or events in the 'real' world; it is abstract and mysterious, with 'meaning' to be found only in its own forms. In this respect the quest for a truly educational rationale for music as a classroom 'subject' in schools has not been helped by the persistent influence of a curiously inartistic academicism that undervalues composers and performers by comparison with scholars and musicologists.[3] Surprisingly, perhaps, these divisions have made themselves felt among concert goers, with the result that a great many people now believe that they are incapable of listening to music without the aid of detailed, analytical programme notes. How often do we hear someone say 'if I knew more *about* music, then perhaps I'd understand it'? Regrettably it is we, the educators, who have misled people into believing that the ability to 'appreciate' music rests primarily upon a knowledge of history and so-called 'theory'.

Yet we cannot help but be aware of the reality of the experience. It is difficult to go through a day without hearing music—from radio and television, in cafés, restaurants, and boutiques, music in the streets, on railway stations, and in airports. In the absence of serious and widespread objection, we must assume that many people find the music helpful. That being so, such universal acceptance suggests that many might be helped towards a deeper involvement with music; one that could revivify and enrich imagination and increase the possibilities for individual fulfilment. In our new technological society we need the arts not only as aids to leisure and relaxation—the majority receiving passively the efforts of a talented minority—but also and most importantly because artistic endeavour, however humble the achievement, calls upon our imagination, sensitivity, and inventiveness, keeping us alive to the world and its opportunities. The 'idea' of music has universal acceptance and seemingly endless formal possibilities; and for that reason if no other, music should have an important role in everyone's general education. Yet, as we have observed, in school we appear to encourage an exclusiveness that preserves music's esoteric image.

Looking for an answer

Since, strictly speaking, music exists only when it is sounding, should we not provide opportunities for as many people as possible to participate in practical music making? Where better to begin than with young people in schools?

---

[3] Cf. Sir Thomas Beecham's sardonic observation that, 'A musicologist is one who can read music but can't hear it' (in H. Proctor-Gregg, *Beecham Remembered*).

This, of course, has been done. From the late 1940s, in Britain and some other countries, funding has been available for instrumental teaching in schools. The result has been a dramatic increase in the number of school orchestras and bands as well as regional youth orchestras organized and often directed by Local Education Authority music advisers. The rise in performance standards among young musicians has been impressive. This is excellent, and no one would doubt that such worthwhile activity should continue. Even so, it would be a mistake to think of this as the principal role for music in education. In the first place, it represents only a small part of the range of musical activity. More-over, successful performance on a musical instrument demands a level of skill unlikely to be attainable by other than a minority of school students. In Britain at the present time [1980s] it is estimated that instrumental teaching provided by LEAs, effective though it is, involves less than 10 per cent of the secondary school intake. Similarly, the number of school students taking courses that will lead them to study music at universities or conservatoires is also small. Naturally, a school should do everything possible to encourage students who are 'musical'—in the widely accepted sense of that word—but we should be wary of persuading ourselves that this is allowing music to fulfil its role in gen-eral education. In that respect, Music is in no way different from any other school subject: in all probability only a few students will go on to study, say, Physics or Mathematics at university—but Physics and Mathematics teachers know that their task is to educate all their students.

Rather more damaging has been the way in which we have allowed the 'musical'/'non-musical' categories to exclude so many students from other and, perhaps, more accessible aspects of practical involvement. We appear to have accepted that, for the majority, nothing can be done other than helping them to become 'informed listeners', and that this will be achieved by way of information and recorded examples. The intention is laudable but Musical Appreciation takes too much for granted. Although analysis and commentary can be stimulating for anyone who has been involved with music practically, for those limited to a moderate awareness of background music no amount of information and extracts from recordings will open doors of perception. Once again, the problem is the gap between what happens in the classroom and the immediacy of musical experience.

The point of decision: music as an education

To a large extent the emphasis upon 'extra-curricular' performance groups derives from the acceptance of 'music as a school subject' rather than 'music as an element of general education'. This may seem like a quibble: is it not a music teacher's task to teach *music*? Of course it is, although, in the context of general education, it might be preferable to say that music teachers educate *through* music; in which case, rather than 'what do I believe my students should know about music?', a more appropriate starting point might be 'what is there about music that is educative?' It may help if we list some priorities:

◆ music should provide an education for all pupils

◆ classroom activities should not lose touch with musical reality

◆ the materials of music are sounds: students should be working with sounds

◆ opportunities for 'thinking and making' in music are of paramount importance

◆ the goal is 'musical understanding'—taking delight in the seemingly endless variety of structural possibilities and the sense of 'finality' (wholeness) that tells us a piece is successful

This last point is central to the idea of 'music as an education'. For, no matter how much information or explanation is offered, the experience of music is different for each one of us. As we have already observed, music exists only when it is 'performed'. The word itself is significant: it tells us that music is truly 'formed' only when it is *presented* ('made present'); and that *performing* ('forming through') involves both those who play or sing *and* those who listen. For both parties there must be a sense of 'making', because it is this that gives the music wholeness and makes us (listeners as well as performers) whole too.

The first step is learning to listen attentively. This can be achieved most easily through the processes of making up pieces of music; working directly with the sounds and using aural judgement to evaluate progress towards wholeness and completion, the point at which the music can be said to be 'a piece'. There is a common misconception—derived from the notion that music's main function is to be soothing and relaxing—that 'enjoying' music means allowing the sounds to 'flow over us'. But surely it is impossible to believe that music's power could persist, continuously in a state of development and renewal, if the audible progress of a piece towards completion matters so little? At the same time, it would be a mistake to assume that 'attentive listening' implies 'analytical listening'. If we expect students to analyse the techniques instead of listening to the 'going on' of the whole structure, almost certainly they will miss the sensation of completeness and finality. That would be akin to concentrating attention upon individual petals rather than appreciating the way in which many elements combine to produce the beauty of the whole flower. For, although music takes place in time, it is not a linear operation (as is language, for example). Many disparate things may be happening simultaneously, in which case our minds must process the continuously changing complexity. Music's *raison d'être* is the delight and sense of wholeness we perceive in the progressive coming together of all the elements of a piece: a 'coming together' that is composed (i.e. 'posed [= set] together' as a unity). Every piece of music is an adventure in a chosen sound-world, and therefore the mental processes by which we receive and understand music cannot be compared with those by which we receive and understand language.

In May 1980, William Mann, music critic of the London *Times*, reviewing a first performance, described himself as 'one whose greatest stimulus in all music is the first impact of a new piece'. Surprisingly, among the vast number of people who would call themselves 'music lovers', there are few who would so uncompromisingly proclaim their belief in the adventure of new music: first performances are usually approached with caution, as though there might be cause to distrust composers! Something very similar occurs with performances of unfamiliar music of any period or provenance: listeners are convinced that they will not be able to understand the music without information. Why can we not have confidence in the composers *and* our own ears? After all, composers do not say that we must like what they have made; they set their completed pieces before us, inviting us to accompany them on journeys in the sound-worlds they create, and to do so without prejudice and unhindered by comparisons with other music we know.[4]

It is this direct call upon attentive and imaginative response that makes music such an important area of creativity and defines its role in everyone's general education. The arts do not have a monopoly of creativity but, because they exploit individual perception and sensitivity rather than pools of agreed information, they may be regarded as areas of special creativity. In the school curriculum the arts offer every student a way of 'coming to know' that is unlike anything else. They do not require justification as culture, education for leisure or anything other than what they are: they justify themselves in their own terms entirely. Educationally, artistic enterprise develops imagination and a sense of wholeness through processes in which individual understanding of the medium is the decisive factor. Nowhere is this more obviously so than when anyone invents a piece of music. Music's abstract nature and freedom from identifiable images, far from being a deficiency, is its strength. In this way

---

[4] Michael Howard, Regius Professor of Modern History at the University of Oxford, has spoken of the need for History teaching to grapple with a similar problem of prejudice: 'We have got to teach people to step outside their own cultural skins and enter into the minds of others.'

music is able to yield 'insight into literally "unspeakable" realities'. [Susanne K. Langer, *Philosophy in a New Key*, 1942.]

Visual arts teachers speak of 'the seeing eye': an intensification of perception that allows whatever is delighting the eye to work widely upon a person's sensibilities. In music education should we not, likewise, encourage students to develop the acuteness of 'the hearing ear'? Once begun, the process furthers itself, just as grammar, formulated in retrospect from language built up by use and necessity, extends the scope of communication by offering more powerful and expressive use of words. In his book *Children's Writing* [1967], David Holbrook refers to the educational importance of encouraging every child's 'perception and the capacity to explore and organize experience, from inward sources, symbolically'. Whatever outward stimulus the teacher provides, it should 'be left to provoke a unique response from each child'. Holbrook is critical of any approach that 'seeks to force children into the same pattern' because that, he argues, produces insincere writing characterized by a 'sameness of "vocabulary" [that] marks a failure of engagement with "felt" meaning'.

A similar theme is explored by D. J. Enright in his poem *Blue Umbrellas* [*Collected Poems*, 1987]. The poet and his little daughter are looking at a peacock. The child asks what it is, 'The thing that makes a blue umbrella with its tail', but her father, aware that his reply will be 'poor and pale' beside the imagery of the question, can only call it 'peacock'. The child has just started to go to school and her father is conscious of the ways in which this may destroy her imaginative vision; in school we learn the names of things and that reduces everything to a grey mediocrity: '... we mar great works by our mean recital'. Henceforth 'The blue-tailed eccentrics will be merely peacocks'; for, as the dictionary opens, so 'the gay umbrellas close'. All too easily teachers have made the mistake of believing that everything needed for understanding can be found within dry, objective facts:

It was not a proper respect for words that we need,
But a decent regard for things, those older creatures and more real.

Poets—like musicians—find 'reality' deep in the world of the imagination. How sad, then, that schooling, which should aim to develop all our humanizing and civilizing qualities, should so often appear to undervalue this precious faculty. Even more unfortunate are the occasions when schools claim to be interested in these things but manage to ignore or avoid the essential imaginative core of art by concentrating upon theoretical exercises—what D. J. Enright, in this poem, calls 'the dubious benefit of rhyme'.

In the final section of *Blue Umbrellas* the poet imagines his daughter, grown now to adulthood and a parent herself, turning to the writing of poetry in order to recover the power of inward experience that schooling had denied her. Through her own verse—'a spell to lift a curse'—she will, perhaps, find again the magic of imagination.

Enright's poem is a warning to all who are involved with the arts in education that a right balance between technical information and creative experiment is essential. The 'rules' should never be allowed to become ends in themselves; and before children encounter 'grammar' they must be allowed to discover the expressive nature of the language. In music education we should not let the standards of our own complex musical training blind us to the inherent value of children's first encounters with music's expressive potential. Listening to pieces they have made up we shall recognize modes of understanding that we thought we had lost, recalling—again in Enright's words—'those older creatures': perceptions that are 'more real' than the visible and tangible reality of the modern world.

It is just such a view of existence that artists retain and blend even with the most advanced techniques. Sadly, although that experience should be an essential part of everyone's education, the traditional modes of schooling, emphasizing the concrete and the factual, have bred distrust of the seemingly insubstantial and fleeting visions of artists; what artists, poets, and musicians *do* is, for many people, a mystery—in which case, it hardly deserves to be taken seriously! Just as those nineteenth-century New Englanders found it impossible to understand how George Ives (conductor of the town band in Danbury, Connecticut, and father of the more famous Charles) could bear:

[the] raucous, bellowing voice of old Alfred Bell, the Danbury stonemason who sang at the Camp Meetings. George Ives used to say to them: 'You'll not get a wild, heroic ride to heaven on pretty little sounds. But look into old Fred's face—look intently, reverently—and you'll hear the music of ages. If you listen to the sound, you may miss the music'.[5]

We should not be surprised by the untutored, natural understanding that children display when they work with sounds and draw upon their inner worlds of imagination. Although more advanced techniques will have their place in later stages, we may find that we have to turn aside, temporarily, from some of the 'benefits of rhyme' that we have come to accept as essential at every level of musical education, and allow the reality of music to show us the way forward.

---

[5] David Wooldridge, *Charles Ives*, 1975.

Keeping music musical:
a British perspective

From M. Comte (ed.), *Music Education: International Viewpoints /
A Symposium in Honour of Emeritus Professor Sir Frank Callaway*[1]

In 1906 that most innovative of British architects, Sir Edwin Lutyens, built his first completely classical country house. His client was a rich Yorkshireman who, understandably, was anxious to see not only that he got value for money but also that he got exactly what he wanted. Touring the unfinished building with the architect, the client was shown the proposed position for a black marble staircase. 'But I don't want a black marble staircase', he said, 'I want an oak one.' 'What a pity', said Lutyens. Some months later they visited the house again and the client was surprised to find the black marble staircase installed. 'I told you I didn't want a black marble staircase', he protested. 'I know', replied Lutyens, 'and do you remember I said "What a pity"?' (Lutyens, 1980: 67–8).

What can explain Lutyens's apparent readiness to ride roughshod over his client's wishes? Was the marble staircase that important? The first Lord Balfour (who, as it happens, was Prime Minister at about the time Lutyens was work-ing on that Yorkshire house) is credited with having said, 'Nothing matters very much, and very few things matter at all.' That might well be a useful maxim for a politician, but for an artist or a musician it won't do: in the work of artists, points of detail do matter—and matter a great deal.

Lutyens' approach to architecture was, in every respect, artistic. *Nothing* could be left to chance: everything had to be decided. In his concept of a building every distinct part (even the door handles and the kitchen sink) was an essential element which in some way had to be related to the whole, and without which the form would not work. And form is everything.

---

[1] (ASME Monographs Series 3, Australian Society for Music Education Incorporated in association with CIRCME, School of Music, The University of Western Australia, 1994), 143–6.

Art is manifest in art objects: completed forms, not half-completed forms. In the concert hall or from a recording we expect a performance—i.e. something 'formed-through(out)'. Mere 'work in progress' would not satisfy anyone. Paintings, poems, sculptures, plays, pieces of music: that is what art is about. Everything else in any way associated with art is either incidental or concerned with the realization and presentation of those art objects.

What do we learn from this about the rôle of music in education?

It may look as though the greatest success of music education in our schools over the past 30 or 40 years has been the shift in emphasis from children sitting in rows listening to recordings of the classics, or copying from the blackboard notes about dead composers, to children being actively involved with music making. Surely no-one would suggest that that was not an achievement; but it tends to obscure the real achievement, which is that we have established music 'as an education' (to use Keith Swanwick's very telling phrase) by accepting that the essential educative force is experience of music as an art.

James L. Mursell puzzled his contemporaries by telling them that 'What educates is significant experience'—without being too clear about just what kinds of experience were 'significant'. Was it, perhaps, the arts he had in mind? The finished form of an art object 'signifies'; and art educates by offering us the experience of art objects, not only those made by the people we call Artists (with a capital A!), but also whatever we make for ourselves. That is to say, we are educated by our own enterprise: by the artistic significance of something, however simple, that we have devised, thought about and 'formed-through' (including musical or dramatic performance), that is our own, and which provides for us the satisfaction of having realized it in its wholeness.

It is the wholeness—the sense of 'rightness' in the completed form—which gives what we have made—or, if we're listening or looking, what we have accepted on its own terms—its significance. It is self-sufficient, self-explanatory; it needs no words about it. As Debussy said of music, 'There is no theory. All you have to do is to listen'.

The Lutyens story with which we began highlights two very important features of artistic working. First, the need for conviction: there is no place in art for timidity. To think artistically—musically—is to make a bargain with yourself to produce some *thing* which, even if it draws upon other people's ideas, ultimately transfigures them and becomes a 'work' or a 'performance' wholly representative of your own point of view. Courage and a sense of adventure in developing ideas is essential; for, as the jazz trumpeter Miles Davis said: 'Music isn't about standing still and becoming safe'.

Commitment like that may be stimulated by the challenge of 'making, out of the ordinary, something out-of-the-ordinary'. This is universal. Storr (1988: 13) points out that

Man's quest for integration and unity seems to be an inescapable part of the human condition. Because of its ability to make new wholes out of contrasting elements, music is the art which most aptly symbolises this quest.

Here, then, is the second of those two important features: the elements of artistic ideas made to work together, combined and contrasted to become the structural forces which sustain the form; and, as we've seen, it is the form which signifies. Incidentally, this may also explain our perception of 'beauty' in nature: disparate elements mysteriously operating together to create something which is more than the sum of the parts. As a medieval translation from the words of the Roman Emperor, Marcus Aurelius Antoninus, has it:

How all things upon Earth are pesle mesle and how miraculously things contrary one to another concurre to the beautie and perfection of this universe.

Thus, we perceive nature functioning like a work of art.

And art is artifice: it is artificial; it is not natural. Unlike science, art does not attempt to explain the natural world but rather to go beyond it, borrowing its shapes, colours, sounds and textures as the raw materials for restless experimentation in the quest for a glimpse of universal form. Art objects are significant not because they show us nature as it might be but because they open windows upon a wholly different level of experience. For that reason, it is the product, not the effort to produce it, that matters.

Stimulating adventurousness of that order, in thinking and making, engaging with great things, and discovering 'harmonies between our inner states and our surroundings' (Giedion, 1967: 430) has been at the root of our efforts, over the past three decades, to revivify the school music curriculum. Today, the most successful examples of music education are not those in which teachers play for safety with a so-called 'balanced curriculum' but where students are encouraged to take risks; to reach for—as someone said of poetry—'a sense of possibility beyond the words.'

It took us 30 years to rescue music in schools from being at best a kind of cultural additive to enhance the performance of the educational machine, and at worst mere entertainment—often justified as a necessary relaxation for students from the 'real' business of learning! In the end what brought music to the centre of the curriculum debate was acceptance of the idea that music as *music*—not as social history or acoustics or 'theory'—has educational potential for all pupils; and in that cause the protagonists were composers: Peter Maxwell Davies, Murray Schafer, Brian Dennis, George Self, and others.

'Anything predictable is not art', declared the always provocative Hans Keller; and, on the subject of his own teaching at one of the London conservatoires, he spoke of 'curing students of their A levels and returning them to music'. Sadly, in the rather grey, examination-oriented culture of the present time, we may be in danger of losing them again. A *fin de siècle* decadence seems to have taken hold, calling to mind Harry Partch's brilliantly simple explanation:

> When things are hopping ... definition: the BIG WORLD, complex in excitement, simple in rules, no analysis. When things are not hopping ... definition: the little world, simple in excitement, complex in rules, utter analysis!

Where has the excitement with music gone? What has happened to imagination? It is *not* musical merely to train students to read guidebooks or follow signposts: 'This way 'sonata', 'fugue', 'baroque', and 'classical'. Whatever significance such information has, it is not a musical significance. Pieces of music can only be understood as individual art objects in their own terms, not by comparing one with another. It is pointless to complain that we can't understand Stravinsky because he doesn't sound like Mozart. The teacher's task is to help students to discover, in every piece they encounter, features which make that particular 'world' whole: the complementariness of elements, revealing their peculiar potential for the developments and transformations which make the music go on in time to create a satisfying form; satisfying because it manifestly fulfils the ideas from which it sprang. In other words, the reason why the black marble staircase was absolutely essential and the oak one would not have worked!

That is the kind of understanding that matters; and in music, it is best nurtured through first-hand experience of working with musical ideas—in improvising, composing, performing, and in relating that experience to a range of other music.

We have come a long way with music education in this century, and the achievements have been real. They may now be temporarily obscured; but that is precisely the reason why we should hold on to our ideals. Now, more than ever, we need to keep music in schools musical.

References

Giedion, S. (1967). *Space, Time and Architecture: The Growth of a New Tradition*, Cambridge, Mass.

Lutyens, M. (1980). *Edwin Lutyens by his daughter*, John Murray, London.

Storr, A. (1988). 'Music in relation to the self', *Music and the Cycle of Life*, British Society for Music Therapy, London.

The composer as educator: things that matter

From H.-W. Heister, K. Heister-Grech, and G. Scheit (eds), *Zwischen Aufklärung und Kulturindustrie/Festschrift für Georg Knepler zum 85 Geburtstag.* (III Music/Gesellschaft, Hamburg, von Bockel Verlag, 1994), 45–54

It is surely a paradox that, although in one way or another we all contribute to change, when it makes itself felt many of us find it hard to accept. How easily almost anything can establish itself in the mind as 'traditional', to be defended at all costs because 'that's how it's always been done!'.

Certainly, as one gets older it may seem that the hazards and problems facing society increase daily out of all proportion to the benefits that new technology brings. Looking back—30, 40, 50 years—wasn't it all so much simpler then? Of course it was not. Even so, are there perhaps aspects of life today that make it more difficult for young people growing up? Is it harder for their parents? Are there now greater problems for the teachers in schools?

Strictly speaking, we should expect education (*educare*—related to *educere*) to 'draw out' pupils' innate abilities, developing sensitivity and imagination, personal integrity and independence of thought: in other words, to be essentially humanizing. In that sense education is not the same thing as instruction—which implies 'constructing', 'arranging' and fashioning in the style of the instructor. There must be elements of instruction in any educational system, but the balance is important. If education draws out ideas and qualities that are within us, instruction does things 'at' us—from outside, as it were. Interestingly, that is also a characteristic application of contemporary high technology, particularly in the field of mass communication which, in the original and limited meaning of the word, most powerfully 'instructs'.

Although there are those who appear to think otherwise, I find it hard to believe that a medium so widespread, so determinedly professional, and so easily accessible as television is not a very strong influence, re-creating us in its own images and generally obliging us—by virtue of its technical superiority—

to accept whatever distortion is placed before us as 'the truth'. That cannot make things any easier for parents or teachers.

Television embraces both the 'communications' and the 'entertainment' industries, frequently with little to distinguish between them. Both appear to manufacture an unreal world in which it is often hard to find a clear distinction between the 'reality' of human behaviour in—for example—commercial advertisements, situation comedies, soap operas, and news bulletins.

Those who produce these things are safely distanced from the recipients; the technology shields them from direct accountability. They are employed primarily to create 'television' (i.e. not even specifially news reporting or drama; 'television' has become a commodity in itself, independent of what it transmits). It is not the presenters or actors who persuade us; not the 'news footage' which convinces us: it is the technology. Precisely because that is so impressive we are ready and willing to believe that it cannot lie.

The veracity of television journalism seems to be beyond question. The news readers and reporters—remote figures, conjured up 'before our very eyes' like the genie from Aladdin's lamp, and as real (or unreal) as the characters in the soap operas or the advertisements—are so obviously 'protected' by the efficiency of the technology. Their 'magic' can instantly show us Moscow, Washington, a battle-torn city, a country in the grip of famine: politicians, terrorists, comedians, charlatans parading before us: it is all 'television', and who is to say what is real or unreal, true or false? The biggest danger seems to be that the very stylishness of the medium itself may stop us thinking altogether. (What does it take to prompt even a tiny, niggling doubt? Enough to want to know who decided to point the camera in that direction? To edit in or out certain pieces of 'evidence'? To link or juxtapose one image with another?)

Does this matter? I think it does—particularly to the extent that its motivating force is the very opposite of education; and, indeed, militates against the best efforts of education. It would be foolish to suggest that we should—or even could—put back the clock and return to some pristine state of technology-free innocence! But is it unrealistic to believe that education should enable people to cope with what technology does 'at' them as well as what it does for them?

If ever we needed a justification for the arts in education, surely it is here. The arts cannot provide a remedy for society's ills, but they are manifestly humanizing and educative because—more obviously than in any other exercise of the mind—*artistic thought is dependent upon what the individual perceives, and what the individual believes about what is perceived.* Art educates by yielding insight through practical, sensory and intellectual participation: hand, heart and mind. Its tools are imagination and sensitivity, and the more they are used the sharper those tools become.

We cannot claim for the arts a monopoly of creativity and inventiveness, but surely this is an area of 'special creativity'? To have worked at an idea; selected, shaped and organized the materials—paint, clay, sounds, words, movements—and to have reached the point where you have made something which is complete in itself, whole and coherent in its expression of what you feel; and, having made it, to know that you must hold to it as your view, your expression: that is a unique experience. In addition to the aesthetic delight such experience brings, educationally it can help to cultivate independence of mind, teaching us that we should not necessarily accept things at face value but that we must raise questions, teasing out what makes sense and rejecting what does not. That significance has long been apparent, but getting it accepted as an essential part of the school curriculum has been a struggle.

Naturally, I write from a British point of view, but I know that the position is not dissimilar in other countries. In Britain, from the first decades of this century, government-initiated educational reports frequently referred to the importance of the arts, but almost always stressed the 'cultural' value; something added on to give the educated person a bit of polish; never artistic experience for its own sake. Those responsible for organizing the school curriculum were suspicious of creativity (some still are!). In the 1920s and 1930s they came to tolerate the visual arts, where at least there was something to show; there could, for example, be exhibitions of children's paintings. By the late 1940s we were beginning to see the development of drama improvisation, and this was soon followed by 'creative writing'. The system began to wake up to its responsibilities: 'The failure to draw out the creativity in each one of us is now spread as widely as the mass media spread the creativity of others. The calls upon the inventive in everyday life are now so rare that the faculty lies withering and when, and if, eventually called on may be found, like our erstwhile tail, to be no longer available. Where stands the home-written song or play against those of the radio or television ... we must provide the conditions for the fostering of all creative talent. Once someone has had a fair taste of his own inventiveness he is unlikely to be satisfied by the inventiveness of others ... Purely academic courses are likely to snuff creativity and, besides, the best way to learn is to do ...' (*TES*. 1965).

Music, however, lagged behind. The reasons were not hard to find: musical education was dominated by music teachers! The profession of 'music teacher' had developed during the 19th century; prior to that, teachers were musicians who happened to give lessons, their own musical accomplishments and success being their 'qualifications' to teach. The institution of diplomas signifying the status of 'teacher' helped to produce a new profession, independent of the 'musician' per se (Abel-Struth 1981, 123–30). This had a far-reaching effect on music in schools. The popular view could not separate music education from its association with private instrumental teachers. There seemed to be no way of incorporating this with the ideals of a general educational curriculum. It was easier to regard music as an 'extra' for those who showed talent in that direction. For others, the best that could be done was to provide 'music appreciation' classes in which they would be given information about music history and facts about the lives of composers. This was unashamedly instructional. That is to say, what was taught was never much more than information about a carefully selected canon of 'suitable' music, the aim being to guide and mould pupils' taste ('appreciation') to match that of the teacher.

Not that music was without advocates for it to be given a more truly educational role. From the early years of the twentieth century there were dedicated and visionary teachers whose work clearly echoed Jean-Jacques Rousseau's view that 'to understand music, it is not sufficient to be able to play or sing; we must learn to compose at the same time, or we shall never be masters of this science' (Rousseau 1763, 1, 223). In Britain there was Margaret Donington (1932) and later Gladys Puttick; and in America the remarkable Satis N. Coleman (1922). But it was not until the 1950s and 1960s that music's potential as 'an education' in which the majority of school pupils could participate began to be vigorously promoted and very gradually accepted.

It was composers who took the lead: in Britain Peter Maxwell Davies (Grant 1963, 108–24), George Self (1967), and Brian Dennis (1970). In 1970 Peter Aston and I published *Sound and Silence,* which was, in effect, a record of work we had been doing in schools over the previous ten years. In 1965 the Canadian composer Murray Schafer had produced *The Composer in the Classroom* (once again, an account of work that had been in progress for several years), and in 1967 *Ear Cleaning:* '... one learns practically nothing about the actual functioning of music by sitting in mute surrender before it. As a practising musician I have come to realize that one learns about sound only by making sounds, about music only by making music ... The sounds produced may be crude; they may lack form and grace, but they are ours ...' (Schafer 1967, 1).

In the three or four decades which have elapsed since we began to question the effectiveness of music in the school curriculum, the philosophy and methodology of music education has made great progress. A lot has been achieved. Thirty years ago very few school music teachers would have been willing to believe that children could compose their own music, and could do so without a background of years of technical training. Now we have a huge body of recorded evidence to show that they can. In Britain, possibly the most striking achievement has been the influence exerted first upon national school examinations (now, any pupil who wants to offer music as part of the General

Certificate of Secondary Education, taken at the age of 16, must both perform on an instrument *and* compose), and more recently upon the National Curriculum for Music, in which, again, composing finds a prominent place.

Worldwide the literature on this subject has grown at an amazing rate. Central to the philosophy is the conviction that music is a creative art in all its modes: improvising and composing (inventing ideas and developing them), performing (interpreting and re-creating music), and listening (re-making the music within yourself; 'making it your own').

Music's most important attribute is its primary emphasis upon form. Whatever else stimulates us to create, play or listen to music, it is ultimately the sound forms themselves that delight the mind and hold its attention; and the best way to understand how that works is to make your own music. The scope for doing this is endless. The results may be of the simplest kind, or they may be extremely complex. Everyone is musical by virtue of being human, and the pleasure we can find in exploring, ordering and making patterns in sound is universal. Beginning at an early age with simple 'generative' creativity—intuitive, largely unconscious and not resulting in final and fixed forms—children can be encouraged to develop their ideas into the realm of 'constructive' musical creativity, where completed forms are perceived as 'artistic'.

The empiricism of the process is vital. At every stage pupils must be able to work directly with sounds, first in small groups (of about five) and later individually, but always 'testing' ideas and completed pieces by performing them to each other in the classroom. In that way they learn why some things are more successful than others (it is not a question of 'right' or 'wrong'), and musical expression develops by hearing how others deal with similar problems. The methodology is based on a process of thinking and making in which the teacher's role is, first, to create appropriate frameworks for experiment and exploration, then to encourage by asking suitable questions about work in progress, and finally to comment positively on the musical achievements of the pieces the children have made (Paynter 1976, 4–10; and 1992, 27–30).

It is also essential for pupils to understand that, with any artistic endeavour, some degree of 'failure' is endemic; that is to say, we should not expect instant success, and we should be wary of accepting the first thing that comes to mind. In any case, it will probably be necessary to explore each idea in some detail, perhaps taking it some way towards a finished composition before we can tell whether or not it will 'work'. Only then may it become apparent that the music—as far as it has gone—will have to be modified substantially, or even abandoned completely; in which case we should have to start all over again. Knowing when to pursue an idea and when to give it up and try a different approach is something that can only be learned by practical means. It is precisely the way in which this teaches us to question and to search and to research (not for nothing was the *ricercare* such a respected musical form among baroque composers; that one word sums up the whole musical thought process!) that 'thinking and making' in music educates. Because there would seem to be no end to what we may do imaginatively with sounds, there can never be a single 'correct' solution; and that at least makes a substantial contribution towards countering the state of unresisting mental numbness that the media producers and journalists so often seem to want us to cultivate.

Testing ideas directly by exposing them to a 'public' (even if that public is only your teacher and fellow students) is important for anyone who makes music. For centuries composers were performers—normally performing their own works; advocates of their own musical inventiveness. Every performance was a credo, every work was a 'meant' gift: and there stood the composer, answerable in person for what was offered. Dowland sang his own songs to the accompaniment of his own lute playing. Handel and Scarlatti were renowned throughout Europe for their keyboard improvisations; Mozart equally so for performances of his own concertos. Operas and large-scale instrumental works were directed, from the keyboard, by the composers; and in spite of the move towards romantic detachment (the composer as 'hero', venerated in his lofty remoteness), the nineteenth century produced a new breed of virtuoso composer/performer—Paganini, Chopin, Liszt—still very much in contact with audiences. During the first half of the present century, Stravinsky, Bartók, Ravel, and others dedicated a major part of their lives to the public presentation of their own music, and in so doing were dependent to a large extent upon their personal executant skills. But of course, like everyone else, they succumbed to the enticement of the gramophone.

It seems that I have returned to my concern over technology! I would be among the first to acknowledge the value of recordings for study, but I have to say that they have never given me anything like the musical pleasure of a live performance; the sense of participation that comes from being close to people moving to make music. Only very rarely will I put on records or tapes for the sake of the music itself: and even listening to a broadcast performance has its association with 'work'!

Like every other invention, there are notable disadvantages as well as advantages in sound recording. On the positive side are the obvious benefits to scholarship: we can still hear Bartók singing a folk song in 1908, and Grieg playing his own piano music; we have Stravinsky's characteristic interpretations of his major works, as well as music from remote parts of the world—perhaps from communities that have by now disappeared or are disappearing: and numerous other examples of similar distinction. But a recorded performance can all too easily assume the status of a touchstone; and we should be wary of giving that too much credence.

Recording creates artificial standards because it produces fixed and unreal performances; presentations that never were, engineered through many 'takes' and created in the studio by careful editing. We all know that this happens; and however much editorial policy may change, music that we receive from loud-speakers can never 'deliver' with the immediacy of live performance. And yet we allow ourselves to be persuaded. Even as I write, my attention is caught by a newspaper advertisement: a record club claiming nothing less than 'unsur-passed audio quality ... technical perfection ... the power and the passion of Beethoven with unmatched clarity, precision, depth and balance'. I thought only the human ear could do all that.

In the first decades of this century composers as well as performers were quickly seduced by the wizardry of recording. Quite apart from the possibility of more or less instant worldwide distribution, it could relieve them of the obligation to test their work directly, face to face, with audiences; and it would reduce, or even avoid altogether, the risk of poor and potentially damaging performances. Henceforth the public could be offered 'perfect' presentations, a concept that opened up wholly new territory for twentieth-century music. Now a composer could produce works solely for highly skilled performers, and there would be plenty of opportunity—in the privacy of the recording stu-dio—to sort out even the most difficult of technical problems in the music; a music designed for professionals, that would not need to make concessions to the taste or abilities of amateurs, and would not require the composer person-ally to put the music before the public. From cylinders to 78 rpm discs to stereo LPs, CDs, and digital tape: the higher the hi-fi the greater the distance between composers and listeners. Moreover, would-be performers are faced with ever greater expectations of technical perfection—unrealistic, perhaps, in concert hall terms, but accepted as a norm by those whose principal contact with music is through the CD player. The sound of music is everywhere, and attitudes to it have changed dramatically (Heister, 1992). Music is now more readily available than at any previous point in history, but at the same time, even for many who like to think of themselves as 'music lovers', the reality of it has never been more remote: not in their wildest dreams could they imagine making it for themselves.

The aesthetics of the recording industry lead to the electronic music studio where the seduction is complete. Alone with a computer, the composer now commands every audible sound in whatever configurations or combinations can be imagined or devised. Is there a danger here of total indulgence? Every fine detail is established and preserved for unlimited repetition without the need of intermediary presenters; without need of public affirmation. Even the recording engineers and editors are obsolete. Of course, there are still creative decisions to be taken, but under somewhat artificial conditions—frequently carried over into presentations of electroacoustic music; even if composers need to appear at all at such events, they can hide behind banks of potentiometers and computer screens, and increasingly it becomes the convention to present this music in total darkness!

It is not my intention to denigrate electroacoustic and computer music; there are many fine works in that genre, and many composers of exceptional talent working in that field. But for some there is clearly an addiction to the technology itself, and dramatic advances in the last few years have spawned commercial initiatives that present a further challenge to music education. Whilst on the one hand we can be grateful for technical resources that enable virtually anyone to make highly convincing and 'professional'-sounding music on a synthesizer keyboard with pre-set rhythm patterns and a wide spectrum of different timbres, there is a danger that the slick 'correctness' will discourage the experiment, speculation and decision-taking which is such an important part of creative work in music education.

Schools are now investing a lot of money in synthezisers and music software, and from some points of view this is a welcome move: it is right that young people should have access to whatever is available for music today. However, unless the equipment is flexible enough to allow genuine exploration of musical ideas, it will ultimately be inhibiting.

I am convinced that the use of natural, acoustic sound sources (including, of course, the voice) continues to be essential in music education. A quarter of a century ago we were concerned to demonstrate that children could make their own music and that there was substantial educational value in this. So much has been achieved, but we must again work hard to ensure that, notwithstanding the benefits of current music technology, we do not lose sight of the primary musical experience: sounds that people make for themselves, which they can explore and modify in the light of their own imagination to discover music which comes directly from them; music which they can themselves present with a feeling of genuine artistic achievement.

References

Abel-Struth, S. 'The professional awareness of the music teacher', in *Musica* XXXV/2 98.

Coleman, S. N. *Creative Music for Children,* New York, G. P. Putnam, 1992.

Dennis, B. *Experimental Music in Schools, Towards a New World of Sound,* London, Oxford University Press, 1970.

Donington, M. *Music throughout the Secondary School,* London, Oxford University Press, 1932.

Grant, W. (ed.) *Music in Education, Colston Papers No. 14* (proceedings of the fourteenth symposium of the Colston Research Society, University of Bristol, April 1962), London, Butterworths, 1963.

Heister, H-W. *Music in concert and music in the background: two poles of musical realization,* in Paynter, J. et al., *A Companion to Contemporary Musical Thought,* London, Routledge, 1991.

Paynter, J. *All Kinds of Music: Teachers Notes,* London, Oxford University Press, 1976.

Paynter, J. *Sound and Structure,* Cambridge, Cambridge University Press, 1992.

Paynter, J. & Aston, P. *Sound and Silence,* London, Cambridge University Press, 1970.

Rousseau, J-J. *Emilius or a Treatise of Education,* first English edition, Edinburgh, 1763.

Schefer, R. M. *The Composer in the Classroom,* Don Mills, Ontario (BMI Canada), 1965.

Schefer, R. M. *Ear Cleaning,* Don Mills, Ontario (BMI Canada), 1967.

Self, G. *New Sounds in Class,* London, Universal Edition, 1967.

TES (The Times Educational Supplement): editorial, London, June 1965.

PART V

STRENGTHENING THE THEORETICAL BASE (1990–2002)

Three Schools Council Projects in the 1970s—*The Arts and the Adolescent, The Musical Education of Young Children,* and *Music in the Secondary School Curriculum*—had argued strongly that active involvement with the arts should be available for all school students. Such proposals helped to strengthen moves towards examination reform, leading through the various modes of CSE to the agreed criteria of the GCSE and the key stages of music in the National Curriculum. However, for some teachers there was still the problem of deciding how best to encourage their students to generate musical ideas and develop them into compositions.

Sound and Silence (1970) had tried to show that, because young people at every level of schooling were used to exploring and creating in the other arts, there was no reason why they should not work in much the same way, freely and imaginatively, with sounds. The influence of new music was important: as the composer Henri Pousseur pointed out later, it was the avant-garde styles of the 1950s and 1960s that made possible developments in school music at that time, a cultural progression that came directly from composers themselves: for example, the achievements of Peter Maxwell Davies at Cirencester Grammar School.[1] The perceived 'difficulty' of modern musical styles prompted teachers to question established patterns of musical education, and that in turn stimulated interest in new possibilities.

By the late 1980s it was clear that we needed to build upon the earlier strategies. Independently of stylistic matters, it was time for a closer examination of the ways in which ideas for music can be developed into complete and satisfying 'pieces'. The crucial question was how to evolve techniques that would help school students to build upon their first thoughts; to hone and clarify ideas in order to obtain the utmost coherence in a finished piece of

---

[1] See Willis Grant (ed.), *Music in Education, Colston Papers No. 14.* London, Butterworths, 1963, 108–24.

music. The theory had to be refined, and that prompted the writing of *Sound and Structure* in 1989.

Later, the theoretical and didactic implications were elaborated further in three articles published in the *British Journal of Music Education:* 'The form of finality', 'Making progress with composing' and 'Music in the school curriculum: why bother?'.

The educational resolve that characterizes the writings of David Holbrook (notably *English for the Rejected* (1964), *The Exploring Word* (1967), and *Children's Writing* (1967)) did much to inspire developments in classroom music teaching in the twenty years between 1965 and 1985. 'Working on one's inner world'—the title is a quotation from *Children's Writing*—considers a range of influences that had brought about change in the theory and practice of musical education during those years, and proposes policy for the future. Written in 1995, it appeared in a collection of essays by his friends paying tribute to David Holbrook on his seventieth birthday.[2]

---

[2] Edwin Webb (ed.), *Powers of Being: David Holbrook and His Work.* Associated University Presses, 1995.

Sounds out of silence

Project 1 from *Sound and Structure* (Cambridge University Press, 1992), 33–8

Sound, time, ideas and technique are the four corners of musical experience. Music results from dynamic relationships between them.

To understand music we need to understand these relationships: to know how sounds work; how they can become musical ideas; and how those ideas, transformed by artistic techniques, can structure time.

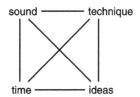

Student assignments

Assignment 1

(i) Sit very still: what can you hear? Identify all the sounds that can be heard where you are.

(ii) Identify only the natural sounds (e.g. breathing, wind rustling leaves). Is this possible from where you are, or do you have to go somewhere else to hear any kind of natural sound?

(iii) Identify sounds that result from human activity, invention and construction (e.g. work sounds, mechanical and electrical sounds, recorded or electronically transmitted sounds).

(iv) Identify sounds produced by natural forces reacting with human constructions (e.g. wind whistling in overhead telephone or power lines).

(v) Identify patterns of sound.

(vi) Identify highest and lowest pitched sounds.

Assignment 2

Understanding a sound from the 'outside': find out how it is produced (i.e. what force reacts with what substance and under what circumstances to produce the sound?).

Assignment 3

Understanding a sound from the 'inside' by imitating it as closely as possible. Record a sound. Listen to it many times to find out how it works. Notice particularly the start of the sound (attack), how it goes on (envelope) and how it finishes (decay). Then try to imitate it exactly with one or more voices. Record the imitation and compare it with the recording of the original sound.

Assignment 4

Understanding sound textures by recreating a sample (a) with voices and (b) with musical instruments. Either individually or in groups (not more than five to a group), sample (by *listening*, not recording) 30 seconds of what can be heard where you are. Note carefully *when* in the 30 seconds particular sounds start and finish; which are high and which are low; which are in the foreground and which are in the background. Remember any special features. By imitating the sounds and the way in which they combine, try to give as accurate a representation as you can of the 30-second 'timescape'. Rehearse it and record it.

Assignment 5

Create in sound an idealized representation of a particular location (e.g. a room in which certain kinds of sounds can be heard, a large hall, a swimming pool, field, wood, seashore, street, alleyway, public square, workshop). The location must be accessible; i.e. it is not sufficient merely to imagine it: its soundscape must be experienced, if possible over a period of some hours either by remaining there or by visiting it from time to time. At the location listen attentively for, say, three minutes. Make careful observation of the qualities and characteristics of every sound heard. Keep an accurate record. Allow a little time to pass, then take another three-minute sample.

Continue in this way for as long as possible, gradually building up a detailed sound-file of that location (like a photograph resulting from many exposures of the same piece of film). Notice in particular the sounds that occur most frequently in all the samples: did those sounds give a special character to the place?

From all this evidence, devise a plan for making a texture of sounds that will suggest to a listener the essence of the place visited.

- How long should the pattern of sounds last? (Bear in mind the things that must be included.)
- Which sounds will start?
- What will be the steady state of the texture? Will some sounds come and go, or reappear?
- How will you end it?

Lay out this organization of the sounds on a piece of paper (you could invent symbols to represent the different sounds and arrange them along a timeline; the higher-pitched sounds above the line, the lower-pitched below). When all the detail of what happens (and when it happens) has been decided and carefully placed, experiment to find the best ways of imitating the sounds. Work at individual sounds and at combinations of sounds until the whole structure can be performed satisfactorily using voices alone or voices and musical instruments. When you can produce a distinctive and definitive sound evocation of the place visited, record it and present it to an audience.

Assignment 6

Create in sound a new and unusual imaginary landscape. Imitate (or use recordings) of easily identifiable sounds but organize them together in a short textural piece that evokes a strange and unreal place.

Teaching points

These assignments are not in themselves musical but, from simple exercises in attentive listening to exploration of how sounds are made and how they evoke atmosphere, the project can develop into a wide-ranging investigation with imaginative use of sound textures that parallel important features of music. It would be useful to draw out these parallels, either in preparation for subsequent projects or (if you have started with other projects) to present previous work in a new light.

An understanding of the inner structure of sounds links easily with the 'opposite corner' of musical experience (see Fig. 1) because the substance of every musical idea rests in the special characteristics of the sounds chosen. Every tiny nuance of pitch, duration, amplitude and articulation can have a momentous effect. Coming to understand the morphology of everyday sounds around us, by imitating them carefully and building up textures of the imitated sounds, is an important step towards evolving and developing musical ideas.

Assignment 5 could be an introduction to the concept of style. First the soundscape is observed as it is in reality, then it is stylized—rather like finding a statistical norm. As with statistics, musical style embodies a generalized truth which does not represent any particular reality. That is why, when we have heard a lot of music from a certain historical period or place (e.g. Vienna in the last quarter of the eighteenth century), we can, without too much difficulty, identify the period (and perhaps the place) by recognizing the general style qualities of composers at that time. Individual works will vary greatly in detail but particular features will stand out—probably because, in one guise or another, they appear most frequently. Those features take root in the mind as the most representative because they have the characteristics most quickly recognised, and so present the generalized view—the statistical norm. It would be possible to take a selection of those features and string them together to make a piece of music sounding passably like a work from the period in question—even of a particular composer. Pastiche composition of this kind is a good way of getting to know how musical styles work.

In Assignment 5 students are asked to focus upon the sound style of the chosen location.[1] An alternative way of tackling this would be to sample the actual soundscape in a series of short tape-recordings. Then, having noted the most significant and frequently occurring sounds, to edit those elements into an idealized version of all that was recorded. In other words, by using the most strongly characteristic sounds—those that immediately evoke the atmosphere of the place—to create on tape the soundscape *as it might be*. This is not nature, in which textures are formed by the accidental coming together of sounds, including industrial sounds; this is art, the tape montage presenting a singular, idealized soundscape.

Now we are in the world of imagination; and Assignment 6, although it uses found sounds, requires them to be structured into what is essentially a musical frame. The sounds must be plotted carefully in time to create the desired effect. If the structure is too short the ideas will be gone before their meaning can be absorbed; if it is too long the mystery and unreality of the imaginary landscape may be dissipated and destroyed.

As a follow-up to this assignment the group could listen to *Visage* by Luciano Berio. Composed in 1961 for the soprano Cathy Berberian, this work combines vocal and electronic music to create what the composer described as 'a sound track for a 'drama' that was never written'. It is based on the shadowy meanings

---

[1] See also R. Murray Schafer, *The new soundscape: a handbook for the modern music teacher* (1969, BMI Canada/Universal Edition London; incorporated with *The thinking ear*, 1986, Arcana Editions, Toronto, Canada). Schafer, one of Canada's most distinguished composers, has written extensively about the soundscape (a term he coined) and its potential in music education.

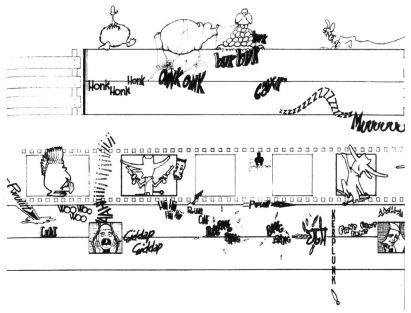

Fig. 1 Part of the score of *Stripsody* by Cathy Berberian

of vocal gestures and inflections (only one complete word is ever used, 'parole'—Italian for 'words'), and it conjures up strange sequences of almost-ideas and almost-events which could have many different interpretations. Berio has said of his use of these ideas in musical composition: 'I am not interested in sound by itself, even less in sound effects ... sighing and breathing are vocal gestures and not sound effects, and thus they carry meaning.'[2]

Cathy Berberian was herself a composer, and her work *Stripsody*—a rhapsody on comic strips, cartoon figures and their conventional onomatopoeic words (Pow! Ugh! Zoom! Splat! Zowie!)—for solo voice, could also link usefully with Assignment 6: 'The score should be performed as if by a radio sound man, without any props, who must provide all the sound effects with his voice.'[3]

Trevor Wishart's *Journey into Space* is a tape composition which uses—and dramatically transforms—an enormous variety of everyday sounds, creating a strangely dreamlike 'imaginary landscape'.[4]

---

[2] *Visage* was recorded in 1967 on TV 34046S (Decca).

[3] Cathy Berberian, *Stripsody* for solo voice (Edition Peters No. 66164, 1966).

[4] Trevor Wishart, *Journey into Space* Parts One and Two. (1972: Realspace Musics, 83 Heslington Road, York). '... the allegorical journey of a man towards self-realization. It begins

The relationship between art and nature is intriguing. At the simplest level, nature supplies the raw materials—sounds, colours, stone, wood, the possibility of controlled physical movement. Nature also suggests shapes, forms, growth of structures and the behaviour of special features (e.g. recession, observable in perspective and audible in the natural decay of sounds). At another level we find artists frequently returning to nature as a source of energy. Some may think of this as inspiration, the natural phenomena stirring the emotions and the imagination. Others emphasize the ways in which art builds upon nature, transforming the raw materials to produce new symbolic structures; forms which stand for a perceived inner reality[5]. Rather than being struck dumb by the overpowering majesty of nature, it is expected that the artist will intervene; and in this sense the musician can enter into the morphology of sounds, transforming them into temporal organizations that 'go on'— and, thereby, engage with the ultimate reality, time.[6]

Certainly the fundamentalism of nature—the way in which it takes us back to first principles—can be a powerful source. For the painter Constable the directness of that encounter was a way of clearing his mind, ensuring that he applied his imagination afresh to his ideas and did not merely rely upon knowledge of what others had done in similar circumstances. 'When I sit down to make a sketch from nature', he wrote, 'the first thing I try to do is to forget

---

in a strange landscape of Birth from which emerges the cry of a baby. The man, as if waking from a dream, sets off in his car with the sounds of a space-rocket launch on his car radio. The two journeys coalesce in his mind as he continues through many strange musical landscapes ... *Journey into Space* was made using the most diverse methods of sound-production and tape-composition. Real-world events were collected via portable tape recorders. Miscellaneous sound-sources were collected from metal workshops, toy shops, builders' yards, etc. Some of the material for the original source-tapes was group improvisation on these collected objects, and/or instruments and voices ... some very free, others less so, and yet other sections strictly notated. Other sound-sources were recorded individually and mixed later in the studio.'

5   The German Romantic writer and music critic E. T. A. Hoffmann believed that a mere copy of nature would be 'as miserable, awkward and forced as an inscription in a foreign language copied by a scribe who does not understand it and who laboriously imitates characters which are unintelligible to him'. By contrast, it was the mission of all the arts 'to seize nature in the most profound expression, in the most intimate sense, in that thought which raises all beings towards a more sublime life', because artists, writers and musicians had received 'the gift to transpose emotions into works of art' (E. T. A. Hoffmann in the story 'Die Jesuitenkirche in G': *Nachtstücke I*, 1816).

6   'That which is within us entering as far as possible into the external reality of things.' (Theodore Rousseau, *c.* 1837). 'The purpose of all musical labour, in thought or in physical activity, is to create and develop the illusion of flowing time in its passage ...' (Susanne Langer, *Feeling and form*, p. 120).

that I have ever seen a picture.' He admired artists who looked for 'perfection at its primitive source, nature', and he had little time for those who were 'intent only on the study of departed excellence or what others have accomplished'.

Exactly the same thing applies in music. We can, of course, benefit from examining closely other composers' ways of dealing with certain kinds of problem, or other performers' interpretations of particular works, but we must also learn to use and to trust our own aural imagination, and to approach every composing and performing opportunity afresh.[7]

---

[7] Music-making is an *intelligent* response to feeling; and the hallmark of intelligence is, as Piaget has shown, 'an assimilation of datum into structures of transformations, from the structures of elementary actions to higher operational structures ... These structurations consist in an organisation of reality, whether in act or thought, and not in simply making a copy of it.'

Wind song

Project 2 from *Sound and Structure* (Cambridge University Press, 1992), 39–43

Poets may use phrases like 'the music of the sea' or 'wind's song', but natural sounds do not really have much in common with musical sounds.

Music is closest to nature in its textures: some sounds in the foreground, some in the background, some growing louder while others fade. In the varying textures of orchestral music we can find some affinity with the way we hear sounds all around us. With timbre too: just as we can recognize and identify the instruments of the orchestra, so natural sounds have their distinctive and memorable colours. Nature also has its regular rhythms: the walking patterns of people and animals; the regular thud of a horse galloping; pulse and heartbeat; waves on the shore; water bubbling over stones in a brook. But none of these sounds and sound patterns is exactly like music; and when we come to consider pitched sounds the link is even more tenuous.

Melody is the most contrived, and therefore the most unnatural feature of music. Pitched sounds in nature are nowhere near as precise as they are in music; the distinctive calls of birds are a long way from the structural completeness of a tune.[1] Notwithstanding this, musicians throughout history have been fascinated by birdsong and other melodic ideas in nature, and have not hesitated to make reference to them in music. To do this they have had to stylize the natural sounds. In other words, they have had to make them more clearly musical.

Student assignments

Assignment 1

On a windy day (or, better still, a number of windy days) record several different examples of wind making pitched sounds. Investigate the various pitches

---

[1] Nevertheless, there is evidence that some birds do extend and develop their songs. The American composer and flautist Robert Dick recalls an occasion when he sustained a

and the ways in which they rise and fall. Make careful notes of all that can be discovered about the character of the sounds. Then, *either* by imitating the sounds with a group of voices *or* by mixing down suitable parts of the recording, invent a way of using the most distinctive features of the pitched sounds to create a short piece called *Windsong.*

Assignment 2

Working as in Assignment I, collect water sounds that have distinctive pitch. Analyze the sound characteristics and identify the pitches as closely as possible (they are unlikely to match exactly any notes on the keyboard, so take the notes nearest in pitch to the water sounds). Then use these notes and the other sound characteristics to make a piece called *Water song.* Once again, this may be done either by tape editing and mixing or by using suitable musical instruments.

Assignment 3

Record the singing of one bird whose song is particularly prominent. If possible, transfer the recording to an open reel tape and—if you can find a tape recorder that will do this—change the speed to lower the pitch. If the original recording is transferred at 19 c.p.s. it can be played back at 9.5 c.p.s. This will lower the pitch one octave and make it easier to hear the individual notes clearly.

Find these notes (or notes as close as possible to them) on a musical instrument. If the birdsong included sliding between notes, think of a way of simulating that on the instrument. Listen carefully to the rhythm patterns in the slowed-down version. Practise playing your version of the bird's song in that rhythmic pattern. Play it at different speeds—some faster, some much slower. Try to play exactly the same shape of tune starting on a different note (i.e. transpose the tune, making sure that the intervals between notes remain exactly the same). Play it at many different points on the instrument.

Then have three or four players (perhaps on one or more keyboards) play this melody together each using a different transposed version. This will create harmony: three- or four-part chords, the parts moving in parallel. Experiment with a number of versions to find the most interesting chords.

Add other instruments (again, all playing the same line of notes in the same rhythmic pattern but each using a different transposed version, high or low). Experiment too with the combinations of the instruments to vary the colour of the chords.

---

lengthy improvisation with two birds, both of which appeared to respond to ideas which he introduced.

Now make up a piece of music based upon these experiments. Perhaps the same idea is repeated several times with different groupings of instruments. There could be interludes in which the rhythm pattern only is played by a group of non-pitched percussion; but the emphasis should be on deriving as much as possible from the birdsong notes and rhythms.

Assignment 4

Collect natural sounds on tape and transcribe and imitate their pitches and rhythm patterns. Few of them will exactly match the notes on standard musical instruments, but in your imitation try to get as close as possible to the main features of the original sounds.

Now, using all or some of these motifs, make an interesting piece of music. Which is the best motif to start with? What will make a good ending? What ways are there of using the different rhythm patterns or (as in Assignment 3) of combining several transposed versions of the same motif to make chords that move in parallel? How can your finished pattern of sounds be made to sound like a whole and complete piece?

Teaching points

These are all relatively long-term assignments. Ideally students should spend some days collecting the natural sounds on tape because this will stimulate greater interest in those sounds and increase the students' powers of discrimination.

The suggested title, *Windsong,* is borrowed from a film score by the American composer Harry Partch (1901–76). Partch was an 'original' in every sense of the word. Self-taught, he turned away from conventional musical ideas to explore monophony (as opposed to the harmonic traditions of European music), natural sounds—including so-called natural tuning systems such as 'just intonation'—and antique and oriental scales. Much of his music was composed in a microtone scale of 43 notes to the octave.[2] Using sometimes the richness of rare and exotic woods and at other times everyday objects such as light bulbs, liquor bottles and vehicle hub caps, he recreated ancient musical instruments and invented new and totally unorthodox ones.

Windsong (later recorded as *Daphne of the dunes*) was composed in 1958 as the soundtrack for a film directed by Madeline Tourtelot. Its melodic material is largely in the form of short, recurring ideas in ever-changing rhythmic patterns; very close in spirit to the natural world depicted in the film.

---

[2] See Harry Partch, *Genesis of a music,* 2nd edn (New York, Da Capo Press, 1974).

The music, in effect, is a collage of sounds. The film technique of fairly fast cuts is here translated into musical terms. The sudden shifts represent nature symbols of the film ... dead tree, driftwood, falling sand, blowing tumbleweed, flying gulls, wriggling snakes, waving grasses.[3]

The Banshee, by Henry Cowell, is not directly connected with the whining of the wind, although that sound may not have been far from the composer's mind.[4] The weird sounds are made by running the fingers swiftly along the length of the piano strings while the sustaining pedal is held down. The piece depends on careful control of contrasts in tone quality and of dynamics. It was composed in 1923, in some ways anticipating the sound world of electro-acoustic music that was to appear much later in this century.

Since the pitched sounds of nature rarely match those of our conventional musical instruments, and natural rhythm patterns (e.g. in birdsong and the calls of wild creatures) are often very irregular, if we want to make use of these ideas in music we must compromise by stylizing the rhythm patterns and matching the pitches to the closest notes. This can often be surprisingly effective, creating exciting short motifs which can be used in many different ways to make musical structures.

It is possible that the motifs of natural 'song' were the starting-point for human music-making.[5] The melody-shapes and rhythms of birdsong in particular could well have suggested simple repetitive musical forms; and the later history of music includes many examples of composers imitating or simulating birdsong. For example, the cuckoo in *'Sumer is icumen in'* (thirteenth century), in Daquin's harpsichord piece *'Le coucou'* (1735), and in Delius's *On hearing the first cuckoo in spring* (1912). In the harpsichord music of François

---

[3] Partch, quoted in Danlee Mitchell's sleeve notes to the recording *The world of Harry Partch* (Columbia Records MS 7207) which includes *Daphne of the dunes.*

[4] Henry Cowell (1897–1965) was of Irish descent but was born and brought up in California. Many of his early compositions were based on Irish traditions and mythology. A banshee is 'a fairy woman, a woman of the Inner World, who comes at the time of a death ... She is uncomfortable on the mortal plane, and wails her distress until she is safely out of it again.' (From the album notes for *The piano music of Henry Cowell* (1963), Folkways Records FM 3349.)

[5] 'Nature's capacity to create, nourish and stimulate is the starting-point for all music; rhythm informs the beat of the heart, the thrumming downpour of rain and the thud of horses' hooves; melody is evoked in the mind by a bird-call or the howl of a jackal; form can be produced quite casually through repetition or memory. The first music was born independently of man, yet it was man who created genuine music from natural sounds ... the two elements of music, pitch and rhythm, were both carried in the human body as natural, cosmic phenomena' (Bence Szabolsci, *A history of melody,* Barrie & Rockliff, 1965).

Couperin ('le Grand') there are several pieces which, in stylized forms, imitate natural sounds ('les sons non-passionnés', i.e. sounds devoid of human feeling). These include the lovesick nightingale ('Le rossignol-en-amour') and the gnat ('Le moucheron'). The nightingale and the cuckoo, along with the quail, also appear in the slow movement of Beethoven's Sixth Symphony. Among other composers who have created birdsong-inspired music are Janequin, Handel, Vivaldi, Liszt, Vaughan Williams and Respighi—whose orchestral work *The pines of Rome* (1924) incorporates a recording of the nightingale.

By far the most extensive and consistent reference to birdsong is to be found in the music of Olivier Messiaen.[6] Rather than merely imitating the songs for atmospheric effect, Messiaen derives fundamental melodic and rhythmic material from a vast range of often very complicated birdsong motifs. The opening section of *Couleurs de la cité céleste* (1963) demonstrates well this use of such motivic material. The form of this work is dependent upon the 'colours' that arise from various combinations of instruments. Here the intervals and rhythms of the New Zealand tui-bird and the bell-bird are used to make parallel chords, vividly contrasting the colours of woodwind and brass, solo piano, and ensembles of xylophone, marimba and tuned cow-bells. This and other works of Messiaen could be used as follow-up to Assignments 3 and 4.

---

6   'In my hours of gloom, when I am suddenly aware of my own futility, when every musical idea—classical, oriental, ancient, modern, ultra-modern—appears to me as no more than admirable, painstaking experimentation, without justification, what is left for me but to seek out the true, lost face of music somewhere off in the forest, in the fields, in the mountains or on the seashore, among the birds' (Olivier Messiaen, *Le Guide du concert*, 3 April 1959).

The form of finality: a context for musical education

From the *British Journal of Music Education*, 14:1 (1997)
(Cambridge University Press), 5–21

*Music is supremely a manifestation of thought and perceptual judgement.
Yet—and in spite of the good intentions of the National Curriculum—because
the importance of these qualities is not generally acknowledged, musical education is in danger of being marginalized. Drawing on the work of W. E. Johnson
and F. N. Sibley in logic and aesthetics, the author formulates a hierarchy of
musical perception corresponding to Abraham Maslow's hierarchy of basic
human needs and suggests that the future status of musical education could
depend upon the extent to which teaching can be focused at a level of perception
where music as thought is most evident.*

The power of music: what are we looking for?

'After a few moments of stunned silence it was greeted with boundless enthusiasm.' This is the critic, Rodney Milnes, writing about Peter Sellars's 'radical
modern-dress interpretation' of Handel's *Theodora*. 'The silence,' says Milnes,
'was a tribute to the overwhelming power of Handel's ... music-drama ... and it
was heart-warming to witness [it] ... being taken to the collective heart of an
audience today.'

Performances which visibly rouse an entire audience are not everyday events;
but, then, why should such things happen at all? What is it that so compellingly
draws us into the music and convinces us that this is the real thing? I recall an
occasion in the mid-1970s: a piano recital by Easley Blackwood which included
Haydn's late E♭ sonata, Schumann's op. 17 *Phantasie*, and Ives's 'Concord'
sonata, the entire programme played with such intensity and musical insight
that all of us quite literally sat on the edges of our seats.

Perhaps we are inclined to take less seriously the demonstrations of
mass approval at rock concerts? It's easy to appear cynical about youthful
enthusiasm being shaped by commercial interests. Yet, in spite of the hype,

appreciation of essential artistic features, such as the formal possibilities of strong musical ideas, may be as evident at a rock concert as at any other musical performance. The critic, Caitlin Moran, writes: 'There are few things in this world more exciting than a genuine Rock Moment'; and she goes on to describe the experience of hearing *Screamadelica*, at Glastonbury, doing 'Step inside this house':

The intro's got a whistle in it—I was just standing in a field, in the dark, listening to 60,000 people whistling. The girl next to me fainted—she said later on that she got so excited thinking about how great the rest of the song was going to sound that her brain overheated. (*The Times*, 24 May 1996)

No doubt these accounts could be matched by examples from other cultures and other historical periods. They all suggest that, as a *complete* experience, music can be deeply moving, intensely meaningful, and totally absorbing. People need music, and there would appear to be no end to ways of creating it, presenting it, and listening to it. Whatever the social, cultural, or geographical circumstances, we are not surprised when we are moved by music. We may even concede that certain composers stand head and shoulders above the rest, and that there is such a thing as 'great' music; and if we go out of our way to be present at, and fully involved with, a live performance do we not hope (expect?) to be affected by the music?

Some years ago, in a pre-concert talk at the Royal Festival Hall in London, the American composer William Schuman took the opportunity to share with those who had come to hear his music some general thoughts on the art of listening. He had noticed a marked difference between what happens in theatres and in concert halls. In the theatre, as the lights are dimmed, people sit up in their seats and lean forward attentively, eager to see from which side of the stage the actors will enter and anxious not to miss the opening lines of dialogue. But in the concert hall, as the conductor lifts his baton, the audience tend to sink back into their seats, waiting for the music to drift over them! Presumably he was implying that, in spite of a being prepared to engage thoughtfully with drama, most of us expect something different from music; a *feeling* experience, perhaps, but not a *thinking* one: on the whole we do not easily recognize music as thought.

If that is so, what kind of 'power' was it that 'overwhelmed' the audience for Handel's *Theodora?* Was it merely sense-experience? And was it anything more than excitement with Easley Blackwood's technical mastery that transported and transfixed us? Or the girl at the rock concert who fainted with thinking about how the music would go on: did she really mean *thinking*, or had she been simply anticipating wallowing in the sensuousness of the sound?

Is there any point in trying to answer such questions? Surely what we experience through music is entirely a matter of individual interpretation; and the only objective explanations of music are those provided by detached technical analysis. If people who see themselves as music enthusiasts are inclined (or reclined!) to settle for something other than what the composer had in mind, is that a cause for concern? Stravinsky evidently felt it was:

Most people like music because it gives them certain emotions; such as joy, grief, sadness, an image of nature, a subject for day-dreams, or—better still—oblivion from everyday life ... Music would not be worth much if it were reduced to such an end. (Stravinsky, 1962: 163)

I shall return to the matter of music's 'worth', but for the moment, I should like to consider Stravinsky's apparent acceptance that not just *a few* people or even *some* people but *most* people believe that music 'gives them certain emotions'. This seems to weaken his argument. For, if there is indeed widespread conviction that the feelings experienced (joy, grief, sadness, etc.) are characteristics of the music—as opposed to associative fantasies imposed upon it by the listeners—then that strong measure of agreement must count for something.

Aesthetic objectivity

Music 'happens' only when it sounds, but that doesn't stop us trying to give those fleeting sensations some permanence in words; perhaps in the hope of confirming the reality of the experience. Baroque composers expected performers and listeners to recognize the symbolic implications of keys (for instance, D major for power and glory, B minor for sorrow), but, as late eighteenth-century classicism focused attention on the subtlety of key *changes*, writers on music expanded the emotive vocabulary in their attempts to capture what they felt were inherent characteristics of keys. Thus, the key of C major was said to be 'pure', 'innocent', 'simple', 'naive', 'cheerful', 'grandiose', 'military', 'serious', 'majestic', 'noble' and 'frank'; whilst F major's properties were 'dead calm', 'complaisance, calm', 'gentle calm', 'noble and pathetic', and—somewhat surprisingly—'majestic, shrill' (Vogler, Schubart, Knecht, et al. cited in Zaslaw & Cowdery, 1990: 126). How accurate—how meaningful—are these descriptions? And do they represent qualities which are *in* the music?

F. N. Sibley (1968) asks whether something really 'can *be*, say, graceful or moving or plaintive', and contrasts disagreements on this matter with the generally unquestioned acceptance that 'things *can* be, say, red'. He suggests that those who are sceptical about this use of language to describe works of art should not lightly 'deny an objectivity, a possibility of truth and error, to aesthetic descriptions which they allow to colour judgements'. Nevertheless, 'with objective matters there must be proofs ... Where proof is impossible, there is no objectivity'. Where, then, should we look for proof? As with colours, if a word such as 'plaintive', used to describe a piece of music, does denote an aesthetic property (i.e. something which is *in* the music), 'a proof ... will make no intermediate appeal to other properties of the [music], but directly to agreement' (Sibley, 1968: 36–37).[1]

And agreement there does seem to be. At the by no means unimportant level of simply liking or disliking what they hear, most people (*pace* Stravinsky) do indeed believe that music 'gives' them certain emotions. This is reinforced by the discovery that others have received similar impressions from the same pieces of music and that agreement in these matters can often be traced back over the centuries (for example, to the doctrine of Affections, applying rhetorical principles of expression to musical figures). In that case, what are we to make of Stravinsky's other well-known assertion that music does not *express* anything?[2] Much the same attitude was adopted by Aaron Copland in his advice to concert audiences in the late 1930s. Aware that people were confused by new music, and that they were looking for stories and messages in music to give them something to hang on to, Copland was adamant that such things were definitely not what music was about. Almost, it seemed, he felt he needed to shout: 'Every composer begins with a musical idea—a MUSICAL idea, you understand, not a ... literary or extra-musical idea' (Copland, 1939/R1957: 23). Other composers too have taken a stand for what Peter Kivy has called 'music alone':

Szymanowski—'I believe that every musical work, regardless of the philosophical concepts, emotions and attitudes which may have inspired it, is always pure music.'

Busoni—'Music remains, wherever and in whatever form it appears, exclusively music and nothing else.'

Harrison Birtwistle—'My preoccupations are about music, and what I *express* is a by-product.'

Broadly, then, we have two clusters of agreement: a musical public, believing that music expresses various emotional states, and composers who would prefer a rather different approach to what they create. There are also those listeners who hunger for information, believing that programme notes are the gateway to musical understanding; but again, this doesn't necessarily please composers. Thus Schoenberg (1975: 378), on the subject of 'Music Appreciation':

Historical facts, biographies of authors and performers, anecdotes of their lives, pathetic, humorous, interesting or instructive, may be of some value to people who are otherwise deaf to the effects of music. But all this cannot help anyone to absorb and remember the [musical] content.

and Hindemith (1921), in a note on his second string quartet:

For people with ears my things are perfectly easy to understand; so analysis is superfluous. For people without ears, such cribs can't help.

Should we leave the discussion there, concluding that the sharp distinction between these nuclei of agreement is proof that differences in aesthetic description arise from different mental conditions represented by completely independent groups of people? Or is there a way of reconciling these apparent disagreements?

For example, is it possible that they could *all* be right? Mozart seems to have thought so, and he consciously designed music to encompass different levels of understanding. On 28 December 1782 he wrote to his father about the piano concertos he was in the process of composing (K.413, 414, and 415):

[They are] a happy medium between what is too easy and too difficult ... There are passages here and there from which the *connoisseurs alone* can derive satisfaction; but these passages are written in such a way that the less discriminating cannot fail to be pleased, though without knowing why. (Mozart, trans. Anderson, 1989, cited in Zaslaw & Cowdery, 1990: 124)

Divergent views would easily be tolerated if it could be shown that they operate within 'a community of principle' which informs all musical perception.[3] It is in this vein that Frank Sibley develops his thesis, arguing that the existence of different levels of perception, giving rise to contradictory opinions about the nature of the alleged properties, does not in itself exclude objectivity:

it certainly applies to much outside the aesthetic that we regard as objective, recognition of faces as smiling, that sentences have meaning, and so on. Indeed it would be absurd to require, for a thing to be *really* ϕ, that ϕ must be discernible by beings lacking the obviously relevant knowledge and experience. (op. cit. 46)

He concludes that:

The group to which the 'is' of attribution is linked is inevitably not homogeneous. There will be a nucleus, and a large and variable penumbra ... exhibiting partial and merging areas of agreement corresponding to what we ordinarily call areas of limited sensibility and levels of sophistication. (op. cit. 46–7)

A hierarchy of musical perception

The concept of nucleus and penumbra, accommodating differences of awareness, experience, and discrimination, may help us to understand the significance of the various modes of response to music and their relative importance for education. It would seem to imply a hierarchy of musical experience at every level of which we find some interest in the *meaning* of music (Fig. 1).

To begin with, there is a general awareness of musical sound. We are drawn in by the sensuous, surface, features: vigorous rhythmic figures; unexpected

Music as Idea: whole—complete—'It speaks of perfection'
Technical understanding: knowing about the details understanding structural devices
Points of special relevance to the listener: social and cultural reference
Preference: knowing what we like and what is popular among those with whom we associate
Awareness of music: sensuous features which immediately capture our interest

Fig. 1 A hierarchy of musical perception

contrasts of pitch, density, amplitude; colourful combinations of instruments; melodies which are elegant, vivacious, plaintive, noble, or whatever. These things excite the imagination.

We enjoy the music, and although attention may focus on the high spots—the loud, exciting passages or the big, memorable tunes—there is also the idea of 'pieces' of music, which presupposes the possibility of dissimilarity in musical effect, and hence different kinds of musical experience.

Liking or disliking is the first stage of perceptual judgement, hinting at something more than mere sense-experience (c.f. Orton, in Paynter, 1982: 217–218; and Johnson, 1921: Introduction, §2). Probably, some measure of preference will emerge, by independent judgement, by association with other people's musical tastes, or through the influence of broadcasting, record promotions, music magazines, newspaper reviews, formal education, and so on. Performers too may be influential, but preference is still most likely to focus upon particular *pieces* of music.

The same kind of influences generate interest in the social, historical, and cultural background of the music, the composers, and the performers. Often people feel they need help and that this will be provided by information or by associating the music with something more concrete: a film or a story, the details of an historic event or a location. It is unlikely that anyone would pursue that kind of knowledge in that particular form were it not for the existence of the music; and, although they may not recognize it as such, the 'way in' must already have been found in the primary attraction of musical sounds: that is an indispensable element of musical perception. Those who believe that they cannot even begin to understand music without additional information may not realize how much and how often they are affected directly by what they hear.[4]

Learning to play a musical instrument will expand our understanding of how music works, as well as providing a great deal of pleasure. Music is a social art, and few experiences can compare with the satisfaction of making music with other people. For many that is sufficient: they *feel* the music as they play, and it needs no further explanation; it is enough that it is per-formed ('through-formed') and present-ed ('made present') in its own terms. Even so, music making generates a specialist vocabulary; for instance, the terminology needed for teaching, for the development of technique, and for the study of interpretation. There is also the language of analysis, helping performers to better understand the challenges of different musical styles and forms but also an intellectual adventure in its own right: a science of music.

Finally, there is something of a very different order: the perception of music as thought; music as the researching of *Idea*. But if indeed we are dealing with a community of principle rather than a number of independent nuclei, then the concept of 'musical idea' will be discernible at every level of the hierarchy. That is to say, in addition to other perceptions, music will always function, in some degree, as a way of coming to know.

Is this the point of reconciliation? Stravinsky's insistence that music is 'powerless to *express* anything at all' was surely no more than a semantic quibble. For, clearly, in its realization music must express—in the sense of 'make manifest'—its own coherence and rationality; the significance of one thing leading to another. As Alexander Goehr has said, 'I write music so that people can follow, from bar to bar; and know that some notes follow and others don't'. Whether or not we interpret what we follow in the music as the expression of emotions will depend upon the level of perception, but that we are able to follow it at all is only possible because *music is thought*. Ultimately this higher order function transcends all else, and it is this that makes music so compelling and so worthwhile.[5]

Music as thought

Walter Pater's frequently quoted assertion that 'All art constantly aspires towards the condition of music' is not so frequently carried to its conclusion. Subsequently he explains that:

in [music's] ideal, consummate moments, the end is not distinct from the means, the form from the matter, the subject from the expression; they inhere in and completely saturate each other; and to it, therefore, to the conditions of its perfect moments, all the arts may be supposed constantly to tend and aspire. (Pater, 1873/1912: 135, 139)

Others have argued the self-sufficiency of musical *forms*; for example, Susanne Langer:

Music ... is pre-eminently non-representational even in its classical productions, its highest attainments. It exhibits *pure form* not as embellishment, but as its very essence ... There is no obvious, literal content in our way. If the meaning of art belongs to the sensuous percept itself apart from what it ostensibly represents, then such purely artistic meaning should be most accessible through musical works. (1942/1969: 209, my italics)

But Pater had already gone further. Music is distinguished by its 'ideal consummate *moments*'; and what the other arts aspire to are 'the *conditions* of [music's] perfect moments'. This would seem to be a reference to the mode of actuality. Was Pater suggesting that music's most important attribute is that it has no history? That is to say, however much we know about previous performances of a work, and important as it most certainly is to study the performance practice of times past, it is only the performance we are listening to (or taking part in) *now* that can affect us. As Stravinsky put it, 'Music is the sole domain in which man realizes the present' (1962:53). What engages the mind is not something extraneous ('what [the music] ostensibly represents'), nor even the sensuous features which *are* present, but the 'now-ness' of music: the immediacy of musical thought.[6]

In his seminal work on logic, W. E. Johnson insisted that the term 'thought' should include perceptual judgements, which 'are commonly contrasted with rather than subsumed under thought':

It is the distinction between sense-experience and perceptual judgement, and not between perceptual judgement and thought, that must be emphasized. The essential feature of perceptual judgement in contrast to mere sense-experience is that it involves activity, and this activity is controlled by the purpose of attaining truth.[7] (Johnson, 1921: xvi–xvii)

This may appear to imply an absolute distinction between sense-experience and thought-as-perceptual-judgement, but, given that our existence is fundamentally sensory, we can assume that, in subscribing to the idea of a community of principle, Johnson would have accepted primary sense-experience as part of a continuum which could lead to perceptual judgement. Thus, in spite of the apparent contrasts between them, an essential link can be discerned between the first stage of musical awareness (sense-experience) and the ultimate higher order function of musical thought where perceptual judgement is the most significant feature (Fig. 1).

Similarly, Johnson's assertions that, 'the aim of the thinking process is not the attainment of truth in general, but always of truth in regard to some determinate question under consideration' (op. cit: xvii–xviii) and that, 'Any thinking process is normally initiated by a question and terminated by an answer' (ibid: xviii–xix), characterize not only the processes of musical composition but also of performance and audition. The 'truth' which every musical work seeks to attain and display is a convincing answer to the 'questions' posed by the musical material and the structural processes as they unfold, the ultimate test of which is the coherence of thought demonstrated by the work in its entirety: 'a substantive proper ... manifested in space and time, or otherwise an *existent*' (ibid: 199).

Johnson divides the category *existent* into two subcategories which he calls respectively *occurrent* and *continuant*: that is to say, *actually occurring events* (which then cease to exist) and *objects* (which continue to exist). This helps us to understand the substantive nature of music. As it is, we may have invested too much in the concept of *form*, not only confusing it with *idea* but also allowing it to stand for both a schemata and a fully worked out and performed piece of music ('realized form'). *Form* is content, and the point at which it is finalized marks the conclusion of the compositional process. It is, in effect, a detailed proposal for musical activity, the result of the composer's artistry and labour, sanctioned but as yet lacking the identity of music. The true identity of music is *occurrence,* unique at every performance. Thus, at the highest level, we encounter musical thought as *event* which presents the 'truth' of the musical *idea.*

'Idea' derives from the Greek ιδεα (ιδειν—to see): it is a matter of how something *looks*: its appearance; the whole view. There is also an element of surprise; perhaps from ιδε—behold!: 'so, that's how it will be!' Stimulated, prompted, inspired, or what you will, by some other aesthetic or noetic experience or interest, the musical *idea* is a sensation of 'how the music will be; how it will go', in whole or in part. Hindemith said that, for him, composition always started with a sensation of the complete piece; like glimpsing a landscape lit up for a split second by a flash of lightning, 'not only in its general outlines but with every detail' (1951: 70). However, this overview is not an impression from nature, or a story, or even a label such as Sonata, Impromptu, Nocturne, Fantasia; nor is it about 'musical ideas' in the limited sense of motifs, melodies, rhythmic patterns or whatever to be extended and developed like building-blocks until they become, eventually, a complete piece of music. Rather it is the perception of a musical argument: the creative task itself, envisaged by the composer as a potential sounding *event.* Without that overall commitment to *Idea* (as opposed to mere technical reasoning about what might be done with motifs) there would be no sense of scale, which, allied to the function of the music, becomes the touchstone of appropriateness in inventing musical materials.

In *The Critique of Judgement* (1790) Immanuel Kant argued that the 'form of finality' by which we recognize beauty in natural objects is the result of chance, whereas in works of art it is achieved by human contrivance. In this process of 'forming' the artist works only with the invented materials, exploring their artistic capacity, selecting and rejecting, devising structural procedures to carry the work forward, thinking with the materials to create the form—the first stage in the realization of the *Idea*.[8] In musical forming there is, again, a hierarchical relationship between the elements:

$$E = \left[\left(\frac{I}{s \times m \times f}\right) \times d\right]^{F}$$

where E = *event / occurrence*; I = *idea*; F = form; s = structural devices; m = musical materials; *f* = *function*; and d = perceived duration.

The overriding consideration is music as *Event*: the music imagined as if it were happening. Working with the mutually interacting modifiers—*structural devices* 'of' (x) *materials* 'of' *function*—the composer contrives the realization of *Idea*, using all appropriate technical means to achieve satisfactory transitions of progression and recession, so that the major architectural features occur at the 'right' moments. *When* things happen in a piece of music is almost more important than *what* happens. This enables the listener's imagination to anticipate the music's direction and to forecast the points of closure, most particularly the final closure. The parameters of musical argument are defined by gratification and/or frustration of the anticipated closures. Everything is governed by the composer's sense of overall 'right' duration: that is, the perception of virtual time demanded by the music itself.[9] Ultimately, the success or failure of the form (i.e. whether, in performance, it appears to have a 'form of finality': a convincingly 'natural'—we might say 'inevitable'—wholeness) depends almost entirely upon the relationship of the worked out *idea* to the perceived duration. This is a matter of sensitivity rather than calculation, and, possibly, it is the element which makes the greatest demands upon the composer's perceptual judgement.[10] For, however long and hard one works on a piece, however many revisions and alterations there may be, and however concrete the completed form may appear in notation, the question will remain: can it succeed as *Event*? Even the most experienced composers misjudge things, and not infrequently works are further revised after their first performances.[11]

Function relates the process of composition to the music's immediate intention: e.g. a projected performance; a response to a commission; an educational work; an 'occasional' piece; music for a film; and so on, considerations which will affect many of the technical aspects of the work. It is also the last vestige of the sense-impression that initiated the *idea*. Once composition has begun, this property of *function* will have been translated into musical energy to interact with the invented materials as part of musical thought, but from time to time it may surface in something like its original shape to nag the composer into questioning the validity of what has been done so far. There are many instances of this. Sometimes the result is the total frustration of the work. Notwithstanding much effort and, perhaps, substantial progress, a match between *function* and *form* cannot be made and a piece has to be abandoned. (See, for example, Schubert's many unfinished piano sonatas.[12]) Most importantly, however, *function* locates music within the general artistic trends of its time and provenance; and this is where titles, background information, and even composer's names can become obstacles for the listener.[13] If we rely too much on other people's thoughts about a piece we may miss the musical thought itself. How should we deal with this? The dilemma is a critical one for education because it affects the way in which we learn from the musical heritage.

'Some sense of possibility beyond the words'

Context defines meaning, therefore every (unique) presentation of an *occurrent* makes sense in its own terms only because the idea of such a 'making sense' is within the context of all occurrent processes in that medium. Johnson (1924: 73), commenting on 'the necessity of referring an occurrence to a continuant', writes:

It is possible ... to conceive of a compound entity which continues to preserve its identity through change of time, although none of the parts, which appear from time to time to constitute the whole, can be said to preserve their several identities ... Thus the law or principle according to which the character of the continuant at one time can be exhibited as depending upon its character at another time, may be the ground for asserting continued existential identity, although the material components of this continuant are not themselves continuant. (op. cit: 81–2, §4)

Accordingly, every musical *event* must be understood, not only by reference to local function (e.g. elements of ritual; association with other art forms; entertainment; etc.), but also in the light of a principle which gives meaning to the existence of music in general. Returning momentarily to Sibley's argument that evidence of widespread agreement is sufficient to endorse objectivity, we can note that human beings' commitment to the *notion* of music never wanes. This suggests an underlying, universal acceptance of a context infinitely greater than any local intentions for particular pieces of music. It suggests a commitment to musical thought per se. Indeed, the very possibility of a process of reasoning conducted, via the imagination, with the abstract materials of music must surely indicate a reaching out for a coherence which cannot be apprehended by any other means. An overview of human history would surely confirm that search for integration and unity.

Explanation is a matter of making connections, and, because the source of energy is *thought*, we all have the capacity to make connections and, therefore, to draw our own conclusions about existence. Generally, though, we leave that to those we regard as specialists: we look to science, religion, and the arts for answers. Obviously, there are other factors to take into account, such as the darker forces which, from time to time, inhibit or distort thought and expression. Then again, although human beings have the potential to ponder the great problems, not everyone is able to realize that potential or is motivated to do so. Yet, whilst we accept that the challenge of other perceived realities is a matter of importance particularly to philosophers, poets, scientists, saints, artists, and musicians, essentially such people are no different from anyone else. The things that concern them concern us all, most clearly—if only we allow ourselves to acknowledge it—the aim of the thinking process itself: the attainment of truth.

Unfortunately, 'truth' is a word that frightens us because it challenges us, not as anonymous members of society, but as individuals; and that makes us uneasy. We should prefer, say, 'verification', which suggests an impersonal, detached, and scientific observation. 'Truth', far from being a vague, unfocused, emotive word, is too definite. It gives us no let-out: it has the ring of commitment and implies a total absence of falsehood and deceit; a state of being in which everything is clear and nothing is hidden.[14] That may seem impossibly idealistic, yet it is a condition to which most of us (secretly, perhaps) aspire. For example, we want the best for our children, and on the whole we would like to have the opportunity to make the most of our own lives: 'to become everything that one is capable of becoming'—which is how Abraham Maslow (1970: 46) defines the term 'self-actualization', the high point of his hierarchy of basic human needs (Fig. 2). Underpinning everything are the biological requirements for existence. The next three levels accommodate needs which must be gratified, at least in some degree, if life is to be worth living. But above and beyond the deficiency needs are growth needs, most notably 'self-fulfilment': the potential for the development of personality; the ultimate possibility for a human being to 'be'.

Combining the diagrammatic summary of Maslow's hierarchy with the hierarchy of musical perception discussed earlier (Fig. 1) reveals some interesting similarities (Fig. 3). Maslow is concerned primarily with formulating a theory of human motivation and, therefore, with the ways in which a 'need' is gratified (or not, as the case may be): 'A person who is lacking food, safety, love, and esteem would most probably hunger for food more strongly than anything else' (op. cit: 37). There is an urgency here that, perhaps, we should not expect to find at the same level of musical perception. Or should we? How could music

GROWTH NEEDS	Self actualization: the need for self-fulfilment
DEFICIENCY NEEDS	Self-esteem: competence, mastery, recognition, reputation
	Love and belonging: affiliation, affection
	Safety needs: physical and psychological security, protection
	Physiological needs: food, liquid, oxygen, constant blood temperature

Fig. 2 A hierarchy of basic human needs (based on A. H. Maslow, 1970: 35–47)

persist were it not fulfilling a genuine need? Offered a Desert Island Discs choice between, on the one hand, simple, tuneful, unsophicticated music we could listen to and, on the other, inert information about 'important' music which we would never have a chance to hear, wouldn't we choose the former? When all is said and done, it is the *sound* of music which feeds the imagination: without that, we should never be drawn to explore it at all.

Maslow's hierarchy provides further parallels. For example, once the fundamental need is gratified:

other (and higher) needs emerge ... And when these in turn are satisfied, again new (and still higher) needs emerge, and so on ... One main implication of this phrasing is that gratification becomes as important a concept as deprivation in motivation theory, for it releases the organism from the domination of a relatively more physiological need. (op. cit: 38)

BASIC HUMAN NEEDS (A. H. Maslow, 1970)	MUSICAL PERCEPTION
Self actualization: the need for self-fulfilment	Music as Idea: whole—complete—'It speaks of perfection'
Self-esteem: competence, mastery, recognition, reputation	Technical understanding: knowing about the details understanding structural devices
Love and belonging: affiliation, affection	Points of special relevance to the listener: social and cultural reference
Safety needs: physical and psychological security, protection	Preference: knowing what we like and what is popular among the people with whom we associate
Physiological needs: food, liquid, oxygen, constant blood temperature	Awareness of music: sensuous features which immediately capture our interest

Fig. 3

Stravinsky may well have misjudged the importance of the simple but essential approaches to musical understanding, but surely he was right in his assessment of relative worth? To adapt Maslow's words: if musical perception can be 'released from the domination of' mere sense-impression, then ability to grasp the real power and portent of musical thought will be very considerably increased. Of course, music can never become what it reaches for, any more than the need for self-actualization can be fully and finally satisfied—at least, not in this life. But, just as creative achievement of one kind or another can give us some sense of personal fulfilment over and above self-esteem, so the most effective experiences of musical thought open windows on a different order of knowing.

Abbs (1989: xii) suggests that the artist's task is 'to fashion aesthetically compelling images of existence, of human meaning and human possibility'; and Willa Cather (1989: 378) defines art as 'an effort to make a *mould* in which to imprison, for a moment, the shining, elusive element that is life itself'. The pursuit of coherence in musical thought is part of that search for connections which will explain the anomalies; the quest for a 'form of finality', comparable to self-actualization, that will help us to find our place in the grand scheme of things, and even, perhaps, to make sense of existence beyond time-bound experience and expression. Storr (1988: 13) notes that this 'seems to be an inescapable part of the human condition', and he suggests that music, 'because of its ability to make new wholes ... is the art which most aptly symbolizes this quest'.

We have come full circle. Undoubtedly there is widespread agreement that people are moved by the properties of music, even though the extent of involvement varies with different levels of perception. Music satisfies a human need and does so most powerfully when presentation and reception are matched; when the conception of a work, achieved in performance, is such that the musical thought is manifest with such convincing coherence that it actuates a similar intensity of perception in the listener. It is the immediacy of this, as *Event,* that overwhelms us: it 'speaks of perfection', we recognize its wholeness, and we are fulfilled by the experience. Most particularly in its higher functions, music is humanizing because, like the concept of truth, the concept of music as *Idea* simultaneously challenges us and raises us up to meet that challenge. This is the *worth* of music.

A context for musical education

I have written at some length here about the nature of music and its significance for us because I believe this is the only base from which to consider the future of musical education. I intend that what follows should include all aspects of music learning, even though different settings have different objectives. For example, it could be argued that instrumental studies are primarily a matter of learning *in* music, whilst schools—at least, in the western tradition—aim to educate children *through* music; that is to say, music is part of the curriculum because we believe it can make an important contribution to every child's general education. Obviously, the 'in' and 'through' modes overlap and interact; the distinction is useful only insofar as it helps us to define the local intention which determines how we proceed. Whatever we do, all music learning should be, beyond doubt, *musical*: if it is not, there is no point in doing it at all. But what is 'musical' in this context? And does a tendency towards trivialization in education make it difficult for teachers of music to maintain the appropriate musical focus?

The hazards

There's an old saying: 'Never teach anything you may subsequently have to unteach'. This means, at whatever level you are teaching, do your utmost to go to the heart of the matter and find ways of presenting 'difficult' topics without watering them down. It's a necessary maxim because the temptation to simplify is always present, especially with subject matter which emphasizes ideas and opinions rather than easily verifiable facts: religious thought, the arts, literature, history, for example. Precisely because these and similar fields present us with views as wide-ranging as human perception itself the prospect for a teacher can be daunting. If I can reduce the extent of apparent differences or controversies and present the main features in outline only, as though they were confirmed facts, will it not be easier to cover the ground and easier for my students to grasp the essential features? This is a persuasive argument, but it doesn't work. Either the time will come when I shall have to explain to those same students that the account I gave them previously was superficial (which could confuse them even further) or—worse still—it is left to someone else to reveal the extent of my over-simplifications. The most damaging outcome would be that some of those students themselves become teachers and, because it was introduced at an early stage in their learning and therefore made a deep impression, the distorted picture they received from me is what they pass on to their own pupils.

An obvious example of this, in musical education, is the notion that children will more easily accept music which 'has a story' or which '*depicts* something they can recognize'. As a teaching strategy this is self-defeating because it points in the opposite direction, suggesting that we value music mainly as a background to other ideas or, at best, as an evocation of a different kind of experience; sound effects rather than musical thought. Even the most deeply committed Romantic composers never thought of music in that way. In any case, the idea that it is a necessary approach is erroneous. Very young children are excited by music: they move to it and delight in it for its own sake. Why, when they go to school, do we allow that lively perception of music *as music* to be spoiled by unnecessary teaching? And what is 'teaching' in this instance? Why bother with words at all? It is much better simply to present children with music to listen to and to enjoy: music of many kinds, complete pieces, and 'live' as often as possible (e.g. the teacher's own playing). Let the experience of music speak for itself. After all, there is wide and compelling agreement that it does have properties which communicate to us if we are willing to receive them on their own terms. *That* is what has to be learned: how to accept music pre-eminently as music. It doesn't require verbal explanation; it doesn't even *require* a title! Pretending that a piece is really a kind of story will not bring children any closer to music than they are already simply by virtue of being human.

Later, and in more specialized musical education—including individual instrumental teaching—there will be things to discuss, but the way in which we talk about music must acknowledge the essential features of music as thought. Among the more common examples of unhelpful simplification at this level is the pervasive and misleading account of the sonata principle as a rule to be followed rather than a starting point for imaginative exploration. In fact, the most striking thing about the sonata *Idea* is the range of inventiveness and original musical thought that it has generated, and the consequent diversity of the repertoire across more than two centuries. It is not a question of the extent to which composers *con-form* but the very opposite (*unform*?). So, why does the simplistic and distorting view persist?[15] Presumably because it avoids what may be seen as time-consuming explorations of music itself. If students learn about 'Sonata Form' as a self-contained fact will they not be able to apply that information to real musical works as and when they meet them? The answer is that they will not: instead, they will retain only the misinformation. Does that matter? On the whole public examinations do not look for much evidence of a candidate's ability to think deeply; and isn't it now more important than ever to ensure that students pass examinations?

Here is the nub of the problem. What we are seeing goes beyond understandable, if sometimes misguided, attempts to make difficult concepts more easily assimilable. Today, the education system as a whole is suffering from a trivialization of its *objectives*. This reflects a general debasing of intellectual values, characterized on the one hand by (possibly misunderstood) ideas about equality and on the other by the elevation of material (principally monetary) ambition. It is said that society gets the educational system it deserves. Much could be written about real and perceived changes in educational practice over the past twenty-five years; about attributing blame for falling standards; and about politicians' attempts to boost public confidence (or their own image?) by means of appraisals, league tables, revisions and re-revisions of curriculum and examinations, and comparisons with other national systems. These devices become ends in themselves, obscuring the real purpose of education, which is the development of reason, imagination, and a spirit of enquiry.[16]

In such circumstances a tendency to trivialize quickly permeates the whole process, in and out of schools. It affects the attitude of parents and children; it affects the way teachers teach, and not least the way in which ideas are expressed. We become afraid of words that imply commitment, and so we allow language to be weakened by insidious jargon: it means nothing and therefore leaves us free of obligations. It is hardly surprising if teachers become wary of making value judgements, cautious of idealism, and afraid to reveal why they believe in what they teach.

The challenge

Believing in what we teach is what it is all about. Shaw's famous aphorism, 'He who can, does. He who cannot, teaches', is nonsense. We cannot expect pupils to undertake anything we would not ourselves attempt. If we are not regularly engaged in writing we are in no position to demand carefully structured and well-argued essays from students, nor shall we be able to help them develop the skill of coherent and powerful expression which is the very life-blood of scholarship. The same caveat applies at every level and in every area of education: what we *teach* we must be able to *do*.

Historically, some subjects in the school curriculum have managed this better than others. It would be hard to imagine art teachers who were not also regular and committed art makers: potters, painters, sculptors, or whatever; but then, we might say, what else would they teach? Precisely! Perhaps our difficulty is that for too long we have had the option of teaching something other than *musical* music. We have got used to eulogizing technique as a goal in itself or filling our teaching with historical and analytical detail, confident that these things have some bearing upon musical experience, as indeed they have; but educating musical perceptual judgement is the greater intellectual challenge.

Maslow (1970: 51–3) shows how certain conditions result in regression from higher to lower levels of the hierarchy of human needs. Similar reversals can occur in musical perception. Feeding young people information without, or even in place of, first-hand experience of music is unlikely to encourage them to respond to their potential to reach for higher levels of musical understanding: instead, they will revert to the most immediate conditions for musical actuality and be satisfied with mere sense-experience. Much the same thing can happen in instrumental teaching when the emphasis is on passing graded examinations rather than on the musical qualities of the works studied, but in this case pupils revert to certificate collecting.

The Performing-Composing-Appraising curriculum makes sense only if its elements are seen to be diversifying an essential unity of creative musical thought. Composing is not an optional extra; in effect it underpins the whole curriculum, and it is the surest way for pupils to develop musical judgement and to come to understand the notion of 'thinking' in music. The composer, Hans Werner Henze, has suggested that:

> If only composition were taught like a language at school, even at primary level, then at least everyone would have a better understanding of music, and the ear would be made more active. (Interview in *Süddeutsche Zeitung*, reproduced in *The Guardian*, 27 March 1992)

In Britain especially, over the past thirty years, great efforts have been made to develop composition teaching in schools—which is why it was adopted for the National Curriculum—but still not enough is done to ensure that all music teachers are as experienced and capable in composing as they are in playing instruments. This is not simply a question of skills: it is also about reviving our ideals. Every aspect of music draws upon creative intelligence, and teachers need to practise thinking compositionally as regularly as they practise an instrument or singing. It also implies a continuous interaction between composing/performing and all other thinking about, and talking about, music. Let us be absolutely clear, we are speaking here of something much more intellectually consequential than sense-impression/expression. The only realistic justification for musical education is that it is active with the higher order functions of perception and with 'forms of finality' which Kant (op. cit: §11) declared were 'The sole foundation of the judgement of taste'. Therefore, the challenge, across the entire range of musical education, is for teachers to cultivate in themselves and their pupils the mastery of musical thinking and making.

Notes

[1] 'Thus, if the sceptic demands a proof that something is graceful, requiring us to cite truths about its properties from which this follows, we must concede that proofs are impossible; *but so they are with colours,* and many other *prima facie* objective matters which he does not challenge' (Sibley, 1968: 37).

[2] 'I consider that music is, by its very nature, powerless to *express* anything at all, whether a feeling, an attribute of mind, a psychological mood, a phenomenon of nature, etc. If, as is nearly always the case, music appears to express something, this is only an illusion, and not a reality' (Stravinsky, 1936: 91–2).

3 W. E. Johnson (1921: xvi), refuting the suggestion that the theory of inductive inference should be excluded from logic on the grounds that 'different criteria of validity apply to different sciences', writes, 'I hold in agreement with most other logicians, there must be a community of principle discoverable in all sciences.'

4 Interviewed by Michael Berkeley on Radio 4 [20 January 1996], the playwright David Hare said he had 'a problem with music's completely abstract nature'. He cited film music as a useful pathway into music because of its association with visual and verbal images. Even so, three of Bach's *Goldberg Variations* were among the first recordings he chose in the interview, remarking that, although at school his teachers had told him that Bach's music was 'difficult', he had found it attractive and it had become important to him because, 'Bach speaks deeply; that is to say, he doesn't attempt to link with other kinds of reality. The music speaks of perfection.'

5 This is, of course, the level of perception for which all serious performance should strive, since, in every instance, including music which is created primarily to serve non-musical purposes, it is the performer's responsibility to 'make present' music as thought, not as image or as narrative.

6 Cf. Edgard Varèse: 'Il n'y a pas d'œuvre ancienne ou moderne, mais seulement celle qui vit actuellement.'

7 Cf. John Dewey: 'Education is active; it involves a reaching out of the mind.'

8 *Idea* both defines and activates the process of composing. Cf. Satie: 'Do not forget that the melody is the Idea, the outline; at the same time as being the form and the subject matter of a work. The harmony is an illustration, an explanation of the subject, its reflection.' (Cited in Orledge, 1986: 157).

9 Cf. Henry Moore (1937): 'there is a right physical size for every [sculptural] idea.' Also Wittgenstein (1975:77, §43), 'for any question there is always a corresponding *method* of finding ... a question *denotes* a method of searching ... To understand the sense of proportion means to know how the issue of its truth or falsity is to be decided.'

10 'The beginning and ending of a composition are only *one* if the music has possessed itself of the interval between them and wholly filled it. For this reason, there is no more crucial test of a composition than the test of its length. The piece that seems long is the piece that has failed to suspend our consciousness of real time.' (Basil de Selincourt, 'Music and duration', in *Music and Letters*, vol. 1, 1920, OUP: cited in Langer, 1953: 110–11).

11 Musicians are not the only creative artists to make such changes. Poets also do this. Indeed, it emphasizes the strong affinity between music and poetry. Properly, poetry—like music—is an *existent occurrent,* to be read aloud, presented, not merely 'observed' as an *object* on the page. Seamus Heaney, in a recent broadcast reading of his long poem, *Station Island,* made a number of significant changes to the printed text. It seemed that, like a composer who felt he had miscalculated the sounding effect of certain passages, Heaney was also conscious of the sound of word next to word, and of duration—for instance, in the length of phrases. One example will suffice to show how telling is the effect of

merely changing the position of a word in a line. Heaney's original phrase (1984: 87):

the one/ patterned with cornflowers, blue sprig after sprig

becomes, in the poet's broadcast reading:

the one/ patterned with blue cornflowers, sprig after sprig

[12] Sonatas D. 157, 279, 346, 557, 566, 570, 571, 613, 625, 655, 840, and 994. The incomplete movements are worth studying in order to consider what Schubert might have done and why he could not bring the ideas to fulfilment. Howard Ferguson's notes (1972–76) in the complete edition of the sonatas (ABRSM, 1980) are very helpful.

[13] The BBC Third Programme used to broadcast regularly record programmes under the general title of 'The Innocent Ear'. No information was given before a piece of music was played; that came afterwards—often providing surprises! It is interesting to note that the technique has been adopted, presumably as a matter of policy, by Classic FM. They seem to have concluded (wisely, in my view) that, if you are trying to attract new audiences for music you should offer the music first and not a lot of extraneous information about it. In musical education we might do well to learn from Classic FM.

[14] Unlike the words which derive from the Latin *verus* (meaning 'true' in the sense of 'real', 'genuine', 'just', 'right', 'reasonable'), the origin of 'truth' is Old Norse *tryg?ir,* implying fidelity, constancy and security (cf. modern Norwegian 'trygg' = secure, safe, confident).

[15] Old chestnut though it may be, it is still trotted out regularly by candidates applying for admission to university. Compare the 'need' for this kind of potted information with William Schuman's comments (cited above, p. 6) on concert audiences who apparently live by programme notes alone and are then able to switch their minds off when the music begins.

[16] Cf. the words of the philosopher, Mary Warnock (1976): 'I have come very strongly to believe that it is the cultivation of imagination which should be the chief aim of education.' Also, G. M. Trevelyan: 'Disinterested intellectual enquiry is the life-blood of real civilisation' (*English Social History,* 1944: viii).

References

Abbs, P. (1989). *A is for Aesthetic: essays on creative and aesthetic education.* London: The Falmer Press.

Cather, W. (1989). *The Song of the Lark,* New York: Virago.

Copland, A. (1939/R1957). *What to listen for in music.* New York: McGraw-Hill.

Hindemith, P. (1951). *A composer's world.* Cambridge University Press.

Johnson, W.E. (1921). *Logic Part I.* Cambridge University Press.

Johnson, W.E. (1924). *Logic Part III: the logical foundations of science.* Cambridge University Press.

Kant, T. (transl. Meredith, J.C. 1928/R1973). *The Critique of Judgement.* Oxford: Clarendon Press.

Langer, S.K. (1942/3rd edn 1969). *Philosophy in a new key: a study in the symbolism of reason, rite, and art.* Cambridge, Mass.: Harvard University Press.

Langer, S. K. (1953). *Feeling and Form*. London: Routledge & Kegan Paul.

Maslow, A. H. (1970). *Motivation and personality (second edition)*. New York: Harper & Row.

Orledge, R. (1986). Satie's approach to composition in his later years (1913–24), in Greer, D. (ed.) *Proceedings of the Royal Musical Association*. 111, 155–179.

Pater, W. (1873/R1912). *The Renaissance: studies in art and poetry*. London: Macmillan.

Paynter, J. (1982). *Music in the secondary school curriculum*. Cambridge University Press.

Schoenberg, A. (ed. Stein, L. 1975). *Style and Idea: selected writings of Arnold Schoenberg*. London: Faber & Faber.

Sibley, F. N. (1968). 'Objectivity and Aesthetics' in *Proceedings of the Aristotelian Society*, supplementary volume 42.

Storr, A. (1988). 'Music in relation to self' in *Music and the cycle of life*. London: BSMT.

Stravinsky, I. (1936). *Chronicle of my life*. London: Gollancz.

Stravinsky, I. (1962). *An Autobiography*. New York: W. W. Norton.

Wittgenstein, L. (1975/R1990). *Philosophical Remarks*. Oxford: Basil Blackwell.

Zaslaw, N. & Cowdery, W. (1990). *The Compleat Mozart*. New York: W. W. Norton.

Making progress with composing

From the *British Journal of Music Education*, 17:1 (2000) (Cambridge University Press), pp. 5–31

Although it is widely acknowledged that composition has a part to play in general musical education, some critics have argued that its place in the school curriculum is not justified by the results. John Paynter finds the evidence still on the whole encouraging and suggests that, where there are shortcomings, these should be seen, not as criticism of classroom composing, but as indications of uncertainty about how to help pupils make progress—a dilemma which, perhaps, reflects lack of conviction about the value of creativity in a curriculum based upon a theory of knowledge and progression more helpful to other subjects than it is to the arts in education.

We accept without question that a school curriculum must show progression, not only in the programme overall but also in the content of each subject. In reality, however, things may not be that simple. In the first place, there are different kinds of progression and what would be a reasonable expectation in one area may not be so in another. Also, to be effective, the scheme must include regular appraisal of students' work, and again that is not necessarily a straightforward matter. Some subjects—music among them—may include group activities, so that defining the nature of the progression becomes part of the larger problem of how to recognize individual pupils' achievements.[1] We are not helped by the continuing confusion about assessment and evaluation; the one an informed judgement which can be challenged and if necessary revised, the other awarding values on a scale representing agreed, and therefore—at least for the time being—fixed, criteria. Either way, there is pressure upon teachers to produce verifiable evidence of progress. If, to do that, it becomes necessary to compromise by making important whatever is easiest to assess/evaluate rather than assessing/evaluating those things which are truly important to a subject, then students' achievements may be trivialized.

In spite of long-standing worries about such matters, I was pleased when, in the mid-1980s, composition became a requirement for the Music GCSE, and even more pleased when, less than ten years later, composing was included in the National Curriculum for Music. At last we appeared to have official endorsement of the importance of composing—something many of us had been hoping to see for a long time. But pleasure was tempered by Piers Spencer's 1993 report on students' opinions of GCSE Music. Although he found that the responses about composing were 'mostly positive', Spencer (1993: 75) was forced to conclude that the notion that 'Creativity should be at the heart of all affective areas of the curriculum—a suggestion I had made in *Sound and Structure*—would have had little meaning for many of these students'. Two years later, in a hard-hitting article on the state of school music, Malcolm Ross (1995: 196) asserted that 'The rush to composition ... has been a completely false trail'.

Ross's opinions did not go unanswered (Gammon, 1996) but they were disturbing, especially when set alongside the earlier objective research, since Spencer himself, as a school teacher during the 1970s, had demonstrated that pupils' creativity could indeed be at the heart of the music curriculum (Spencer, 1981). Not surprisingly, in collating the results of his survey, he had found it:

uncomfortable to read that so many felt that the GCSE had failed to promote their musical learning in a useful way ... [and that] ... those who have gone on to pursue the subject at degree level should be so lacking in any conviction about the aesthetic essence of music. (1993: 75)

Like many other teachers, I have long believed that all school pupils should be encouraged to compose music, not only because it is an essential element of musical education but also because it benefits the general development of imagination and inventiveness. As the years have gone by, that belief would appear to have been borne out by developments in a number of countries. In addition to the British National Curriculum (from age five) and GCSE syllabuses, composition now features in the IGCSE, the International American Schools' Music programme, the International Baccalaureate, the IB Middle Years Programme, and in a number of other national curriculum guidelines. The teaching techniques have been evolving over a period of more than forty years and the evidence now available to us worldwide in articles, books, films, and recordings of children's compositions is impressive. Have we been deluding ourselves? Has it all been worthless and misguided, as Malcolm Ross seems to suggest: 'a completely false trail ... [where] compositions owe more to the teacher's skills as an arranger than the pupil's as a creator'?

I am sure we have not been wasting our time, and I am equally certain that, by and large, pupils' attainments in composition are real. Yet I am conscious of a difficulty which could explain why the students Piers Spencer interviewed (and others like them) seem to have got so little sense of achievement from their GCSE composing and therefore failed to build upon that activity a wider understanding of music. It is simply that, whilst we enthusiastically encourage pupils to be musically creative, we are far less sure of ourselves when it comes to helping them to *get better* at composing.

Why do we compose?

It is the most natural thing for human beings to make up music. Even now, as we look back on the twentieth century with its extraordinary record of scientific achievement, all over the world people continue to create songs and dances intuitively more or less as they have done for thousands of years. Only a small part of the daily outpouring of music is made by those we would call 'trained musicians'. Unfortunately, this very fact causes problems for us in musical education. If inventing music is intuitive, who are we to interfere? Why should we even try to help pupils to get better at composing? Surely it's enough that they do it at all? Isn't it obvious that children make up whatever is in their imagination? They are not concerned with high-flown things like 'structure' and 'form'; they are simply responding imaginatively to a stimulus. They like the sounds they discover, they enjoy playing with them and making patterns, and they can fashion little musical 'pictures' to represent incidents, animals, or whatever. Isn't it all a matter of feeling and emotion, not something that a teacher should attempt to influence? Even renowned composers appear to have supported that view; Ravel, for instance, in pointing out that 'Sensitivity and emotion are the real content of a work of art'.

That is true, but the mistake is to conceive of emotion and feeling as being entirely divorced from and in opposition to 'thought'. It has tended to make teachers of younger children wary of discussing musical details, on the grounds that what the children have made is simply 'what they feel'; whilst with older pupils the tendency is to avoid reference to what is felt by concentrating upon technicalities which are presented as 'rules'. Neither way are pupils being helped to get better at inventing their own music.

Our feelings may appear to be involuntary and irrational but they are, of course, activities of the mind. Even the simplest intuitive piece made up by a very young child is recognized as music only because it is heard as music: that is, as a *process* which starts, goes on, and stops and in which sounds follow one another or are combined in various ways. Spontaneous and natural though the music may be, there are points where things change: some things happen that are not heard again; some things go on for a short time and others for much longer; some passages are *progressive*, so that we feel the energy and forward 'drive' of the music, others are *recessive* in effect, the music calming or becoming quieter or slower until it seems to want to stop of its own accord. These things are the result of decisions—not necessarily conscious decisions but decisions nevertheless—taken by whoever makes up the music, and the precise moments when changes occur are crucial to its success. Since—as I shall try to show—all musical expression, simple or complex and of whatever style or cultural background, behaves like this, we could conclude that the surest way to help pupils to get better at composing is to encourage them to think about the essentially *musical* process, not as abstract rules, but directly in relation to what they themselves create.

Teaching from what is offered

The differences between instruction (*instruere*—to build into [the child's mind]) and education (*educere*—to lead out from [the child's mind]) have been rehearsed often enough. As archetypes of attitude and practice they are used frequently to support or decry changing fashions in schooling. However, in the development of musical aptitude these terms do not represent positive or negative attitudes, according to your point of view, but a necessary duality.

Instruction is appropriate for teaching someone to play a musical instrument. The techniques exist independently of the pupil, deriving equally from the ergonomics of the instrument and the changing conventions of performance practice. The teacher's task is to ensure—as far as that is possible—the pupil's success in acquiring those techniques. Although, later, in matters of interpretation, pupils must learn to develop their own ideas, in the initial stages at least, the teacher is the arbiter of success—along with others, such as examiners and competition adjudicators.

Composing is different. From the start, pupils must try to judge the success of what they make. Their composing decisions are, therefore, vitally important. Indeed, the teacher cannot even begin until students bring something which they have made.

The word 'composing' means 'positioning [things] together', and when anyone has tried putting sounds together and is pleased with the results, enough to remember them, then the teacher can start to teach—mainly by asking questions about what is presented. It may be no more than a brief melodic pattern or a progression of chords discovered, remembered and rehearsed until fluent. It does not have to be notated, and even if there were only two notes the teacher could ask, 'Why did you put that note there and the other one *there*?' We are not imparting received techniques because what is presented to us did not exist until the pupil(s) invented it. Of course, there are bound to have been influences—all the music the pupils have ever heard, and their musical preferences: what they think of as 'music'—but even if it is derivative, what they produce is *what they have made,* and to do that they had to take decisions. By focusing on those decisions, and by pressing students to discover as much as possible about why they have made the music as it is ('I just like it like that' is not good enough!), we start them on the path of asking the questions that every composer must ask about every piece: 'Where are these musical thoughts leading? What are the possibilities? Why should I choose that path rather than any other? How do I know when this piece is completed?'

Listening and commenting

On the subject of children's poems David Holbrook (1967: 8) says, 'The least piece of writing, if the teacher has established the context for proper 'giving', will be a 'meant' gift. We can apply that to school pupils' composing. The music they make is 'offered' to us and should be received in that same spirit. In my experience there is always something of genuine musical worth to be discussed as seriously as we would with recognized masterworks. Talking with younger children we shall use simpler language but we must not be afraid of dealing with essentially musical matters.

To demonstrate these principles I have selected two pieces of music for comment: one a group composition by three ten-year-old girls, the other a well-known piano piece by Robert Schumann. My reason for choosing these is, quite simply, the availability of recordings—because it is essential that readers listen to the music. The children's composition can be found on an existing *BJME* tape,[2] and the Schumann piece is one which I hope may be found, without too much difficulty, on CD.

It is important to comment on what we hear rather than on what we see notated. In the case of the children's composition there is no other possibility. This piece may or may not have been notated but, in any case, we don't have a score and therefore we must trust our ears. Likewise, I hope readers will resist the temptation to look at the Schumann score. The 'music' is what we hear, and in each case we must listen to the whole piece. As it ends we should ask ourselves, 'What can I say about this as *music?*' In the classroom this would be the moment when we must teach. You will have your own answers to the question: I offer mine, for what they may be worth, as one possibility.

What can we say about ...

The children's piece

The first thing I should want to say is that this seems to me to be successful and memorable music. You may be surprised, at the moment when it finishes, to find just how successful it is, since some slightly odd things happen along the way; things which at first might make us wonder if the composers had indeed conceived this music as a *piece.* The silence halfway through, the abrupt ending, and the unexpected dissonances are all such striking features that they immediately beg questions. True, the silence marks the end of music which is then repeated, but why such a long pause? Is it misjudged or can it be justified? The dissonance is attractive, but why here? Merely as variation? And, at the end, why do they not feel the need to do the conventional thing and slow down? Puzzling as these features are, they do seem to belong with the distinctive qualities of the melody, producing music that has a strong sense of direction and purpose.

I am not implying that three ten-year-olds engaged in technical discussion about every twist and turn of the music they were making. Probably most of the things which I find interesting occurred intuitively; they liked what they played and it became fixed as 'the piece'. But that itself was a decisive action. It could hardly be otherwise. Music can only be the outcome of a mental process which determines, at the very least, how to begin, what to do next, and how to stop. Every experienced composer knows that, as a composition grows, the music itself appears to take over, and when the work is finished it is often difficult to remember how it came into being. By listening attentively to the processes in a piece, and commenting on what appears to be happening, a teacher can help pupils to understand the nature of what they have created intuitively and to build upon that experience.

What we do know is that the girls' *intention* was to make music for dancing (see note 2), and this is apparent in the musical style: a brief drum pattern to set the tempo and a repeated phrase in octaves lead into the dance proper with its bouncy piano accompaniment. Whatever we say at this point about the music's success we should not confuse that with the mere fulfilment of intention. Rather, the evidence of success is to be found in the quality of the invention and the way in which the musical materials are extended, transformed, and developed to create the whole piece.

This is an important distinction. A composer's Intention is part of the Context: the starting point, 'stimulus', 'inspiration', or whatever we wish to call it. That may be literary, historical, political, sociological, topological, or even zoological!—as with Saint-Saëns's *Carnival of Animals.* It may be a musical procedure—e.g. fugue or the sonata principle—or a stylistic convention, such as Stravinsky's neoclassicism in *Pulcinella,* or a particular combination of sounds, performers, their instruments, and their technical accomplishments. In principle anything could be a starting point for a new musical work, but that is *not* what the music is 'about': it is merely the Context from which a composer starts to think about making a piece.

Context, then, is pre-musical, and although it might be described as 'an idea for music' it is not the same as a musical Idea! Unfortunately, some of the most commonly employed terms are often used rather loosely. 'Musical idea' may be applied to a melody or motif (perhaps better described as *musical materials*), and 'form' is used indiscriminately for what is notated as well as what is heard, or—most frequently—to refer to abstract schemata (ternary, rondo, sonata) irrespective of any musical reality. Those terms appear to describe independent objects, but a composition is not an 'object': it is an event presented (i.e. *present*-ed: literally 'made present') for us. The teacher's task is to focus pupils' attention on the music in action. We may, in passing, refer to the pre-musical Context—in this case the decision to compose a dance—but only to draw attention to what the composers have invented: i.e. the Idea and the materials (melody, rhythmic patterns, instrumentation).

Idea is the outcome of thinking about and around Context. It is entirely musical and may be a sudden revelation: a feeling for the completed piece and what the whole thing will be like (Paynter, 1997a: 11). Crucial musical features may suggest themselves at this stage, but most importantly there should be some sense of the wholeness which the piece must have if it is to fulfil (i.e. 'fully fill out') the Idea. First, pupils need to ask themselves what kind of piece it will be. Do they have a general view of the *character* of the music and why it should be like that? If, as with the piece we are considering now, that results in a decision to make a dance, then the next stage is to define the Idea: what kind of dance? Slow and solemn? Fast and wild? How will it start, go on, and end?

In the Dance as we hear it, the second part effectively develops the first, and this must surely have been a feature of the Idea. Initially the composers may have thought of it simply as a repeat, and it would be interesting to know if they could remember when, in the course of their composing, it became something more: a realization that, in the repetition, there could be subtle changes. There are a number of other questions I should like to ask. Did they invent the tune first? That is possible since, when we think of 'a dance', a certain style of music comes to mind. Was the introduction added later? If so, we might take note of its structural importance in causing us to expect something to happen—an expectation quickly satisfied by the way in which the introduction leads us to anticipate the appearance of the tune.

The silence, longer than would normally be expected before a straightforward repeat, is similarly full of anticipation; surprising and, in a way, disturbing. Possibly it was this that led the composers to their boldest stroke: the decision to avoid a *ritardando* at the end. That seems to characterize the music's daring; for, surely, every listener's first reaction must be to wonder why the piece doesn't continue. Yet the music's own authority seems to tell us that the composers have got it right. Earlier (at 29 seconds into the piece, the end of the principal melody), what sounds like an abrupt change of key also creates a moment of surprise. When this passage reappears in the second half it is coloured by dissonances and contrary motion. The effect is both pleasing and disquieting. On the one hand the dissonance is *progressive,* maintaining the excitement by means of a new and unexpected transformation, but at the same time it has a *recessive* quality, the original texture represented in a darker and denser version. The surprise of that conclusion is such that it forces us to recall the other surprises and to notice how those decisions have worked together to produce a satisfying piece which, in its completed form, is so much more than a tune heard twice over.

Before we consider what else we might say about this music, let's see what happens if we ask similar questions about the Schumann.

Schumann: Eusebius (no. 5 from Carnaval op. 9)

It is easy to take a piece like this for granted. Even if it is very familiar, we must try to listen as though we were hearing it for the first time.

It lasts for just 1 minute 43 seconds but a lot happens in that short time; so much so that we are hardly aware of the music 'taking time': it is as though we hear it all at once. If we ask, 'What makes this a work of art? What makes it *music*?' the answer might be, its *control* of that 'all-at-once-ness': the seamless unfolding and refolding.

So much here depends upon the nature of the materials the composer has invented. That should remind us to encourage pupils to be wary of settling too quickly for the first things they think of. They must learn to press imagination ever harder until they are absolutely sure that what they have invented is as good as it can be. Whether or not the Eusebius motif came, with Mozartean ease, fully fashioned or, like Beethoven's thematic materials, had to be wrestled with over a period of time, the quality of Schumann's invention is manifest at the outset in the seven-note turn. The chameleon-like character of this motif pervades the whole piece. Melodically memorable but hardly a 'tune', its ambivalent rhythmic features give rise to the series of short sections. Sectionalized music can sometimes sound bitty and lacking in overall coherence, but Schumann achieves a remarkable wholeness in this piece by slowly transforming the material and then gradually restoring it to what it was. Obviously, repetition helps to create coherence but here that is compromised by continuously fresh views of the motif. Even the final note-for-note reprise of an earlier passage has small differences in its presentation, and in general the listener's mind is focused not on similarities but on surprising motivic changes within a framework of repetition.

Indecision is the overriding characteristic of this music, but to achieve that the composer cannot afford to be indecisive! The apparent diffidence and self-contradiction can work only if the musical process is carefully controlled. Harmonic engineering plays a big part in this. There are very few root-position chords, with only one root position of the tonic—and that's not at the end! The piece opens with a first inversion and concludes on a second inversion, unsure but nevertheless resigned. A particularly important harmony at internal cadences is the dominant ninth, wistful but dispirited after moments of hopeful energy.

All this apparent instability is precisely regulated, the transformations of the motif becoming agents of progression and recession, causing (or allowing?) the music to forge ahead, to hold back, or to cease altogether. We can hear this right at the start as the subdued melodic line moves with an odd combination of grace and gaucheness against the apparent 'security' of the left-hand crotchets. Every aspiring rise falls back again; should it take this path or that? We cannot tell. The recessive effect is strong and we feel the piece could stop altogether after only one phrase. But just when that seems about to happen the music picks itself up with a new, slightly agitated figure in which the shape of the motif is recognizable even though the notes are faster and the upward leaps are wider. The progressive quality continues until, at its most passionate moment, rich and flowing, this variant resolves on to a grand restatement of the opening phrase. Thereafter, every retransformation is recessive, little by little losing its energy until at the end it fades completely.

Thinking and making

The children's piece: Dance

We can now look at the details of what the young composers invented. At first hearing, the piece appears to consist of four, more or less independent, episodes: a rhythmic pattern (drum alone), a short introductory phrase in descending octaves, the dance tune, and a brief coda—most of which is then repeated with minor changes. Yet there is a powerful impression of wholeness, suggesting that the composers were intuitively aware of an underlying unity. Can we find anything to confirm this?

If we go straight to the main tune we notice that, in spite of its springy dance rhythms, it has that 'serious' quality often associated with minor keys, but nowhere do we find the expected minor-key features—upward movement to a tonic by way of sharpened submediant and leading note. In fact, this tune is *modal* and exploits typical Dorian mode melody-types—in this case on C—which help to make the tune memorable (see Figs 1, 2, and 3).

Fig. 1

Fig. 2

Fig. 3

The combining of these non-harmonic modal patterns with a chordal piano accompaniment is interesting. It is obvious that the girls will have heard a great deal of harmonic music but we can only guess at where the 'folksy' modal influences may have come from.[3]

The tune, in two broad phrases, lasts for a mere twenty-one seconds, after which there is an abrupt change to the mode on A (with E♮, A♮, and B♮) for a coda: a brief stepwise rise and fall accompanied by other instruments with some contrary motion, the finality of the concluding note emphasized by repetition. This sounds like entirely new material but when we hear it again, in the second half of the piece, it is played three times and the notes in contrary motion are an octave higher, giving them greater prominence. Suddenly we are aware that the 'new' and unexpected rising and falling figure is related to the opening of the piece by means of a simple counterpoint which is, in fact, the introduction transposed down a minor third.

Other melodic elements undergo subtle changes to become unifying features. Thus,

in the first phrase of the tune becomes, in the second phrase,

the changes opening up possibilities for further transformation:

Similarly, in the first phrase

—a traditional modal melody-type—is echoed in the second phrase by

The beginning and ending of the tune is also of interest. At both points we hear the same material with its characteristic syncopation:

but whereas, at the start, it is set off vigorously by an anacrusis and there is a resolution of the syncopation—which also acts as an anacrusis to what follows, in effect pushing the tune onward

—at the end, this same motif but without the additional notes sounds convincingly final: an important factor in the surprise created by the coda which also appears to be 'new':

There is rhythmic as well as melodic unity in the piece. The pattern played by the drum alone at the start does more than merely set the tempo: it focuses attention on the syncopation and is the rhythmic model for the beginning and ending of the tune and also the variant of that motif (Fig. 4).

Many examples of similarly 'clever' transformations can be found in traditional music worldwide, reminding us that such things happen intuitively. Their structural importance is fully revealed only at the moment when the performance finishes, and even then their significance is *felt* rather than

Fig. 4

understood in a logical way. (A satisfaction not unlike that which we can experience even with mundane household chores: the sense of orderliness and completeness at the moment of finishing.)

Of course, it is possible that these ten-year-old composers consciously organized the links and developments in the melody, but it would seem much more likely that they acted instinctively. Experienced composers are aware of how much musical construction goes on in the subconscious mind, and of how they can develop their techniques by 'observing' work in progress, noting these processes, and then consciously exploiting them in other musical circumstances. By teaching from what is offered we can draw attention to possibilities in children's music which, because it is their own, will be important to them, but which can also help them to discover similar things in other people's music.

Schumann: Eusebius

The unifying features are immediately apparent. Even so, Schumann would almost certainly have had to experiment with a number of options before finalizing even the principal motif. Assuming he decided at an early stage that the music should have a vague, uncertain and indecisive character; he then had to think of a way of achieving that *generally.* There were, of course, the harmonic possibilities. On the other hand, he may well have settled first for the duple metre and the divided beats: seven quavers rather than eight giving rise to the main motif. Later, individual beats are divided into fives and threes and, to thicken the plot, that same semiquaver-quintuplet plus quaver-triplet melody line subtly outlines the *duple* metre whilst, in the left hand, *three* crotchets replace the by now established two.

Eusebius has certain things in common with the children's Dance—unifying melodic and rhythmic features, for instance. It also gives the impression of being in two halves, the second a modified reprise of the first. We've seen already how Schumann creates unity by drawing everything melodic from the seven-note motif and its transformations, but in addition, harmonic, dynamic, and textural changes, often of a dramatic nature, are integrated with the melodic developments to create progression (diversity and forward movement) and recession (unity and closure). The miracle of this music is its completeness in every detail; clearly and carefully composed but also deeply felt. For it would be wrong to suppose that intuition is for the musically naive and that 'real' composers construct music always with an almost scientific detachment.

Buried treasure

Whatever place music has in our lives—the reassurance of a familiar repertoire; the challenge of new pieces; a relaxation from the demands of hectic schedules; something to match a mood or raise our spirits; or to create an exciting atmosphere at a party—the only reason why we have anything to do with it is because we want something to happen: we expect in some way to be moved by the music. There are so many things that might attract us: memorable melodies; 'big' orchestral sounds; the overwhelming excitement of a rock band; unusual or exotic instruments; the virtuosity of solo performers; the combination of words and music. Yet none of these would even begin to excite our attention unless it were found in a 'piece' of music.

This is the one thing that everybody knows about music—that it comes in pieces! The word suggests a musical actuality; an event completed and accepted entirely on its own terms. It may be prepared-composed or instantly-composed (improvised), notated or held in the memory, but if the music is 'all of a piece' we experience a flow of sounds such that unexpected developments simultaneously surprise us and sound quite natural—inevitable, even; as though it could not possibly be otherwise.[4] The question of what makes a piece 'a piece' brings us closer to understanding why, whatever diverse sensations we experience in composing, performing and listening, the feeling of self-sufficiency and completeness in the music is of paramount importance.

The wonder of it is how everything comes together and sounds right, pleasing our aesthetic sense: in the words of a medieval translator of Marcus Aurelius Antonius:

How all things upon Earth are pesle mesle; and how miraculously things contrary one to another concurre to the beautie and perfection of this Universe.[5]

How is that concurrence, that sense of *belonging*, brought about? The sculptor, Austin Wright, spoke of 'the points at which things legitimately stick together', arguing that, in sculpture, those points 'should show [because] they are the strength of the structure'. Something very similar occurs in music: the mind engages with the flow of sound and, subliminally, we notice the *changes* that occur. We are aware of the music transforming itself—making itself whole—and we too are transformed, made whole, by it.[6]

The children's piece: Dance

I said at the outset that this struck me as successful music, and I have tried to show how that opinion might be supported by the quality of the musical invention, the melodic and rhythmic developments, and the underlying unities—all the result of decisions taken by the composers. Those decisions were to do mainly with the nature of the materials and what happens to them. We've now begun to touch on another level of decision-taking: the matter of *when* changes and transformations occur.

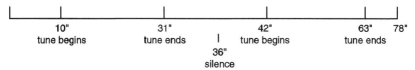

Fig. 5 The Dance: positioning of the tune

The Dance lasts for 78 seconds, of which the most memorable element is the tune itself, placed more or less centrally (Fig. 5).

Between the end of the tune in the first part and its reappearance in the second part is a passage which seems to act like a pivot. It is occupied by the coda, the silence, and a reprise of some of the introductory material—the drum solo but *not* the descending octaves. Why is that last element, so important at the start, omitted here? Did the girls discuss this? Did they at first include it and then decide to leave it out? If so, we still have to ask why. And did they know why? (Perhaps because initial improvisations had given them an impression of how that would feel in relation to the overall duration?) Or was it simply a feeling that the tune had to start again when it does? But there is more. The durations of the opening and closing sections of the piece are *not* symmetrical. The first section (before the start of the tune) lasts for 10 seconds and the final section (the dissonant coda and its repetitions) lasts for 15 seconds. This has the effect of positioning most of those significant changes close to Golden Section points (Fig. 6).

Now, before you howl, 'Not the Golden Section again!', I am well aware that a great deal has been written about it already and that many people must be heartily sick of it.[7] Identifying precise or close coincidences between members of a mathematical sequence and what appear to be important developments in a piece of music will add nothing whatever to anyone's enjoyment of that music, but we should not too hastily dismiss the evidence of a ubiquitous delight in *a*symmetry. If we are interested in developing our own or our pupils' abilities in composition, noting how long this or that lasts, and when it might

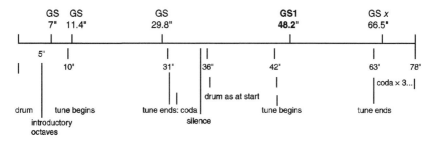

Fig. 6 The Dance: Golden Section points

or might not be the right moment to introduce something different, can reveal why certain things appear to weaken the form whilst others strengthen it. In consequence we may want to reconsider the durations of some sections, although we should bear in mind that there's no such thing as a recipe for a composition, and no one can make 'good' music merely by arranging for 'the climax' to arrive at precisely 0.618 of the overall duration!

Nor should we be influenced by the fact that some great painters—Vermeer, for instance—undoubtedly did calculate in advance these 'special' points on their canvases. Music, because it takes place in time and is subject to subtleties of performance, is an entirely different matter: the relationships are complex and may be sensed but not reckoned. It is not a question of measuring in advance precisely when one particular high point should occur but of realizing that all the elements in a composition interact to produce what we *feel* as a 'rightness' of form which complements the character of the musical materials and is confirmed by the varying strengths of progression or recession at different points in the musical flow.

Figure 6 shows that, in spite of what appeared at first to be a symmetrical form of two more or less equal parts, placing the various sections within the overall timescale reveals an *a*symmetrical form. This tendency applies to the dance tune on its own as well as to the piece as a whole. We have already noticed how a simple stepwise rising of repeated notes in the first half of the tune reappears, modified, in the second half. Although this tiny figure may seem relatively unimportant, the changes it undergoes have a strong effect. Perhaps this is because, whilst we recognize the notes, the metrical displacements and the silent beats unsettle us, engendering expectation and preparing the ear for even more drama as the tune dips and then reaches up to its highest point. Will it continue upwards? But no, it pulls back and drops, to end on the note from which everything sprang. The final silence occurs at the principal GS point and powerfully provokes our expectations, but it is not the climax of the tune. Likewise, the recession *from* the climax, rather than the climax itself, coincides with the Golden Section of the duration between GS1 and the end—which I call GS x: the moment, in numerous pieces of music, when something unusual happens which strengthens the finality of the ending (Fig. 7).[8]

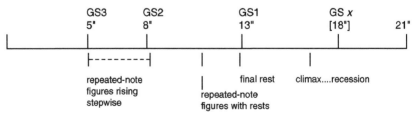

Fig. 7 The Dance: use of repeated-note figure

Schumann, Eusebius

Asymmetrical proportions are evident from the start. In the first statement of the motif, the moment of reaching up to the highest note (E♭) coincides with GS1 of the duration of that seven-note figure, and in the first phrase as a whole other structurally important features occur at Golden Section points (Fig. 8). Why does the high G appear so soon? It is strongly progressive and sounds like a climax point, but its power is immediately dissipated, the melody falling back by way of the F and then the low A♭ to G (so far the lowest pitch in the phrase). If we examine how this works proportionally we find that the pre-emptive 'climax' coincides with GS2 while the low G is at GS1, creating an impression of impulsive action all too quickly running out of steam: when we *expect* an emotional high point we hear instead the music begin to decline. The retreat from the climax is confirmed just three seconds later by that same note G, now clearly signalling 'it's over' (although, in fact, it isn't!), coinciding with that other important point, GS *x*. As in the children's Dance, something of significance at this moment enhances the finality of the closure.

It is inconceivable that Schumann would have calculated the tiny durations which create these asymmetrical proportions—and in any case, there would have been no point in doing so: clearly, he *felt* that these proportions were 'right'. In that first phrase the coincidence of GS1 with a strongly recessive moment characterizes everything that happens subsequently. High points there are in plenty—climaxes of the kind the ear expects—but the essence of this piece is its ambivalence: trying so hard to be outgoing and optimistic but never quite making it; always falling back to introversion and self-doubt. The piece could not be on a larger scale because the 'big' moments cannot sustain themselves. Surely this must be in the nature of the 'possibility' that Schumann sensed in the Idea? It is achieved largely by means of the $\frac{2}{3} + \frac{1}{3}$ unit that permeates the entire form: in every instance, the progressive qualities are developed in the larger part only to be dashed again in the much shorter downward slide to closure.

Particularly striking is the GS1 point of the whole piece. This—marked once more by a languishing dominant ninth—occurs in the midst of the most passionate passage, but is again a moment of 'doubt'. Although it is followed by a final attempt at extrovert passion, ending on the one and only root position of the tonic chord (putting a brave face on it, perhaps?), the tendency towards

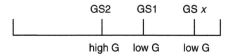

Fig. 8 *Eusebius*: proportional 'markers' in the first phrase

recession is now so powerful that the music can never rise again: it can only fade gently into oblivion.

A universal principle

Francis Bacon wrote that 'There is no excellent beauty that hath not some strangeness in the proportion',[9] seeming to suggest that this maxim would hold good anywhere. Certainly the paradox of a piece of music sounding well balanced because it is in fact *un*balanced is by no means restricted to Western art music. That other cultures also find asymmetry attractive is demonstrated by the following two examples:

1. 'Maharo Jalalo Bilalo Ghar Kad Avasi' (Awaiting the Beloved). A folk song from Rajasthan (recording: *The Songs of The Desert Sands* NRCD 0059 DDD (1995)). The singers are accompanied by *ravenhatta* (long-necked fiddle) and the *dholaka* (double-faced barrel drum). Figure 9 shows that all the important changes are close to, and in one case—the first time we hear the full ensemble—precisely coincident with, Golden Section points. Although we do not consciously listen for such things, there is no doubt that these structurally significant moments are 'the points at which things legitimately stick together', creating the hierarchy of asymmetrical proportions which produces a unified and satisfying piece.

2. *Bubaran Hudan Mas* (Golden Rain), Pélog Patet Barong. Javanese Court Gamelan from the Pura Paku Alaman, Jogyakarta (recording: Elektra Nonesuch Explorer Series, CD 7559-72044-2 (1991)). A *Bubaran* concludes an entertainment and is played as the audience is leaving. *Hudan Mas* is a

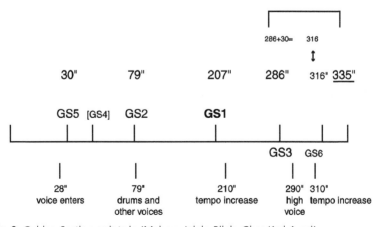

Fig. 9 Golden Section points in 'Maharo Jalalo Bilalo Ghar Kad Avasi'

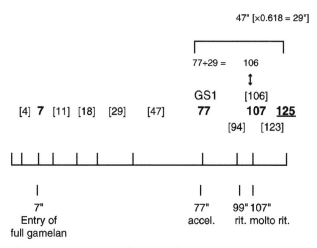

Fig. 10 Golden Section points in *Bubaran Hudan Mas*

well-known piece in the conventional gamelan form. A brief melodic introduction heralds the entry of the full gamelan and develops into a major section establishing the musical material. Later this is transformed by an
accelerando signalled by the drum which controls every change of tempo
and style, and then—again, at a signal from the drum—the pace slackens,
finally changing, at a precise moment (i.e. not gradually) to an even slower
tempo as the end is approached (Fig. 10).

This is not a matter of calculation or analysis but rather of *the perception of
wholeness in what is heard:* the intersection of virtual time with 'real' time,
apparent in the *proportions* of sectional durations to overall duration, the former marked by varying intensities of change (Paynter, 1997a and 1997b). The
control of proportion is what Carter means by 'manipulating the flow of time'
(see note 4). This has nothing to do with musical academicism. It is the most
natural thing in the world and is experienced, not only in the so-called masterworks (prepared-composed or improvised-composed), but also in the hum-
blest of pieces made up by musically untutored people, including the
spontaneous music of children.

How do we know when it's 'right'?

I've had a lot to say about recognizing the 'rightness' of important moments in
music. How can we help school students to develop this sensitivity—possibly
the most important technique in composition? A painter, standing back from
work in progress, might ask, 'Does it look right on a canvas of that size?' In

music the question would be, 'Does it sound right if it goes on for that long?' Composers have to make things work together satisfactorily in a timescale and must judge by what they *hear*, either in the imagination or directly from the sounds.

In fact, this process is not at all unusual. In many areas of life decisions are taken when a number of conditions must be met at the same time. You weigh up all the possibilities, reach a conclusion, and probably say, 'If I do that, I've only myself to blame', accepting that the one person you have to convince is yourself! That is the essential element, learned largely by trial and error. The more familiar we become with the characteristics of what we are judging the more confident our decisions will be. In musical education—from the viewpoint of the teacher—the greater the variety of music we know, and the more we practise listening to the way combinations of musical materials work, the easier we shall find it to discuss pupils' compositions. That discussion will encourage them to think for themselves about what sounds right and why it might be considered to be so, and to know that they have *only themselves to convince.*

They must also understand that, in spite of feeling satisfied at the moment when a composition is completed, they may, nevertheless, have misjudged it. There are many examples of famous works which have been revised after the initial performances because the composers felt that they had taken the wrong decisions. Sometimes this has involved a substantial alteration, such as removing one whole act of an opera. Beethoven's notebooks record his struggles to organize musical materials successfully, and to fashion, by many small changes, the 'right' character of themes and motifs, whilst Schubert's unfinished piano sonata movements show him *failing* to find satisfactory ways of maintaining the flow of the music.

There are two things we should learn from this. First, that composing can never be a mechanical process; it is entirely a matter of judgement and there are no rules other than what the ear tells us is right. Second, even for very experienced composers, until the music is performed, it can be difficult to know if the judgements are correct. So much depends upon that first presentation of the completed piece. We see this happening in the classroom: it isn't until the moment when a finished piece is presented that the teacher and the composer(s) know whether or not it succeeds as music. That is why this is such an important moment in which to comment on what everyone now hears as a 'piece'. By paying careful attention to what happens in their music—and, in particular, *when* certain things happen—the teacher highlights for the students judgements they have made and decisions they have taken.

It is not the purpose of musical education to make children musical: they are already musical, since that is part of their human nature. Our questions draw attention to what they know intuitively—that musical material has potential to *go on*—so that, by taking stock of what they have made up already, the imagination can begin to explore in new directions. As we listen to pupils performing a composition we should try to remember melodic and rhythmic figures and interesting combinations of voices and/or instruments, especially where these are associated with moments of change. We can also have in mind general considerations such as unifying features; whether the music makes sense as a whole; the relationship between duration and the character of the music (how long does it last, and does that seem too long or not long enough?); whether the composers attempt to expand and transform musical materials or merely go on inventing new things; and, not least, the strength and quality of the ending. These are the things to discuss.

As soon as the performance concludes we must be ready to comment. For example, we might ask 'How do you feel about this tune / this rhythm pattern / those particular instruments—do we hear enough of it/them so that we can really enjoy what happens? Or is it over too soon? How would you describe the *character* of this music—serious? solemn? light-hearted?—does it need more—or less—time? Do you think you've got it right? Shall we get tired of it if it goes on too long? What about the beginning? Should that music go on longer so that we really get to know what it's about? Does it change too suddenly to something different? Or does it take too long to get anywhere? Are you sure about the beginning / ending? Why is it like that? Listen to yourselves as you play what you've made: do you think the important things happen when they should? How can we tell? We have to try to feel when it sounds right. Why do you think *that* sounds right? What could you do differently? Would that be better? Why?' And so on. These questions should be directed at the composers. Other members of the class learn from that discussion.

It's unlikely that we shall want to talk to pupils about the Golden Section, and we should certainly not propose that as a 'method' for making a successful piece, but it does show us that durations and proportion—*felt* rather than calculated—play a big part in the success of many different kinds of music. We should not underestimate children's sensitivity to these effects. They may not have listened to as much music as we have but they will have *heard* a lot. Children become aware of music from birth (possibly before birth) and by the age of six they may be experimenting with spontaneous songs of their own (Davies, 1986 and 1992). We can talk with them about those songs or about their experiments with classroom instruments, and as they get a little older we can begin to ask questions such as, 'What do you think that tune might do next?' or 'How do you think this piece should end?' The teacher's task is to help pupils to think about the way music works, and to *realize* that they are thinking about it.

Musical meaning

Music can mean whatever anyone wants it to mean. If, while you listen, you imagine landscapes, seascapes, interplanetary travel or anything else, no one can say that is wrong; but, then, another person's entirely different literal interpretations would not be wrong either! What about the composer's intention for the music: surely that takes priority? We might think so, but that has never stopped film directors and choreographers, for example, from making use of music to support interpretations which probably would never have occurred to the composers. I remember the scornful response of a class of fourteen-year-olds in the mid 1950s who told me I was quite wrong about Holst's 'Mars': they knew the music well, they said, and it had nothing to do with planets; it was from the film *Quatermass*! (Not music *for* the film, you understand, but music *from* the film: a significant difference.)

Does it matter? I doubt it. There is a widespread desire for explanation, but information about the composer's intention and the circumstances in which the music was first performed is unlikely to enhance appreciation substantially: the majority of people believe that music is doing its job if it stirs emotions or suggests images. The possibility that it may represent emotions and 'real world' events, in spite of differences of interpretation, seems to provide at least some kind of answer to the question, 'What does this music mean?'

Yet we could go further. Consider the success of muzak. Those who produce it know that supermarket shoppers' minds can be conditioned by music in the background and that no one needs appreciation lessons or information about composers before they can be moved to make purchases! If we follow that line of argument we might conclude that there is another level of meaning which unites the enormous diversity of interpretation, and *that* could be easier to apprehend if we had no information at all; not even the composer's name and the title of the piece. There's a lot to be said for the innocent ear.

The musical present

The immediacy of music is its most potent property. Even the obvious indicators of meaning—the words of a song or the specific functions of, for example, liturgical music—can be overtaken by the singularity of the musical event: you don't have to be a believer to be deeply moved by religious music. Could it be that every piece, simply by functioning as music, speaks to us of the possibility of the perfection of a single, all-encompassing moment beyond Time? Stravinsky (1962: 53) argued that, because humanity is 'doomed to submit to the passage of time', only in music are we able to 'realize the present'. Does music, then, temporarily alleviate a restlessness which is at the heart of the human condition?

Certainly, if there is such a thing as 'real time' (which some doubt!), we experience it as 'passage', although individual events appear to have margins of varying duration. Thus 'the present time' can mean different things. It could be this very moment—'a split second', as we say—or it could take in a much longer stretch of time: this year; this century. Presumably the 'present' that Stravinsky had in mind would not change in that way: it would have the same (or a very similar) significance for everyone and would be without past or future.[10]

Clearly, some kind of duality is at work here, and that brings us back to the notion of a 'piece'. Everything we need to know about the music is there in what we hear; a unique sound-world the purpose of which is, literally, to entertain us—*inter tenere* 'to hold [us] between' two experiences of existence: chronometric time and psychological time; reality and imagination; the finite and the infinite. An entire audience will be aware simultaneously of the beginning and ending of a piece but during the course of the performance everyone will feel differently about how the time is passing—or, perhaps, not passing: often there is a sensation of time suspended.

The 'normal' present of our quotidian lives appears to be an emergent event; a *becoming*, the inner nature of each 'present' shaped by past conditions and suggesting an as yet unrealized future (Mead, 1932: 19). The occasion of a concert or a recital is just such a present: it has 'become'—i.e. it is conditioned by its past (preparation and anticipation: the performers have rehearsed and advertised the programme and the audience has bought tickets) and it forecasts a future (reaction, reflection, and understanding or rejection)—but there is a qualitative difference between that and the making present of the music on the programme. Each piece remains a putative form until actualized as an *occurrent event* at a designated point in the *continuant* 'present time' of the concert. The special present of the musical event is not a 'becoming' but a singular occurrence in which all the elements are organically related to each other and only to each other, 'for nothing else exists there' (Langer, 1953: 109, 262). In other words, it functions as music only at the point in time and space when and where we receive it.

Musicians and poets are keenly aware of this unique quality, particularly at the moment of a work's conception. For Hindemith it was like seeing a landscape lit by a flash of lightning. Seamus Heaney speaks of 'the poem as a ploughshare that turns time / Up and over'[11]—in effect, exposing and holding up a piece of time for us to contemplate—and Elizabeth Jennings describes vividly that moment in the composition of a poem when, suddenly and perhaps unexpectedly, everything comes together: 'in the large flights of imagination / I see for one crammed second, order so / Explicit that I need no more persuasion.'[12] Likewise, when we perform or listen to a piece of music, what ultimately persuades us that this is worth doing is not information about the cultural/historical context nor even the possibility of the music representing something else, but the *musical thought* itself concentrated in the special present of the performance. To recognize that we must also be aware of the 'normal' present in which all of this is happening.

The importance of this duality was illustrated by György Ligeti some years ago in a filmed discussion of his *Lux Aeterna* for sixteen voices. In 1966 Ligeti had broken new ground with this work. The challenge he had set himself was to create a dense micropolyphony which would produce little or no feeling of movement but which, like all other music, would satisfy listeners' expectations of conclusion and completeness. This meant that the interdependence of psychological time and chronometric time was particularly significant, and Ligeti described how, whilst 'listening' to the piece in his imagination, he used a stopwatch to confirm the 'right' performance duration. Instead of the melodic lines and clearly audible words of conventional choral music, a fragmented text is slowly unfolded with subtly increasing and decreasing intensity in a web of vocal colour. It is hardly surprising that such highly atmospheric music was later used as part of the film score for *2001: A Space Odyssey*. The voices enter gently, one by one, on a unison (*Sostenuto, molto calmo:* 'from afar'), moving outwards very gradually in intricate canons to form shimmering note-clusters which spread and draw together, little by little reaching up to a high point and then descending to end an octave lower than the opening. It lasts for just under eight minutes, but it *feels* timeless.

Music as a model of possibility

Much of this has to do with the mind's ability to flip backwards and forwards between the two time modes, testing the 'rightness' or otherwise of the experience. This is rather like those images which can be interpreted differently according to how one chooses to view them (Fig. 11).

It also has something in common with that other familiar sensation when two trains, heading in opposite directions, are stationary side-by-side. One starts to move, but passengers in the other have the impression that it is *their* train that is moving. By looking away from the window they can tell immediately that their train is stationary, but looking out of the window again reverses the sensation. In other words, the mind occupies two linked existences: one in motion, the other at rest (cf. Mead, 1932: 80). Einstein observed this and similar phenomena as he travelled by tram to his work in the Swiss Patent Office, and from those experiences he derived his General Theory of Relativity which

Fig. 11

has had such a profound effect upon the course of science. Could it be that the relativity of time perception which we experience in music awakens, somewhere deep in the unconscious, a feeling of encounter with forces that drive the universe?

Perhaps too, it resonates with humanity's attempts to reconcile the evidence of physical change with perceptions of an unchanging existence. The Hindu *Trimurti*—the triad of Brahma, Vishnu, and Siva: the unity of a single body with three heads—has only superficial resemblance to the Christian Trinity but the resonance of a threefold perfection is striking. The essential Trinitarian quality is its indivisibility: 'The Utterer, Utterèd, Uttering'[13]—that which exists outside Time (*Idea / Logos*) manifesting itself in history (*Event / Incarnation*) and continuing to enlighten (*Spirit / Meaning / Understanding*). Here, change and unchange are two aspects of the same thing. Parallel with this—in religious thought, mythology, science and art—is the doctrine of interacting opposites: death and resurrection, the Chinese yin-yang; Siva symbolizing simultaneously destruction and renovation; Pandora's box of evils sent by Zeus to offset the fire which Prometheus had stolen to save the human race; Empedocles's conviction that the four elements—earth, air, fire and water—whilst individually immutable, were combined and separated in various ways by the opposing forces of Love and Discord, continuously making, destroying, and remaking; the protagonist and antagonist of Greek tragedy; and even our somewhat jaundiced, contemporary view that 'life rubs along on hostilities!' Each of these, in its own way, is a response to the question, 'What makes existence *possible*—what makes it work as it does?' Does musical 'possibility' both ask and answer the same question? If so, that could explain why human beings seem unable to do without music.

'Somewhere in the memory there is always music'

It may seem that we have strayed a long way from the question of what to say to children about their compositions, but this has not been a diversion. Speculating on the roots of our music-making points us towards the *necessity* of what we do. For in whatever way we interpret the fundamental motivations—psychological, spiritual, or biochemical—it is clear that they apply universally. All the world makes music and, as Curt Sachs (1944: 20–21) says:

> However far back we trace mankind, we fail to see the springing up of music ... for [it] has little to do with the mutable surface of life, and nothing with the struggle for existence. This is why music is one of the steadiest elements in the evolution of mankind.

If, then, the need to create music plays such a major part in human life why do we not recognize that necessity and capitalize upon it in education? Why do we so often leave students with the impression that 'real' composing is what other, specially talented, people do? Partly, I suspect, it is because we take for granted the natural magic of making up music. The sheer quantity of music now available makes it difficult for us to convey to pupils the sense of adventure, and like so many other magical things in nature we expect music to be there whenever we want it. It is 'the daily doing which takes off the admiration'.[14] But this is also the key. Music is able to mean anything anyone wants it to mean only because *at root* it means the same thing to everyone: we assume that all music will behave musically. Does not this underlying universal sensitivity to music as *music* suggest very strongly that composing and performing are, jointly, the true basis of musical education?

Knowledge: the dilemma of education

Yet, in spite of what everyone knows intuitively about the nature of music, on the whole its place in the school curriculum is justified still, not by the educational potential of musical activity—unique and unlike anything else we may encounter—but by the body of knowledge it appears to represent.

Knowledge comes in many different guises and occasionally we may wonder why anyone should think it worth the effort of gathering the information. Some years ago, in an article for *The Times*, Bernard Levin wrote, with barely disguised scorn, of research designed to discover whether lobsters moved faster across the seabed in single file or line abreast. Yet even if we can't see the point of such a project, or find it amusing, we might conclude that, in the grand scheme of things, it must be useful because all knowledge is equally valuable.

To a large extent the school curriculum is based on that unspoken belief. In whatever way we define education, schooling seems to be about imparting and receiving knowledge, and in this we prefer conformity rather than discriminating between different ways of coming to know. That is justified by a curriculum which takes its validity from the standards of its component parts but at the same time judges the credibility of subjects by their intellectual comparability. It is hardly surprising that students want to feel that they are mastering skills and learning something quantifiable, but is the one-size-fits-all model of the curriculum necessarily the right one? Even accepting that no knowledge is entirely without value, should we not be asking what kind of knowledge is *appropriate* to the subject? We could then consider how that appropriate knowledge might command respect by being dealt with in a way comparable with the most intellectually demanding subjects.

Educational theorists in the late eighteenth and early nineteenth centuries argued that music should be part of every child's elementary schooling. What they had in mind was singing, which they believed could have wide-ranging benefits for general education (Rainbow, 1989: 175 *et seq.*). As this idea became established it was supported by the tonic sol-fa methods of Sarah Glover, John Hullah and John Curwen, leaders in an amazing popular movement which introduced some thousands of people, many from among the poorest groups, to the pleasures of music-making. Tonic sol-fa is a means to an end: a notation devised specifically to help singers pitch intervals accurately and to enable them to achieve results faster than they could with staff notation. But by the 1870s the use of tonic sol-fa in the schools had become a step towards theoretical knowledge: 'the scientific study of music' (Rainbow, 1989: 253, citing Heathcote Statham). And there, perhaps, we have the seeds of a music curriculum in which inert facts can take precedence over active musical experience.

The Appreciation lesson, central to school musical education from the 1930s to the early 1950s, tended to equate meaning with the pre-musical Context (which usually included anecdotes of the composer's life) and Intention (e.g. to compose a sonata—*cue* information about sonata form). The National Curriculum has continued in that vein. In spite of including performance and composition as classroom activities it tends to support the belief that intellectual rigour is provided by historical/cultural information, notation skills, and 'bar-by-bar' descriptive analysis. This also appears to raise the status of music by giving it parity with subjects such as history, mathematics and languages, but it does little to develop students' interest in their own creative efforts. Indeed, it may have the opposite effect, students being inclined to undervalue their composing because the approved curriculum appears to value the other things more.

In his recent book, *Musicking*, Christopher Small suggests that the well-established view of musical knowledge has been detrimental to the way in which concert audiences listen, its continuing influence due to musical historians, not least among them:

the doyen of contemporary German musicologists, Carl Dalhaus, who tells us, flatly that 'the subject matter of music is made up, primarily, of significant works of music that have outlived the culture of their age' and that 'the concept 'work' and not 'event' is the cornerstone of music history'. (Small, 1998: 4, citing Dalhaus, 1983)

I have argued elsewhere that music's most compelling quality is that it has no history: 'nowness' is of its essence (Paynter, 1997a/1997b). The study of musical history is not the study of *music* because, regardless of the culture of the age in which it was composed, a piece of music has no relevance except for those who perform it and listen to it at the moment when they perform and listen—i.e. within their own time and culture. The differences between live and recorded performances are also significant.[15] Indisputably we experience every work of music as an independent *event* not as a musical object: the score (which is what Dalhaus means by the concept 'work') is no more than a sign of potential music. Notation is an imperfect science and composers have a habit of making alterations or leaving things in a sketchy state.[16] And in any case, an improvisation is just as much a 'work' as is a notated composition.

The tendency which Small identifies among concert-goers has also influenced musical education. In spite of the attention we pay to other cultures, the highest achievements of Western art music still seem to represent a body of *knowledge* by which we may assess the worth of any music. By comparison with that canon of acceptable, stood-the-test-of-time musical works the compositional efforts of school pupils are bound to appear primitive. It seems hardly possible that we should develop a worthwhile level of discourse around such pieces. All too easily we may leave students with the impression that, whilst we believe it is good for them to 'have a go' at composing, that is not on the same intellectual plane as learning about 'great' music.

Yet the 'learning about' could be appropriate were it linked purposefully to creative and artistic questions arising from students' composing and performing. For example, in the children's 'Dance' discussed earlier, their intuitive Dorian tune might have started them on an exploration of modes generally (including Indian rāgs), leading to the conscious use of that knowledge to create more modal pieces. Or again, the strongly characteristic folk dance style (Greek?—hinting at the syncopations of the *kalamatianos*; or Israeli? e.g. the tiny decorative downward movement at the end of the first phrase which we do not hear the second time round[17]) could lead to further compositions deliberately exploiting characteristics of other ethnic musics, much as Bartók and Janáček did.

Music stemming from literary or visual contexts presents particular problems when it comes to deciding what is appropriate knowledge. It is tempting to think that if we tell students 'the story' they will understand the music more easily. Unfortunately, that has the opposite effect. Beethoven was certainly aware that, by imitating birdsong in the slow movement of his Sixth Symphony, he might be giving listeners the wrong idea. In his own programme note for that work he made it clear that this was 'more an expression of feeling than a painting'. Similarly, an evocative title, even when it is meant to help, may send us in the wrong direction. Liszt, in spite of being the inventor of 'programme music', would not have expected listeners to hear 'Les cloches de Genève' (from the first set of *Années de Pèlerinage*) as nothing more than a representation of bells.

What appropriate knowledge could we derive from listening to Schumann's 'Eusebius' in the way I have suggested above? The piece might be played and discussed as follow-up to a composition project involving the combining of contrasting characteristics. In that case it could be helpful for students to know that *Carnaval* is a collection of twenty-one 'characteristic pieces', a genre which, although not in any sense 'programme music', often displays strong associative links between Context and Idea. Here the background is the *comedia del'arte* with its Pierrot-like figures, to which is added the dual persona of Eusebius and Florestan symbolizing Schumann's view of his own personality, by turn introvert and extrovert. The Context could be the basis for thinking about how a musical Idea might be derived from thoughts about introversion and extroversion.

Inevitably the school curriculum will always be under review and subject to change. Whatever the reasons for such changes—demographic, ideological—it is the teachers who have to try to make sense of what is to be done. A curriculum which cannot allow for differences in the kind of knowledge and progression appropriate to individual subjects makes every teacher's job harder. In music, even an unwitting emphasis upon 'the scientific study of music' and an onwards-and-upwards notion of progression seems to have influenced students to think of composing as a relatively unimportant aspect of their education. In such an atmosphere it is very difficult for teachers to help students to get better at composing.

My principal concern here has been to show that, aside from the enormous quantity of information that has grown up around the study of music, and irrespective of variety in style and interpretation, it is the essentially musical properties—that is to say, the ways in which we recognize it as music—that draw us in and persuade us to become involved with it. Therefore, it is what can be learned from musical *activity*—composing and performing—that makes most sense of the subject as an element of the school curriculum. Music-making offers students a chance to encounter a kind of knowledge different from that which characterizes the majority of curriculum subjects. Unless, in the first place, we can capitalize upon that there would seem to be little justification for including music in the curriculum at all. Historical information, the techniques of harmony and counterpoint and analysis are important and worthwhile so long as they are directly related to musical activity, but when such things become ends in themselves, hurdles to be overcome or a mere gathering of knowledge because it is felt that this gives the study of music academic validity, then, inevitably, imagination and creativity are downgraded and real musical understanding goes further beyond reach.

Notes

[1] As we enter a new century it is interesting to note that, in spite of curriculum changes designed to restore standards allegedly lost in the 'freedom' of 1970s schooling, more and more business operations are calling upon education to develop students' collaborative potential. Twenty-five years ago we were demonstrating that musical education in schools could provide opportunities for the kind of creative 'team' working that is now so highly valued. Why has that been forgotten? (See Grenville Hancox, 'Music Education and Industry', in Paynter, 1982:239–40.)

[2] The cassette tape accompanying *BJME* 8 (1991). The piece I have selected can be found in track 37. It was composed by three girls participating in a Durham Summer School for Young Musicians. The recording is associated with the article 'Music and Play' by the late Richard Addison (*BJME* 8/3: 207–17. See also *BJME* 10/1: 2). Detailed commentary on the music was not a consideration in that article because Addison's principal concern was with composing as an example of 'play'. He noted only the circumstances in which the piece was produced and used ('The next piece also was composed by a group of three girls. It was intended in the first place as a dance, but was later fitted with words. The dissonant ending is entirely intentional (drum and piano)'). See *BJME* 8/3: 311n. from which the position of the piece in track 37 can be identified.

[3] These children appear to have done quite naturally what one famous British composer did deliberately—to spite his teacher! In a broadcast talk given towards the end of his life, Ralph Vaughan Williams spoke of how he had begun to be interested in modality during the 1890s. His composition teacher, Charles Villiers Stanford, had little time for such experiments and, trying to steer VW back to classical harmony, told him to compose a waltz: 'So, I wrote a waltz', said VW, 'I wrote a *modal* waltz!'

[4] Cf. Alexander Goehr, 'I write music so that people can follow from bar to bar, and know that some notes follow and others don't' (BBC broadcast talk). Also Elliot Carter, 'to me composing consists in dealing with the flow of music rather than with particular instants of sound ... Music is the only world in which you can really manipulate the flow of time ... so that how you make the stream flow

and what obstacles you put in to stop it from flowing ... become fundamental.'
(Alan Edwards, *Flawed Words and Stubborn Sounds: a Conversation with Elliot Carter* (New York: W. W. Norton & Co., 1971: 37.))

5 'Pesle mesle'—pell-mell, confused, disordered.

6 For well over 2500 years—certainly from Plato onwards—this important property of music has been discussed and written about. It underpins the now standard paramedical practice of music therapy. In addition, almost all 'alternative' medicine makes use of music for what is seen as its power to *calm*. However, another interpretation might be more accurate: that music, rather than calming (in the sense of disengaging the mind from its immediate concerns), actually *engages* the mind with the musical processes and transformations, transporting us, as it were, into a different state of awareness; notably our awareness of how time is passing.

7 I confess to having written about it myself in a number of publications, beginning with *Sound and Silence* (1970: 197–9). In 1965 I had come across Ernö Lendvai's article, 'Duality and Synthesis in the Music of Béla Bartók' (*New Hungarian Quarterly*, 3/7, 1962)—the first exposition of a theory he subsequently developed in *Béla Bartók: an Analysis of his Music* (London: Kahn & Averill, 1971). I was greatly influenced by his ideas, but later came to feel that, in a basic feature of his method, Lendvai was mistaken: he calculated the durations in numbers of bars whereas, in reality, we are concerned with the durations we *experience*. About such a crucial matter the score can tell us nothing: everything depends upon the duration of a piece in *performance*.

8 To give just one example, the completely unexpected rising demisemiquavers [thirty-second notes] in the two final bars of the first fugue (C major) in Book 1 of Bach's '48'.

9 *Essays or Counsels Civill and Morall* (1612), no. 43.

10 Metaphorically, that is, since this could not strictly be true. It would be possible to conceive of a present that included the whole of temporal reality, but 'Whatever else it would be it would not be a present, for that out of which it had passed would not have ceased to exist, and that which is to exist would already be in that inclusive present' (Mead, 1932: 1).

11 Seamus Heaney, 'Poet's Chair' 3 (*The Spirit Level*. London, Faber and Faber, 1996).

12 Elizabeth Jennings, 'I count the moments', *Collected Poems 1953–1985* (Manchester: Carcanet Press, 1986).

13 Gerard Manley Hopkins: unfinished poem on *Margaret Clitheroe*.

14 John Donne, Sermon XXII, St Paul's Cathedral, Easter Day 1627: 'the ordinary things in Nature would be greater miracles than the extraordinary, which we admire most, if they were done but once; The standing still of the Sun, for *Josuahs* use, was not, in it selfe so wonderful a thing, as that so vast and immense a body as the Sun should run so many miles in a minute; The motion of the Sun were a greater wonder than the standing still ... And onely the daily doing takes off the admiration.'

15 Much is made (by BBC Radio 3, for example) of 'live' broadcasts of concerts, suggesting that this offers something substantially different from recorded

concerts. But apart from the fact that the broadcast is taking place at the same time as the event in the concert hall (a fact which is of no musical import whatsoever), what we hear through our loudspeakers is what the engineers want us to hear, and that may include all manner of acoustic modifications to make the broadcast sound 'more acceptable'. In this way it is the *broadcast* which is made important, not the music. The 'live presence', which is an essential part of musical experience, cannot be transmitted.

[16] Handel and his contemporaries routinely altered the scores of major operatic and choral works to take advantage of new performance opportunities. Mozart would deliberately leave details to the chance of the concert occasion: for example, the piano concerto in D major K.537 (known as the 'Second Coronation' concerto) was composed in 1788 but the score was always incomplete. When Mozart performed the concerto in Frankfurt in October 1790 much of what the audience heard would have been improvised. No cadenzas were written down, some melodies in the piano right hand were in outline only, and *the entire left-hand part was left blank*—it was completed in 1794 by an anonymous hack so that the score could be published. Concert audiences listening to this concerto today are not generally aware that a substantial amount of what they hear is not by Mozart.

[17] Cf. the two Druze dance tune examples in the *New Grove* article on 'Israel'. (Stanley Sadie, ed., *The New Grove Dictionary of Music and Musicians* (London: Macmillan, 1980), 9: 358–9.)

References

Dalhaus, C. (trans. J. B. Robinson, 1983) *Foundations of Music History*. Cambridge: Cambridge University Press.

Davies, C. (1986) 'Say it till a song comes (reflections on songs invented by children 3–13)', *BJME*, 3 (3), 279–93.

——(1992) 'Listen to my song: a study of songs invented by children aged 5 to 7 years', *BJME*, 9 (1), 19–48.

Gammon, V. (1996) 'What is wrong with school music? A response to Malcolm Ross', *BJME*, 13 (2), 101–22.

Holbrook, D. (1967) *Children's Writing*. Cambridge: Cambridge University Press.

Langer, S. K. (1953) *Feeling and Form: a theory of art developed from Philosophy in a New Key*. London: Routledge & Kegan Paul.

Mead, G. H. (1932/ed. A. E. Murphy, 1959) *The Philosophy of the Present*. La Salle, Illinois: The Open Court Publishing Company.

Paynter, J. (1982) *Music in the Secondary School Curriculum: trends and developments in class music teaching*. Cambridge: Cambridge University Press.

——(1992) *Sound and Structure*. Cambridge: Cambridge University Press.

——(1997a) 'The form of finality: a context for musical education', *BJME* 14 (1), 5–21.

——(1997b) 'Che cosa si può dire sulla musica?' *beQuadro*, 66/67. Fiesole: Centro di Ricerca e di Sperimentazione per la Didattica Musicale.

——& Aston, P. (1970) *Sound and Silence: classroom projects in creative music*. Cambridge: Cambridge University Press.

Rainbow, B. (1989) *Music in Educational Thought and Practice*. Aberystwyth: Boethius Press.

Ross, M. (1995) 'What's wrong with school music?' *BJME*, 12 (3), 185–201.

Sachs, C. (1994) *The Rise of Music in the Ancient World East and West*. London: J. M. Dent & Sons.

Small, C. (1998) *Musicking: the meanings of performing and listening*. Hanover: University of New England Press.

Spencer, P. (1981) 'Different Drummers: the case for Afro-American music making in the school curriculum'. Unpubl. D.Phil. thesis: University of York.

(1993) 'GCSE Music: a survey of undergraduate opinion', *BJME*. 10 (2), 73–84.

Stravinsky, I. (1962) *An Autobiography*. New York: W. W. Norton.

Music in the school curriculum: why bother?

From the *British Journal of Music Education*, 19:3 (2002) (Cambridge University Press), pp. 215–26

This article is a revised and expanded version of the text of the Third Annual Bernarr Rainbow lecture, delivered on Wednesday 17 October 2001 at the Guildhall School of Music and Drama, London, and reproduced here by kind permission of the Bernarr Rainbow Trust.

In spite of centuries of experience and experiment, the practicalities and benefits of general education (schooling) remain uncertain. Can we sustain the spread of subjects that now make up the curriculum? In particular, can we justify time spent on music, which to many would appear to be a specialized study for the talented? The evidence of past practice suggests that the content of classroom music teaching has not done much to help the majority of people to understand music. Yet making music is manifestly an important feature of our humanity. Are there principles at work deep in the nature of music which explain this, and can those features be exploited as the basis of a musical education which will have value for everyone?

In his *English Social History* (1942: 582), George Trevelyan revealed a disappointment with formal education. It had, he said, 'produced a vast population able to read but unable to distinguish what is worth reading'. Twenty-two years later the American psychologist B. F. Skinner, writing in *New Scientist* (1964: 484), suggested that 'Education is what survives when what has been learnt has been forgotten'—a maxim echoed in his book *The Technology of Teaching* (Skinner, 1968: 148), where he asserts that 'one of the ultimate advantages of an education is simply coming to the end of it'.

So much, then, for 'schooling'; for that is what Trevelyan and Skinner had in mind: not an abstract theory of education but the practicalities of the curriculum. In effect they both seem to have been suggesting that school probably doesn't do us much harm but neither does it do us a great deal of good. How, then, can we justify the content of the school curriculum? Should it include anything other than the basic skills of literacy and numeracy? And if there should be other subjects, can we justify time spent on music? Does music have identifiable educational benefit?

Knowledge and understanding

The word 'curriculum' suggests 'a course to be run'; a voyage of discovery, perhaps—although in practice the emphasis has tended to be on the challenge rather than on the experience. A curriculum very easily becomes a summary of knowledge to be passed on, established skills to be acquired and well-attested facts to be memorized. Thus Roger Ascham (ed. Arber, 1927: 25) in the late sixteenth century:

After the childe hath learned perfitlie the eight partes of speach, let him then learne the right joyning together of substantives and adjectives, the nowne with the verbe, the relatiue with the antecedent.

Applied to schooling, prescribed learning became the norm, notwithstanding other possibilities demonstrated by visionary teachers such as Pestalozzi (1746–1827) and Froebel (1782–1852), who believed that it was important to build upon pupils' experiences and personal discoveries (cf. Rainbow, 1989: 135; Kendall, 1986). Given the incidence of reforming views, it is, perhaps, surprising that legislation in nineteenth-century England enacting 'universal education' merely reinforced the tendency to prescription and conformity. Clearly the notion of 'education for all' implied that the school curriculum should be *accessible to all pupils,* but often that was achieved by reducing everything to mechanical tasks which could be practised by pupils en masse under the teacher's direction. Paradoxically, those tasks—regarded, presumably, as 'simplifications'—were distilled from relatively advanced practice and either took for granted or ignored natural starting points for the development of understanding. The twentieth century saw more carefully refined notions of education and the ways in which children learn. For example, the compilers of the 1931 Hadow Report were quite clear that:

A good school ... is not a place of compulsory instruction, but a community of old and young, engaged in learning by cooperative experiment ... The essential point is that the curriculum should not be loaded with inert ideas and crude blocks of fact ... It must be vivid, realistic, a stream in motion, not a stagnant pool. (Hadow *et al.*, 1931: xvii, xxiii)

Similarly, the 'Butler' Education Act of 1944 recognized the need to educate children according to their 'age, aptitude and ability', and today it is readily acknowledged that not all children learn in the same way. That, together with the increasing variety of curriculum opportunities, suggests at least a tacit acceptance of 'other ways of coming to know'. Yet, notwithstanding the educational developments of the second half of the twentieth century the corpus of factual knowledge to be *passed on* has retained its primacy not only because correlations of right/wrong and success/failure make it easy to evaluate pupils' progress but also because there are now more and more demands upon schools to provide evidence of the efficacy of their teaching. Unfortunately, league tables and performance criteria tend to play down the difference between assessment (informed but nevertheless subjective *judgement*) and evaluation (definition of a precise—and, therefore, presumably, indisputable—value). We seem to have reached a point where we accept without question the possibility of *evaluating* all learning in terms which will have the same meaning across the curriculum. As a consequence, we may all too easily allow ourselves to be trapped by compromise, making important what can most easily be evaluated rather than valuing what is important. In which case, why do we bother with 'other ways of coming to know' which although they may be assessed, cannot be evaluated—notably, anything that relies upon the exercise of imagination, creative response, and the expression of independent views.

Music is different

Music has no past; it exists only at the moment when it happens, and no two performances are identical.[1] This is not a disadvantage. On the contrary, it is music's greatest asset because, perhaps more than anything else in our experience, it evokes the essential 'now' without implications of a past and a potential future. Thus, Stravinsky (1962: 53) pointed out that only through music are we able to 'realize the present'. Musical 'meaning' cannot be separated from the act of presentation. However, the necessity of *present*-ing music—making it present here and now, without which it will not be music at all—does not sit easily with a concept of education that rests mainly upon received factual knowledge and which, by tradition, uses the past to make sense of the present.[2] If we want music to have a rôle in general education it would seem logical to acknowledge this difference and give prominence to activities that will involve all pupils working directly with music. Yet, in spite of numerous attempts to develop a more *musical* music curriculum for the majority of school pupils, the 'immediacy' of the experience is given scant attention in the classroom, the emphasis being still, as it has been for so long, on pupils absorbing inert information about music.

The reasons for this are not hard to find. Probably very few people would regard music's distinctive 'nowness' as a property of the art itself. Doubtless, the majority would see it simply as the most obvious result of musicians per-forming to audiences. During the middle decades of the twentieth century a new sense of purpose began to be evident in grammar-school music teaching with the development of orchestras, bands, and choirs. The advent of LEA peripatetic instrumental teachers had made it possible for grammar school 'directors of music' to emulate the positive and characteristic features of music in independent schools. Subsequently, the comprehensive schools inherited this practice but, understandably, insisted that the music-making should be seen as part of the curriculum even though rehearsals were normally scheduled 'out-of-timetable'. With rare exceptions, such activities still cater for a minority of pupils—it could hardly be otherwise—but the ultimate justification is that the ensembles *give concerts*. That, in a roundabout way, influenced the programme-note style of timetabled 'music' lessons which, over many years, has subtly emphasized the difference between the concert-giving minority's activity and the musical *in*activity of everyone else. It gave rise to the theory that, although the 'unmusical' majority might not be able to participate in music-making, if their education provided them with enough information *about* music, they could become 'good listeners'. Have we realized that aim to any greater extent than Trevelyan, 60 years ago, thought we had done with literature? Might it not be more honest to forget the general 'music lessons' and allow music-making to be an option for those who show the appropriate inter-est and practical talent? Or again, should we not bother at all with music in schools, providing instead dedicated facilities for those who want them in local music schools or conservatoires?

Words as a substitute for experience

Given the curriculum's focus on factual knowledge it is hardly surprising that there has been so much 'talking about music'. In the memories of some of us who were at school in the 1930s and early 1940s Musical Appreciation may well be associated with Walford Davies's legendary broadcasts (Rainbow, 1989: 294, 309, 346). By contrast, the regular classroom music teaching at secondary level tended to lapse into formula, feeding pupils 'facts' about music often without them hearing any music at all—as, for example, in the teaching of so-called Form. As a result, so many concert-goers now believe that they must have infor-mation before they listen to music. Yet at the same time they may find them-selves alienated by what they read! As Bernard Levin famously wrote, in an article in *The Times,* after attending a performance of Bach's *The Art of Fugue*—and having been thoroughly bemused by the programme note references to 'fugues by augmentation and diminution', and 'canons *rectus et inversus*'—'The problem with this stuff is that those who can understand it don't need it, and those who need it can't understand it!'

It does seem unfortunate that, in the name of education, people have been brought misguidedly to believe that they need such detail. Originally intended simply as background support, this information is transformed into essential knowledge which, although it may be interesting in itself, has nothing directly to do with what is experienced. Rather, it appears to suggest that, in spite of all the careful artifice of those who labour to create it and present it, *music has to be explained.* People truly believe that they will not appreciate what they hear without words of explanation. And what are they offered? Either a description of what is being 'portrayed', on the assumption that this will give the music some kind of tangibility—even though we all know music cannot 'portray' anything except by association—or else an impenetrable technical analysis plus an account of the composer's life. That kind of information reinforces the conviction that music cannot speak directly to us; which is tantamount to saying that composers and performers don't know what they are doing.

Composers themselves have frequently made it clear that such marginal information is neither helpful nor necessary. For example, Beethoven, in the announcement of his 'Pastoral' symphony, warned listeners that he was not offering them anything so crude as an attempt to imitate the sounds of nature: rather, they should hear it as a 'recollection of feelings'.[3] Debussy, irritated by analysts, remarked, 'You don't capture the mystery of a forest by counting its trees!'—and, on another occasion, 'Insensitive rabble! Can't you listen to chords without demanding to see their identity cards and characteristics? Where have they come from? Where are they going to? Is it really necessary to know this? Just listen. That's enough'[4] (Boucourechliev, 1972: 84).

And, of course, he did mean *listen:* that is to say, listen attentively to the progress of the music, immersing yourself in *what happens.* Here are some others:

What I would like to achieve is music that is self-contained; music determined to free itself from any suggestion of the picturesque; completely non-descriptive and unassociated with any particular locality in space. (Albert Roussel in 1929, cited in Hoérée, 1938: 66)

Most people like music because it gives them certain emotions; such as joy, grief, sadness, an image of nature, a subject for day-dreams, or—better still—oblivion from everyday life ... Music would not be worth much if it were reduced to such an end. (Stravinsky, 1962: 163)

I believe that every musical work, regardless of the philosophical concepts, emotions and attitudes which may have inspired it, is always 'pure music'. (Szymanowski [1933])

... every composer begins with a musical idea—a MUSICAL idea, you understand, not a ... literary or extra-musical idea. (Copland, 1957: 23)

I write music so that people can follow, from bar to bar; and know that some notes follow and others don't. (Alexander Goehr, in a broadcast talk introducing a new work)

If you've gotta ask, you'll never know! (Louis Armstrong when asked to define jazz)

Again, if composers themselves doubt that music can be 'explained', should we be devoting precious school time to providing mere information?

Making the most of our musical nature

If music is to make a worthwhile contribution to general education we must look beyond its potential for sentimental association; beyond historical and technical information; beyond cultural, sociological or political reference. None of these things truly *explains* music, for, even without them, music itself is a form of knowledge; not of the same kind as (say) historical or scientific knowledge and only tenuously connected with the observable, measurable world we call 'reality', but an important 'way of knowing', nevertheless. The very existence of music in our lives is evidence of something we cannot afford to ignore; how otherwise would it have persisted as such a powerful and necessary element in every human society? As Curt Sachs (1944: 21, 22), pointed out:

However far back we trace mankind, we fail to see the springing up of music. Even the most primitive tribes are musically beyond the first attempts.... [Music] has little to do with the mutable surface of life, and nothing [to do with] the struggle for existence. This is why music is one of the steadiest elements in the evolution of mankind.

Since the invention of sound recording the number of people who are consumers of, rather than participants in, music must have increased enormously, but although those we regard as 'musical' may now be in a minority, musical *understanding* still belongs, quite naturally, to us all. John Blacking (1959: 8) made the point plainly:

'My' society claims that only a limited number of people are musical, and yet it behaves as if all people possessed the basic capacity without which no musical function can exist—the capacity to listen to and distinguish patterns of sound.

This is important because when we begin to consider why music might have a place in the school curriculum we must believe that a teacher's commitment is to all the pupils, not only to those with conventional talent. Music may have a rôle in school life socially but, if it is to be a valuable *curriculum* subject, what is done in the classroom must reach out to every pupil; that is to say, it must exploit natural human musicality.

How, then, is this inherent musicality manifest? Not, I think, in the first instance by listening to music, nor even by learning from someone else how to play on an instrument, but by *making up music*. Across the ages most of the world's music has been made up—invented and performed—by musically untutored people. There are still people like that in every culture, and they are still making music. It may be that most of us have come to think of music as something to be *listened* to—in the same way that we think of paintings as objects to be *looked at*—yet, in essence, both music and paintings are what human beings *make:* it is the act of making that justifies the art.[5]

Here is something everyone can do, using whatever means are most suitable to the immediate purpose: voices, conventional instruments, 'classroom' instruments, or indeed any other ways of making and controlling sounds musically. In schools this idea began to be explored seriously in the mid 1950s and early 1960s,[6] although, prior to that—indeed, going back to Jean-Jacques Rousseau in the mid eighteenth century—composing had been advocated as an essential element in basic musical education.[7] Today numerous recordings from many countries provide abundant evidence of children's intuitive musical creativity.[8]

The principle is simple: to teach from what is offered. Even quite young children will make up spontaneous songs which the teacher can encourage and receive as what David Holbrook (1967: 8), referring to children's poems, has called 'meant gifts'.[9] Coral Davies (1986, 1992) has described how she regularly invited children to tell her, day by day, about things that mattered to them or things that were happening around them—and to do the 'telling' by *singing* what they wanted to say. In one such example Mary, aged six, sings about trees in autumn:[10]

Leaves are falling off the tree,
turning colours and ... blue—
When they coming down the tree,
different colours as well.
One is purple and one is blue and
one is green and one is brown and
ONE IS YELLOW!
When they're falling down the tree.

What do we learn when we listen to this song? First, that it behaves like a piece of music: it could not conceivably be mistaken for anything else. If that seems obvious it is nevertheless important to remember that the one thing everybody knows about music is that it comes in 'pieces'. Moreover, everyone understands that the word 'piece', applied to music, means not a *bit* of something but rather a *whole* of something, self-contained and experientially complete. Common to every piece is what Immanuel Kant (1790: §§10, 11) called 'the form of finality'. Although we may never give that a thought, it is what the mind expects and what we find satisfying. 'Understanding' a work of art implies perception of a 'common sense' relationship between the work as a whole and its materials—for example, in music: melodic motifs, harmonic and rhythmic figures, timbres, varied textures and densities, and so on. Either as listeners to or as makers of music, if we are attentive we shall sense the coherence that is achieved, largely by intuitive ways of 'working' the materials *together*—hence the notion of 'com-position' = positing or 'putting-in-place-together' the invented materials so that expectations emerge and are fulfilled or postponed and brought to ultimate closure in a way which says, '*that's* how it should be: *that* makes sense'.

In six-year-old Mary's spontaneous song about the falling leaves we can hear how she works the materials towards a particular point. In spite of her hesitation before singing 'blue' at the end of the second line, it is clear that she feels the rhythmic pattern of '*turn*ing colours and *blue*' because she reinforces it with the phrase '*different* colours as *well*'. The manner and impetus of that rhythmic reinforcement continues in '*one* is purple and *one* is blue and ...', so that the thought flows on with even greater vigour in a larger pattern combining the two short phrases ('*one* is purple and *one* is blue and *one* is green and *one* is brown and ...'), all of which leads to the singular 'ONE IS YELLOW!' Here is an obvious climax, but that effect is not achieved solely by the powerful high and *fortissimo* delivery. Rather it is the musical thinking-through that ensures that we receive the full impact of this moment.[11] The process begins with '*one* is brown'. That is truly the song's crucial point because everything else takes off from there; and, as it does, we realize how all that has gone before now makes even more musical common sense. Having reached this point, the possibility of an ultimately satisfying wholeness becomes apparent. It is the power of the passage from 'one is brown' to 'one is yellow' that gives to the contrastingly gentle phrase that follows ('When they're falling down the tree') a finality of closure that seems both inevitable and 'right'.

It would not be necessary to explain to this child what she has achieved, even if one could think of a way of doing so. What matters is that she has been encouraged to create a musical event which has been received with interest and enthusiasm by the teacher. Simply by making this song, Mary has discovered things that she could not have learned in any other way. It might be said that she is following well-tried and deeply rooted patterns; after all, she's six years old and no doubt she's already heard a lot of music which works more or less in the same way as her song. But she is not singing a song she already knows or has been taught, one made up by someone else: this is *her* invention, words and music; she has made the shape of the song 'her own' and has related that to words which simultaneously generate the melody. Moreover, it seems clear that she understands intuitively the way in which the wholeness of the song—its

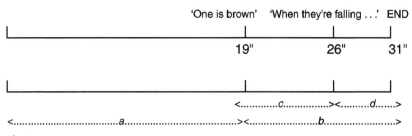

Fig. 1

'common sense'—depends upon precisely when certain things happen: a precision that is felt, not calculated.

Austin Wright (cf. Hamilton, 1994: 142) suggested that a piece of sculpture should be explored 'like a building, a ruin, a landscape, a town. Think how you would cross it, climb it; where you would rest and where you would want to get in the end.' He also described those important intersections as 'the points where things legitimately hang together': moments, so to speak, of achievement which 'add up' and validate the piece by giving it an overall logic. This too is how music works. Changes of direction, unexpected extensions and additions, moments when we feel something important happens: all are crucial, in the strict sense of the word, because they mark time and, by so doing, create significant proportions within the overall timescale of a piece. It is the proportions that make sense of what happens. Listening to Mary inventing her song as she goes along, we too can feel instinctively the rightness of the proportions she creates. Her intuitive 'thinking in music' governs the repetition of phrases and words which engineer that repetition. Thus, the cardinal point ('one is brown'), from which the wholeness of the musical event springs, occurs at about 19 seconds into the song: a pivotal moment in a piece which, in total, lasts for a fraction over 31 seconds. Likewise, in the passage from 'one is brown' to the end of the song, the same proportional relationship occurs at 26 seconds with the start of the closing phrase ('When they're falling down the tree') (see Fig. 1).

Models of perfection

The asymmetrical relationship of one-third to two-thirds in measurements of duration or space has immense significance in the history of the world's poetry, literature, visual arts, architecture and music.[12] We have seen how such relativity occurs naturally in a child's spontaneous song. It is found the world over, in music of every kind, old and new. It is a proportion that is especially satisfying when we observe it in nature—in the shapes and patterning of seashells and fir cones, for example—and, perhaps for this reason, it has been consciously emulated in painting and sculpture. It is discernible in numerous ancient man-made structures and in the 'magic' shapes of the pentagon and five-pointed star. Even in architecture that at first sight seems to be celebrating symmetry (for example, Palladian buildings) it is the vertical *a*symmetry in the positioning of horizontal features such as string courses that fascinates and delights the eye. In poetry, as in music, it is again a matter of durations and rhythmic units. The sonnet, for example, makes its most telling division with great subtlety somewhere between the eighth and ninth lines—where it frequently marks a new departure or a striking development of the poem's idea. For the same reason, the iambic pentameter intrigues and satisfies us with its merest hint of emphasis approximately two-thirds of the way through each line.[13]

'There is no excellent beauty that hath not some strangeness in the proportion', wrote Francis Bacon (1612/1825: 145); and, indeed, it would appear that the human mind does find greater satisfaction in asymmetry than it does in symmetry. Perhaps this is because, compared with the somewhat static properties of 'binary' symmetry, the 'trinitarian' dynamics of asymmetry—acculturation/realization/revelation—lead the brain, via eye or ear, most powerfully to a sensation of well-being and *wholeness*. Our hope is evident in that word: to be kept inviolate in spite of the worst that life can do to us. Thus, to be whole is to be hale is to be healed is to be holy—the realization of the quality that, however we express it, makes us truly *human* beings.

Obviously, the processes of thinking and making that we now call 'art' go far back into the origins of humanity. The medium is indeed the message, and the characteristic 'making sense in its own terms—that necessary feature of every art object or event—is surely a response to those things which, because we cannot take hold of them, ultimately trouble us most: time and space and their mysterious relationship with life and death. Even in our modern world we confront and accommodate these problems by making models of perfection—although we may not recognize them as such, nor be willing to acknowledge that that is what we are doing. Our predecessors constructed temples and cathedrals to make space graspable; we build skyscrapers and geodesic domes. We also, of course, continue to make sculptures and paintings, and, notwithstanding the 'subject', an artist's primary concern will always be the careful handling of scale and proportion to offer glimpses of perfected space. Likewise, in poetry and literature we are conscious of a similar *pacing* of the thought to fulfil ideas in forms which themselves (i.e. in addition to their literary substance) give satisfaction and make sense. Of all mankind's attempts to model perfection, music is, perhaps, the most subtle. Its meaning is manifest not in objects viewed or touched but in *events* that can only be experienced in the time it takes to make each one audible. Music lifts off from the surface of life: it cannot be concerned with depiction or description of worldly reality even though its points of departure are frequently found there.

This should not prevent us from using music in whatever ways we choose, worldly or otherwise! We can make it mean whatever we want it to mean—and undoubtedly it does inspire an infinite number of different uses and interpretations; but that is possible only because, at root, *music means the same thing to everyone.* Whatever the overlay of cultural or sentimental reference, stylistic decoration or technical virtuosity, what finally convinces anyone that a piece 'succeeds' is the music itself. That is achieved, not by what other people write or say about it but through our experience of, and perception of, structural proportions in the piece *as it progresses.* The longer, more extensive sections are assimilated first, the mind establishing the relationship between Idea and materials. That brings realization. Now it is clear what is happening, but there is more to come; and often this can be surprising, particularly as we approach the ultimate point of closure. The moment of revelation which puts the seal of finality on a work must not be too long delayed; nor should it appear too soon: hence the shorter section, related to the first in a proportion we recognize intuitively.

Walter Pater (1873/1912: 135, 139) believed that 'All art constantly aspires towards the condition of music'; to that state in which 'the end is not distinct from the means, the form from the matter, the subject from the expression'. It could, however, be argued that, rather than merely aspiring to that end, all the arts do in fact achieve it. For some, the means of expression—language, visual forms and images—may seem to be tied to mundane existence; yet all, like music, are concerned with perceptions of proportion and completeness which suggest an 'other' reality. In the strict meaning of the word, art 'entertains' us, in that its principal function is to 'hold [us] between' (*inter tenere*) two levels of experience: two kinds of reality. Thus, music operates in virtual (psychological) time, although we are aware of it taking place in 'real' (chronometric) time.[14] A similar perception of the precise points at which significant things happen in time or space applies in our appreciation of every art form.

A place for music in the school curriculum

Schools today have to fulfil a variety of needs, social as well as educational, but the core of their responsibility is, as it always has been, the learning that takes place under the guidance of teachers in classrooms. That core is increasingly under pressure, not only from the demands of testing and appraisal but also from expansion (e.g. 'literacy' hours and the reintroduction of 'citizenship' lessons). We ought to be sure that everything we put into the curriculum has educational justification. Time was when we were content to accept music as a relaxation from the rigours of seemingly more demanding subjects! That was not good enough then, and it won't do now. Neither will it suffice to impose on music a spurious academicism to make it appear rigorous in exactly the same terms as some other curriculum subjects. Apart from anything else, that is unnecessary: music has its own rigour in the demands of sensitivity, imagination, and inventiveness common to all artistic endeavour—qualities which are sorely needed in the modern world. This, I suggest, is what we should expect, first and foremost, from musical education in the classroom—an education accessible to all pupils. The justification for music in these circumstances is not more information to be assimilated but a very important human quality to be exercised and developed: the potential we all have to make art by making up music. There could be no better illustration of the old maxim that 'You cannot teach anyone anything she or he does not already know'. It calls to mind Herbert Read's (1958: 298) often quoted words:

Appreciation is not acquired by passive contemplation: we only appreciate beauty on the basis of our own creative aspirations.

Composition (I prefer to call it 'making up music') is the most natural thing in the world. The only stimulus it requires is the opportunity and encouragement to do it. It is quite simply through 'doing the art' that not only do we learn about the nature of music itself—thereby achieving understanding of what more experienced musicians have been able to do—but also we use and develop, in many subtle ways, our powers of judgement, the confidence to take decisions, and the courage to stand by those decisions. Up to now, the principal hurdle has been music teachers' lack of experience in composing, perhaps because of an emphasis, in their training, upon performance skills. By contrast we would be hard pressed to think of art teachers we have known who were not active in their own right as creative artists.

The first thing is to develop the right atmosphere: one in which it is assumed that what students do in 'music lessons' is to make up pieces, present them, and discuss them. At least in the early stages, such pieces will not be notated. Like the bulk of the world's music they will be invented directly through experiment and improvisation, confirmed by repetition, and remembered. This is as it should be because it places the emphasis on what is heard rather than what is seen on paper. For the teacher, the essential quality is an ability to comment purposefully and encouragingly on pieces which pupils produce, either in small groups or individually. The teacher's observations must follow on immediately from the presentation of the music, drawing in all other members of the class in addition to the composers themselves to recall what happened in the piece: the relationship of materials to Idea, and the extent to which the Idea was fulfilled—that is to say, 'fully filled out'. Much of this will be achieved through appropriate questioning, with occasional reference, preferably by demonstration, to compositions by other composers who have explored similar ideas. These teaching techniques have been extensively documented over the past 35 years, but still many teachers lack confidence, not only in their own ability but also in students' potential to respond. The tendency to revert to instruction is understandable. Collaboration with other arts teachers could be helpful. Apart from the constraints of time, this need not preclude other aspects of musical education, either in the classroom or in out-of-timetable activities such as choirs and orchestras. In general, music in schools would benefit by closer association with the other creative arts and with those things that underpin their place in the curriculum—the age-old natural processes of 'thinking and making' which manifestly produce such worthwhile results in the visual arts, creative writing, dance, and drama. Only on that basis shall we ever realize a school music curriculum which really can involve everyone and justify the time we give to it.

Notes

[1] This is true even for 'concert' presentations of electro-acoustic music which consist in the diffusion of works created in a recorded format. The property of 'nowness' is evident in the differing circumstances of each presentation (different venues with different acoustic qualities; the changing composition of audiences; make-up of the programmes; etc.).

[2] Cf. Quennell (1945: 83) on Edward Gibbon's studies in Roman history: '[for Gibbon] ... the past gave to the present the justification that it needed, suggested a continuity in human affairs that, at first glance, seemed often strangely lacking, supplied the perspective essential to a clear and dispassionate view'.

[3] See Crowest (1904: 175–6) and Kerman & Tyson (1980: 2.383[a]). In his sketches for the symphony Beethoven had noted, 'A recollection of country life ... a matter more of feeling than of painting in sounds' (Forbes, 1964: 436). In this context the parallel between Beethoven and his exact contemporary Wordsworth is not without interest. The latter, in his 1800 preface to *Lyrical Ballads* (Littledale, 1924: 246), defined poetry as 'the spontaneous overflow of powerful feelings ... [which] takes its origin from emotion recollected in tranquillity'.

[4] 'Foule ahurie! N'êtes-vous capable d'écouter des accords sans demander à voir leurs cartes d'identité et leurs caractéristiques? D'où viennent-ils? Où vont-ils? Faut-il absolument le savoir? Écoutez. Cela suffit.'

[5] David Hockney talks about 'doing the art'. Similarly Giotto, early in the fourteenth century, described his work thus: 'Da capo a fondo ogni pennellata è comporre' (From beginning to end, every stroke is composition).

⁶ Cf. Schafer (1965); Self (1967); Dennis (1970); Paynter & Aston (1970), all of whom record work undertaken with children during the 1950s and 1960s. For appraisals of these developments see Metcalfe (1987: 97–118); also Pitts (2000).

⁷ Cf. Rousseau (1762/1979: 149): 'in order to know music well, it does not suffice to transmit it; it is necessary to compose it. The one ought to be learned with the other; otherwise one never knows music well.' (Cf. the first English translation (1763): 'or we shall never be masters of this science'.)

⁸ British examples include pupils' compositions from the 1970s which can be heard in the films, tape–slide programmes and recordings produced by the Schools Council Project, *Music in the Secondary School Curriculum* (1973–82) and, among more recent examples, those on tapes and CDs issued with the *British Journal of Music Education* (Cambridge University Press). Over 40 pieces made by children and young people in Italy can be heard on the tape that accompanies vol. 66/67, September 1997, of *beQuadro* (Journal of the Centro di Ricerca e di Sperimentazione per la Didattica Musicale, Fiesole, Italy). Similar compilations, on tape or CD, have been produced in Japan, Norway, and many other countries.

⁹ 'The least piece of writing, if the teacher has established the context for proper "giving," will be a "meant" gift.'

¹⁰ Track 20 of the tape accompanying *British Journal of Music Education*, vol. 9, no. 3, November 1992.

¹¹ Similar to the process that produces a climax in a discussion or a presentation, and that has been characterized as 'thought occupied with indicators of what is common in the passage from one attitude to another'.

¹² The precise point in space or moment in time—the so-called 'Golden Section'—is the product of n × .618 (where *n* is length or duration). The Fibonacci sequence expresses the same relationship (1, 2, 3, 5, 8, 13, 21, etc.).

¹³ I am indebted to Mr R.T. Jones, formerly Senior Lecturer in the Department of English and Related Literature in the University of York, for pointing out so concisely that, of all the rhythmic patterns in the English language, 'It is the one we like to *hear* the most, / And we can also *speak* it if we try.'

¹⁴ For example, all those present at a concert could agree on the time when a piece began and the time when it stopped, but everyone would have a different impression of how the time passed during the course of the piece.

References

Ascham, R., ed. Arber, E. (1927) 'The first booke for the youth'. In *The Scholemaster* (1570). London: Constable & Co.

Bacon, F. (1612) *Essays or Counsels Civil and Moral, XLIII*: 'Of beauty'. In *Lord Bacon's Works*, vol. 1, 1825. London: William Richardson.

Blacking, J. (1959) *How Musical is Man*, Washington, D.C.: University of Washington Press.

Boucourechliev, A. (1972) *Debussy*, Paris.

Copland, A. (1957) *What to Listen for in Music*. New York: McGraw-Hill.

Crowest, F. J. (1904) *Beethoven*. London: J. M. Dent.

Davies, C. (1986) 'Say it till a song comes (reflections on songs invented by children 3–13)'. *BJME*, **3**, 3, 279–93.

Davies, C. (1992) 'Listen to my song: a study of songs invented by children aged 5 to 7 years'. *BJME*, **9**, 1, 19–48.

Dennis, B. (1970) *Experimental Music in Schools*. Oxford: OUP.

Forbes, E. (ed.) (1964) *Thayer's Life of Beethoven*. Princeton, NJ: Princeton University Press.

Hadow, Sir W. H., *et al.* (1931) *Report of the Consultative Committee on the Primary School*. London: HMSO.

Hamilton, J. (1994) *The Sculpture of Austin Wright*. London: The Henry Moore Foundation, in association with Lund Humphries Ltd.

Hoérée, A. (1938) *Albert Roussel*. Paris.

Holbrook, D. (1967) *Children's Writing*. Cambridge: CUP.

Kant, I. (1790), trans. Meredith, J. C. (1928/R1952) *The Critique of Judgement*. Oxford: Clarendon Press.

Kendall, S. (1986) 'The harmony of human life: an exploration of the ideas of Pestalozzi and Froebel in relation to music education'. *BJME*, **3**, 1, 35–48.

Kerman, J. & Tyson, A. (1980) 'Beethoven'. In S. Sadie (Ed.), *The New Grove Dictionary of Music and Musicians*, vol. 2. London: Macmillan.

Littledale, H. (ed.) (1924) *Wordsworth and Coleridge: Lyrical Ballads 1798*. London: OUP.

Metcalfe, M. (1987) 'Towards the condition of music: the emergent aesthetic of music education'. In P. Abbs (ed.), *Living Powers*. London: The Falmer Press.

Pater, W. (1873) *The Renaissance: Studies in Art and Poetry*. Repr. 1912. London: Macmillan.

Paynter, J. & Aston, P. (1970) *Sound and Silence*. Cambridge: CUP.

Pitts, S. (2000) *A Century of Change in Music Education*. Aldershot: Ashgate.

Quennell, P. (1945) 'Edward Gibbon'. *Four Portraits*. London: Collins.

Rainbow, B. (1989) *Music in Educational Thought & Practice*. Aberystwyth: Boethius Press.

Read, H. (1958) *Education through Art*. London: Faber & Faber.

Rousseau, J-J. (1762) *Émile, or, On Education*. Trans. A. Bloom, 1979. New York: Basic Books.

Sachs, C. (1944) *The Rise of Music in the Ancient World/East and West*. London: Dent.

Schafer, R. M. (1965) *The Composer in the Classroom*. Don Mills, Ontario: BMI Canada.

Self, G. (1967) *New Sounds in Class*. London: Universal Edition.

Skinner, B. F. (1964) 'New methods and new aims in teaching'. In 'Education in 1984', *New Scientist*, **22**, 392.

Skinner, B. F. (1968) *The Technology of Teaching*, New York: Meredith Corporation.

Stravinsky, I. (1962) *An Autobiography*, New York: W. W. Norton.

Trevelyan, G. (1942) *English Social History: A Survey of Six Centuries: Chaucer to Queen Victoria*. London: Longmans, Green and Co.

Working on one's inner world

From E. Webb (ed.), *Powers of Being: David Holbrook and His Work* (Associated University Presses, 1995), 125–41

The charm of impossibilities

A full stop at the end of the world. It's a comforting thought; not only shall we not slip off the edge but also things won't come apart. Existence will be *contained*.

Believing that geography could have an authenticated end was always likely to provoke a desire to find it. The Greek navigators of the fourth century before Christ were precise in their description of Ultima Thule: an island of volcanoes, in the northern seas, 'six days sail from the Orcades,' where day and night were always equal. Whatever the reality they had in mind (Iceland, perhaps?), as a poetic allusion the image still had currency in the early years of the seventeenth century; for example, in a madrigal of Thomas Weelkes:

Thule, the period of Cosmography,
Doth vaunt of Hecla, whose sulphurious fire
Doth melt the frozen clime and thaw the sky;
Trinacrian Aetnae's flames ascend no higher.
These things seem wondrous, yet more wondrous I,
Whose heart with fear doth freeze, with love doth fry.[1]

Although the conceit is primarily that travellers' tales of farthest Thule are as nothing compared with the simultaneous freezing and frying of a lovelorn heart, there could be also a suggestion that the full stop at the end of the world, somewhere over the rainbow, will not be discovered by voyages through the world or even through the universe because that kind of 'finality'—answering the ever-present, nagging questions of existence—is actually to be found within oneself; in the 'yet more wondrous' inner world of feeling and imagination.

The flow of human history is marked by many powerful symbols of the desire to understand 'reality'. Columbus's voyages were, in the widest sense, spiritual journeys, as important in that respect as the search for spices, trade routes, and territories; and Neil Armstrong's 'one small step for a man, one giant leap for mankind' is clearly confirmation of much more than purely scientific achievement. However far back we trace mankind we find very similar dilemmas being raised by the diversity and temporaneousness of experience. Glimpsing the possibility of a different order somehow, somewhere, 'beyond,' humanity responds with models of space and time; images of what might be, to make sense of life as it appears to be.

In their technical realization, the immense spaces of the Gothic cathedrals offered medieval Christians foretastes of eternity; light filtered through coloured glass, the full height of the soaring vault only dimly visible, and yet the whole manifestly controlled by the unshakeable strength of the huge stone pillars. Today, the cool objectivity of high-profile technology is just as likely to produce a public reaction which is in large measure 'spiritual' or 'artistic': multimillion-dollar space probes are as much symbols of a graspable and contained universe as were the contrived and fully equipped 'worlds' of the Egyptian pyramids, neolithic and iron-age round- and long-barrows, and the Viking burial ships.

Objects and ideas; the examples could be multiplied endlessly. All tell the same story: in our search for an ultimate coherence, what speaks to us—what moves us—is *form*; new structures, the product of imaginative speculation, again and again revealing hitherto unnoticed relationships and 'some sense of possibility beyond the words'.

A capacity for inward symbolism

In all of this the work of poets, painters, musicians, sculptors, dancers—indeed every kind of creative artist—is crucial, principally because they all try to come to terms with what is sensed, what is felt, rather than with what is merely measured or calculated. Isaiah Berlin[2] described artists as people 'blown through' with the spirit of their time and place and society; each work of art conveying 'a total human experience, a world'. Sigfried Giedion, in *Space, Time and Architecture*[3], reminds us that, but for this, much of our world would 'lack all emotional significance' because the artist's chief mission has always been 'The opening up of such new realms of feeling.' And Wilfrid Mellers shows that there is indeed no end to this activity: the potential is there in each one of us, so that, in a healthy society, all people 'should be artists to some extent and in some way, in proportion to their capacity to live creatively'.[4]

It is evident now that, in addition to those people we are accustomed to think of as artists, there could be many more who would welcome opportunities to explore their own creative ideas. This is as important for them as being on the receiving end of artistic enterprise. The surprising thing is how long it has taken us to recognize this—and its implications for formal education.

From time to time in the 1920s and 1930s exceptional teachers would find opportunities to present new points of view about the arts in schools.[5] But it wasn't until much later that we began to see a wider professional acknowledgement of the contribution the arts can make to everyone's general education. The 1951 Festival of Britain had successfully punctured the post-war gloom, and, in spite of continuing austerities, heralded a renaissance; at last there was room for innovation and initiative. By the mid 1950s a growing number of teachers who were themselves active as poets or composers or who were working creatively in dance and drama began to question the established methods, and to look for new ways of educating what, twenty years later, Robert Witkin was to call 'the intelligence of feeling'.[6]

Changing attitudes

Inevitably there were pockets of suspicion and, perhaps, resentment. Persuasive advocacy was needed; and in David Holbrook we had the pioneer. Although he may not have intended to do so, in effect he spoke for all arts teachers, producing—in *English for Maturity* (1961), *English for the Rejected* (1964) and *The Exploring Word* (1967)—the evidence of children's creativity and the justification for encouraging it in the classroom. The doubters began to be reassured.

In *Children's Writing* (1967) he establishes the universality of the context:

When anyone is really working on his inner world, he becomes excited—for he is making important discoveries and gains, as between his ego ... and threatening shadows within. He sees connections and relationships, and possibilities of structures, patterns, richness of content: and in these, joy and beauty. Expression will convey the bodily feelings of experience, and the 'inscape' of an inward effort.[7]

Then, bluntly, he addresses the problem:

The least piece of writing, if the teacher has established the context for proper 'giving,' will be a 'meant' gift. Of course, it depends on what the teacher's attitude is to human beings. If he cannot believe that every human being has an inward need to find himself, in a struggle with love and hate, and between the subjective and objective worlds, then he probably won't get given poetry. But how can anyone read poetry and not see that these problems are universal? Of course, you can deny the whole area with which art deals. A colleague was told by a scientist in his staffroom, 'Children from decent homes don't write poetry.' This man meant that it was possible to live without 'working on one's inner world.' But it isn't![8]

For those of us who had been trying to move in new directions *Children's Writing,* with its inspiring Introduction and its unique approach, offered just the encouragement we needed. It was such a surprising book, taking us far beyond anything we might at first have expected from its matter-of-fact subtitle, 'A Sampler for Student Teachers'. Music education in particular benefitted immeasurably from this brilliant study of how teachers can handle meaning in children's creative use of language.

In passing, we may note a nice irony in the tangential link with *language;* for the phrase 'the language of music' has been something of an obstacle to the development of children's musical creativity.[9] A forced equation between expression and notation (not notation in general but just one form of notation) has been especially unhelpful; quite apart from which, similarities between music and language are hard to justify. Of far greater significance are the crucial ways in which music and language differ.

Constructing experience

There are no logical models for music; in fact, to a large extent every piece has its own 'grammar' which must be defined as part of the process of composition. Then again, music is nonconceptual, and in spite of an amazing expressive diversity it lacks entirely the power of description (other than in a very crude fashion, and then only by association). Every piece is self-justifying; it does not need to be explained. It cannot be paraphrased or shortened: either you have it all or you have nothing. Whilst, in language, a single word retains its meaning(s), in music a single note (or even a group of notes) has no meaning at all aside from its relationship with the larger, and autonomous, musical context. In other words, music is pure form, as Langer has maintained:

Music ... is pre-eminently non-representative even in its classical productions, its highest attainments. It exhibits pure form not as an embellishment, but as its very essence; we can take it in its flower ... There is no obvious, literal content in our way.[10]

At root surely that is true of every work of art in every other medium? All art is 'abstract' in that its elements are abstracts from a perceived order presented as statements of a 'felt' ideal. And the prime concern of every artist must be the variety of ways in which structural forces can be made to work together to produce coherent forms to embody these statements. Indeed—and not least in an educational context, as David Holbrook so convincingly demonstrates—even when *language* itself is the medium, it is as necessary as with any other medium to be reminded that the principal creative consideration is the relationship between ideas and form:

Once the point of a 'creative' approach to children's work has been grasped, a teacher becomes concerned with the germ, the gist of a piece—its content, *first*. Of course, matters of spelling, punctuation, layout and handwriting are important.

But the most important thing to get is the message.[11]

To study their [children's] work confirms the impression expressed by Sir Herbert Read that each human soul is impelled to seek order and beauty within by what he calls 'ikons' ... Thus, creativity is a matter of relationship with oneself ... [12]

Children as composers

The things that stimulate children to improvise and compose music are essentially those things that motivate all composers: personal experiences, things seen and heard (including other works of the imagination: literature, poetry, paintings and sculpture) or heard about; significant events past and present, things of joy and things of tragedy; sounds themselves; shapes and patterns. Eventually the piece, as it begins to grow through working on the ideas, takes over and dictates its own directions. In a sense, then, starting points are not all that important. What is important is that they should stimulate *musical ideas* of distinctive character that can be worked upon and developed (i.e. made to 'go on' in time). Experiment with ideas will reveal their potential for variation or transformation or combination with other ideas to drive the musical form on to the point where it is memorable as a coherent sound pattern. That is really what music is 'about,' regardless of images that may be evoked by a starting point or a title.

We can see how this works by examining some music made by children at a primary school in the Yorkshire dales.[13] It started with a walk near their school on a windy autumn day. Back in the classroom the teacher talked with them about what they'd seen, and they wrote about it:

We have been outside to see what the birds were doing in the wind. They seemed to be dancing on the wind. They flew in a pattern, they glided for a while and then they flapped to keep themselves up in the air. The gulls were wheeling in the sky. They went a little way gliding then they rocked. To turn a corner they banked like an aeroplane. The little finches were being driven back. They flapped their wings rapidly. The wind made the finch jerk and it seemed as if it was teasing the finch by making it hop.

Wind constantly rushed into me. Birds manoeuvered gliding then darting. Gulls flew on like aeroplanes then banking and finishing by steadily rocking. The ferns blowing seemed as if they were stuck in ice and the wind was in vain trying to pull them out. The spring rippled in the wind. Wind whistling through the trees was like the sea. Another kite-like bird flew on—it was a rook. A small finch, rapidly beating its wings, then gliding in a small way, then flapping again, seemed to hop along.

The children had enjoyed the clear, bright atmosphere of the day, and were excited at feeling themselves carried along by the wind, almost as though they were flying like the birds:

As soon as we came back we talked about the manoeuvering birds. Then we acted the birds. At first we acted the rooks. Some thought that they wobbled some didn't. Some thought that they went high, some thought they went low. The seagull I liked best. The seagull had more movement than the rooks. We banked and wobbled, we turned round we went low and high. It was nice to be the seagull for once. The finch was nice, it hopped, it swooped, it dived. But we did not see it much. We talked about making some music. Someone suggested that we would have tambourines to be the beating of the rook's wings. We agreed. We thought what we would have for gliding. Someone tried top c and g [on recorders]. It goes c then the tambourines, then g and so on. The leaves were falling all the time. The leaves were the xylophone. We had to think of something for the banking of the seagull. Pamela thought four notes on the piano, I thought it was an excellent idea. As well we had recorders and a drum for the wind. I played a part in the finch music. I played the swooping of the finch. Guy played the flapping of the finch by tapping the drum. I had the piano. Then we replayed the first line.[14]

As we shall see, possibly the most important part of this account is the very last sentence. It had been entirely the children's idea to repeat the opening of the piece, presumably because they felt that this literally 'rounded it off' and strengthened the impression of it being fully contained by its form.

The music was built up in a series of group 'improvisations'; working over each until everyone agreed it was right, gradually developing the sound texture by adding layers, repeating sections or creating new ones. One child described the fast swooping movements of the rooks, and tried to capture the sensation in a musical idea played on a recorder; but another thought a double bass would be better 'if we had one!' (He seemed to have some idea of a string glissando). That prompted someone else to describe the kind of music he would make 'if he had a harp'. The teacher showed them the strings inside the piano, which of course looked like a harp, and stroked them with the sustaining pedal held down; this produced the effect the children wanted. There was a lot of discussion about the music for the finches; something was needed that would adequately represent the short, jerky movements. Someone suggested tapping a drum lightly with the fingernails rather than with sticks, although he couldn't control the sounds well enough to his own satisfaction. But another child did succeed. And in this way—trying out each other's ideas—the music grew.

The classroom discussion had begun with the overall impressions of the walk they'd taken. Then, guided by the teacher's questioning, attention began to focus on the birds they'd seen, and the movements of the birds. When it came to making music, the children's first aim seemed to be to 'copy' those movements musically. Thus, the musical ideas became symbols of each style of movement, following the action—flapping, hopping, swooping, or gliding. Nevertheless, *they were inventing musical ideas;* and we must ask now why those ideas take the forms they do.

At the start the rook-tambourines flap their wings, transferring to recorders to 'soar' on the notes d-G-d. But while the rooks flap and 'manoeuvre' the leaves are falling 'all the time' to a pentatonic ostinato played throughout on a

Birds Flying[15]

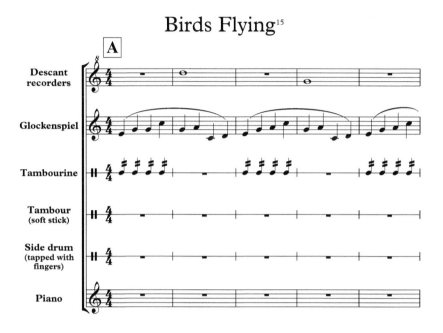

*Piano: glissando with finger-nail across the strings, sustaining pedal depressed.

glockenspiel and effectively holding the entire piece together. This is particularly interesting because musically it is very different from the obviously imitative symbolism of the bird ideas. Nothing in this pattern of eight bell notes repeated over and over could, of itself, suggest 'falling leaves.' True, there is the continuity: apart from one short section where the glockenspiel is silent, this idea is present 'all the time,' like the falling leaves. But why *these* notes rather than others? The child who thought of this figure had not been told about 5-note scales or ostinato patterns, yet, playing on a chromatic glockenspiel[16] with all the possibilities of that full range of notes, he selected a 'white key' pentatonic set and used it to make a phrase of considerable character which works splendidly as an ostinato. The aspiring third plus fourth falls back lightly, first to the G and then through a yearning downward sixth to the low C, from where it neatly curls upwards by step to ease the repetition of the phrase.

The loud, strong opening gives way to what ultimately became a middle section in two parts. The first of these (inspired by the banking and gliding of the gulls) contrasts dramatically with the start of the piece. This is simple but beautiful music: rocking back and forth in surprisingly gentle consecutive seconds on the piano, and then 'floating' on the recorders' smooth octave Cs against the background of a quietly rolled drum, rising and falling like the hum of the wind. This leads into the second part: the finches with their curious hop and swoop and the return of the 'falling leaves' ostinato.

Revelation

It was at this point in the process that the musical structures themselves took over. The children were wondering how they could continue; they'd run out of birds to imitate and no one had suggested either further elaboration of the existing ideas or the addition of new material. It was then that they hit upon the very satisfying idea of repeating the opening section. It is important to realize that this was their idea: the teacher did not suggest an ABA form! Indeed she had not prompted them at all in the shaping of the music other than to ask questions such as 'what should happen now?' Instinctively they felt they had to bring back the glockenspiel as an accompaniment to the 'finches' (letter C in the score above). That was a clever musical judgement because not only did it make a subtle link with what had been heard earlier, accompanying other material, but also—and this was the point of revelation—it would link perfectly with a straight repeat of the 'rooks' music that began the piece.

They were immensely impressed with this discovery and the evident wholeness it produced when they played the piece through. No longer need they cast around for other ways of continuing, but—and much more importantly—the repetition was clearly 'right.' They reinforced their conviction about this by adding two features of purely musical structural significance: a tiny crescendo figure on the drum (immediately before letter $\boxed{A}$ in the score) which lifts the middle section forward into the reprise, and a single loud drum beat at the end. A more decisive 'period' to the 'cosmography' of this piece is hard to imagine, characterizing—literally at a stroke—the completeness of this little world of sounds they had created.

Widening musical horizons

An important feature of David Holbrook's work has been 'to train students in being able to see opportunities for links with literature, as children's poetic needs become apparent from their own expression'. Time and again in *Children's Writing* he asks, 'what do you do about following this up by other literature?' or 'say what literature (poems and stories) you would give the children' or 'what will you read to the class to match this pupil's interests?' and 'what then can we supply for Paul from literature?'[17] In just the same way we might now ask, à propos of *Birds Flying*, 'what can we supply for Pamela, Christopher, Guy, and their friends from the literature of music?'

Possibly the first thing would be to match the overall atmosphere of the piece (with, perhaps, a special reference to the glockenspiel ostinato). In which case we might play to the children Martin Peerson's *The Fall of the Leafe*.[18]

Later it could be useful to listen to music that uses direct imitation of natural sounds; birdsong, for example. Here we're spoiled for choice because bird songs and bird calls appear in so many works. Noticing how Delius, in *On Hearing the First Cuckoo in Spring*, makes the bird's two-note call a musical motif from which a longer melody is spun and developed, would be a reasonable place to begin (incidentally, it would be essential to listen to the work in its entirety; extracts can never tell us what a piece of music is about, and merely to point out the cuckooing clarinet would be totally inadequate). There's also a cuckoo piece for harpsichord by Daquin; and, among a number of harpsichord pieces by Couperin in which he imitates natural sounds (*'les sons nonpassionnés'*), there is a *Nightingale in Love*. (There's also a gnat!) A mechanical or recorded nightingale takes its place in the orchestra for Respighi's *The Pines of Rome;* and the nightingale, quail, and cuckoo make an ensemble appearance at the end of the slow movement of Beethoven's *Pastoral* symphony. Messiaen used stylized forms of birdsong as the basis of very many of his works. Going far beyond simple imitation, the resulting motifs became important structural features of the music.

The Fall of the Leafe

Martin Peerson

This is precisely where we should be heading. The simplistically imitative examples make musically superficial 'matchings'; and David Holbrook quite rightly insists that 'matching needs to be done sensitively, governed by an understanding of the deeper implications of a child's work, not its mere explicit meaning'.[19] The deeper implications in every piece of music are to be found not in correspondence between ideas and stimuli but in the structural features of the musical ideas and their development within the timespan of the piece; that is to say, in what the sounds themselves *do*.

In *Birds Flying* we have a pentatonic ostinato which is structurally the backbone of the whole piece; a strongly contrasting middle section featuring gentle consecutive seconds together with the twitching 'finch' figure (fingernail-tapped drum and fingernail-stroked piano strings, an interesting combination of unusual sounds); and then a modified reprise of the first section for which we have been subtly prepared by the return of the glockenspiel ostinato in the second half of the middle section. It is these characteristics we need to match: their musical nature and the force they exert by driving the music on to a completed form. All have, of course, been worked out intuitively, so the teacher's task is now to draw attention to why certain features are so successful in creating the overall piece. As David Holbrook might say 'The point is that these children need to discover more pieces which are 'about' similar *musical* ideas'.[20] Bartók's *Mikrokosmos* exploits a range of techniques, figures, and patterns, and is such a rich source of characteristic pieces that we shall very likely find there what we are looking for.[21] Vol. III, No. 78, 'Five-tone Scale' is based on an entirely 'white note' pentatonic set; not the same set as that used in *Birds Flying*, but Bartók's arching melody lines have a lot in common with the children's glockenspiel 'falling leaves' ostinato. From there we might move to *Mikrokosmos* Vol. II, No. 61, 'Pentatonic Melody.' This uses yet another 'white' five-note set, and the first nine measures have an ostinato figure as the lower part. Although that doesn't continue throughout, other ostinato-like passages appear in both upper and lower parts as the piece goes on.

Mikrokosmos Vol. V, No. 132, 'Major Seconds Broken and Together,' provides a useful link with both the musical ideas and the dreamy, slightly unreal, atmosphere created by the middle section of *Birds Flying*. Bartók's piece opens with a slow, wandering melody in the lower part; a gently meandering line, moving by steps never larger than tone or semitone, accompanied above by quiet 'cluster' chords which are also built of tones and semitones and which gradually resolve on to a unison G (structurally very similar to the way in which the rocking consecutive seconds in *Birds Flying* resolve on to the purity of the recorders' sustained c-c-octave). A middle section lifts the whole texture up into a higher, brighter register, the meandering melody now in the upper part and the accompanying cluster-chords below. Then—a useful comparison with the overall form of the children's piece—the opening ideas return in a modified reprise: as always in Bartók, he never repeats anything exactly.

A revolution in school music

A leading article in *The Times Educational Supplement* for 8 January 1965 observed that 'The failure to draw out the creativity in each one of us is now spread as widely as the mass media spread the creativity of others'. It went on to urge that we 'provide the conditions for the fostering of all creative talent'; but even as those words appeared things were happening.

We've come a long way in the twenty-six years since that small group of children in Yorkshire composed *Birds Flying* and other pieces like it. The creative arts have been brought more and more into the educational debate as those responsible for curriculum planning have recognized that, whilst it is of course important to see that everyone has good basic communication skills, we must at the same time ensure that they realize how much they do indeed have to communicate.

In this respect music as a school subject has been totally transformed. In the 1960s and 1970s two major projects under the auspices of The Schools Council[22] looked at ways in which creativity could be encouraged; and in the 1980s the new examination at 16+—the GCSE—provided the essential formal framework within which to develop these ideas. Now, for the first time, we had an examination rooted in classroom work and for which candidates would have to submit original compositions. The impetus has carried forward to the implementation of a National Curriculum where music—fundamentally practical and including both performing and composing—figures as a foundation subject from the start of a child's schooling.

The education pendulum will continue to swing, producing the inevitable changes, orthodoxy becoming heresy and vice versa.[23] But we've had the revolution in music education, and the achievements of the past thirty years, together with the influences that triggered them, will not easily be forgotten. Even so, it has never been more necessary than it is now to keep such things in view. Increasingly human potential for thought and reflection is being destroyed; young minds dulled and desensitized by unremitting noise and ever more frequent images of violence. Opportunity for what Dewey would have called 'significant experience' may not counter entirely the battering of sensitivities we have to suffer in the modern world, but it could nevertheless be the very thing that pulls us through.

It was Schiller's view that the elements of a successful work of art are incapable of effecting anything: only through form are we *wholly affected*.[24] Form is wholeness; and we learn the truth of that by exercising our own inventiveness. Music with all its subtleties and possibilities for nuance is an especially apt medium because the sounds themselves are our only guide.

One thing that everybody knows about music is that it comes as 'pieces': forms which satisfy us precisely because each is 'all of a piece.' Whenever we make music there will be a moment when it is necessary to decide whether the piece is indeed complete: 'Is this now really what I *mean*?' The decision is a crucial one because at that point in the process we come full circle. Here, in a sense, we get our first glimpse of farthest Thule, and know with reasonable certainty that the music we have made is safely contained; it won't come apart, and our efforts are no longer in danger of collapsing. A satisfying and comforting moment. A full stop at the end of the world.

Notes

1. Thomas Weelkes, *Madrigals of 6 Parts* (London: 1600), ed. E. H. Fellowes, rev. T. Dart (London: Stainer & Bell, 1968), no. 7.
2. Quoted in Herbert Read, *Art and Society* (London: Faber and Faber, 1945), p. vi.
3. Quoted in C. A. Patrides (ed.), *Aspects of Time* (Manchester: Manchester University Press, 1976), p. 82.
4. Wilfrid Mellers, *Music and Society: England and the European Tradition* (London: Dennis Dobson, 1946), p. 10.
5. For example, Marion Richardson, in the preface to the catalogue of the Children's Art Exhibition at County Hall, London in 1938, wrote, 'The artist discovers in the world around … relationships, order, harmony. This cannot be done by the conscious scheming, *planning* mind. Art is not an effort of will but a gift of grace—the simplest and most natural thing in the world.'
6. Robert W. Witkin, *The Intelligence of Feeling* (London: Heinemann Educational Books, 1974).
7. David Holbrook, *Children's Writing: A Sampler for Student Teachers* (Cambridge: Cambridge University Press, 1967), p. 3.
8. Ibid., pp. 8–9.
9. My comments have, of course, no bearing upon or reference to the ideas expounded by Deryck Cooke in his distinguished and influential book *The Language of Music* (Oxford: Oxford University Press, 1959). His use of this idea is of an altogether different order. Rather I have in mind the woolly thinking of those who, ignoring the ways in which major cultural differences produce substantially different musics, glibly talk about music as 'a universal language'. Often the very same people confuse things further by using the term 'musical language' as a synonym for 'rules' of what is also widely and mistakenly described as 'music theory' (= certain conventions of western classical style distilled into bland and anonymous 'examples' that have little or no connection with musical reality). In fact there could not possibly be a single theory of all music; it would, though, be quite correct to talk about 'the theory of *a* music' (e.g. the theory of Javanese gamelan) or 'theories of musics'.

10. Susanne K. Langer, *Philosophy in a New Key: A Study of the Symbolism of Reason, Rite, and Art,* 3rd. edn. (Cambridge: Harvard University Press), p. 209.

11. Holbrook, *Children's Writing,* p. 115.

12. Ibid., p. vii and p. 2.

13. This piece is a group composition dating from 1966. Although the methodology of classroom composing has been considerably developed since then and many excellent and more recent examples of children's compositions are now available, I have chosen this one because it is more or less contemporaneous with the books by David Holbrook discussed here which had such a powerful early influence upon music education. I have written about this, and other pieces by the same children, elsewhere (John Paynter, 'The role of creativity in the school music curriculum,' in Michael Burnett [ed.], *Music Education Review Vol. 1* [London: Chappell & Co., 1976]), but have taken this opportunity to revisit it and to think my way afresh through its implications. That in itself has been an interesting and worthwhile experience.

14. Readers who are familiar with *The Exploring Word* and *Children's Writing* will no doubt be feeling that these examples of children's writing contradict all David Holbrook's principles of 'engagement with 'felt' meaning.' ('It is not mere *vocabulary* we wish to develop—but perception and the capacity to explore and organize experience, from inward sources, symbolically.') Clearly there is an uncomfortable 'sameness' of vocabulary (e.g. the birds 'manoeuvre'). But the work described took place a year before the appearance of *Children's Writing,* so that the teacher had not had the benefit of reading Holbrook's comments on 'Mr Rowe's approach' (pp. 17–21). I do not doubt that, had she read them, she would have acted upon them. For although there is not the scope here to explain in greater detail the background to *Birds Flying,* I feel I should say that, notwithstanding the apparent 'insincerity' of these pieces of writing by her pupils, this very experienced teacher, then quite close to retirement, was one of the most remarkable educators I have known. She really did encourage the children to generate and develop their own ideas, and to do so in several ways more or less simultaneously; that is to say, they talked, they made pictures, and they worked out their ideas in dance and drama and music.

15. The score printed here is a transcription from a tape-recording. It has to be remembered that the composing process was empirical, the music created through improvisations that were then worked upon until the structures were defined and could be remembered by the whole group. When it was completed the children made their own score on a large sheet of paper, a mixture of pictograms and staff notation surrounded by bird pictures (of the children's own making). Not everything that children invent musically can be notated in the standard 'staff' system, but even if they have to devise their own signs it is worthwhile; notation gives a sense of permanence to a piece of music.

16. The reference to 'xylophone' in the child's description of how they made the music is an error. They found it difficult to remember the difference between the two instruments!

17. Holbrook, *Children's Writing,* pp. x, 17, 36, 37, etc.

18. Martin Peerson (1571–1651), *The Fall of the Leafe.* This impressionistic piece appears in that great early seventeenth century collection of keyboard music, *The Fitzwilliam Virginal Book,* edited by J. A. Fuller Maitland and W. B. Squire, reprint of 1898 edition (New York: Dover Publications Inc., 1979).
19. Holbrook, *Children's Writing,* p. 15.
20. Ibid., p. 16.
21. Béla Bartók, *Mikrokosmos: 153 progressive pieces for piano* Vols. I–VI, 1926–39 (London: Boosey & Hawkes, 1940).
22. The Schools Council Curriculum Projects, *Arts and the Adolescent* (University of Exeter 1968–1972) and *Music in the Secondary School Curriculum* (University of York 1973–1982).
23. Cf. Charles Carter et al., *Swings for the Schools: an Essay on Demographic Waves in Education* (London: Policy Studies Institute, 1979).
24. J. C. Schiller, *On the Aesthetic Education of Man,* ed. and trans. E. M. Wilkinson and L. A. Willoughby (Oxford: Oxford University Press, 1967), p. 155.

Selected Publications
by John Paynter

Books

(with Peter Aston) *Sound and Silence*. Cambridge: Cambridge University Press, 1970
Hear and Now: an introduction to modern music in schools. London: Universal Edition, 1972
(with Elizabeth Paynter) *The Dance and the Drum*. London: Universal Edition, 1974
Music in the Secondary School Curriculum: trends and developments in class music teaching. Cambridge: Cambridge University Press, 1982
Sound and Structure. Cambridge: Cambridge University Press, 1992

Teaching materials

All Kinds of Music. Oxford: Oxford University Press, 1976/9
Sound Tracks. Cambridge: Cambridge University Press, 1978
Oss komponistar imellom: når barna gjer som Grieg. Oslo: Rikskonsertene, 1993
Invenzioni Musicale—seven projects ('rubriche'): 'Creare un inizio', 'Titoli', 'Non perdiamo tempo', 'Solo musica', 'Gesti', 'Una passeggiate con le note', 'Una fortunata di avvenimenti', in *Musica Domani* nos. 122–9. Turin Società Italiana per l'Educazione Musicale, 2002/3

Articles

'Music and imagination' (six articles), *Music Teacher*. London: Evans, 1972
'The relationship between music and the other arts in lifelong involvement', in Kraus, E. (ed.), *International Music Education*, ISME Yearbook III, Mainz, B. Schott's Söhne, 1975/6
'The role of creativity in the school music curriculum', in Burnett, M. (ed.), *Music Education Review: A Handbook for Music Teachers*, Vol. 1. London: Chappell, 1977
'Music education and the emotional needs of young people', in Bontinck, I. (ed.), *New patterns of musical behaviour of the young generation in industrial societies*. Vienna: Universal Edition, 1974
'Music for all', in Spence, K. and Swayne, G. (eds), *How music works*. London: Macmillan Co. Inc., 1981
'Wilfrid Mellers—the man and his music'. *Performance*, No. 4. London: Brevet Publishing Co., 1981

'En mer virkelighetsnaer musikkundervisning: noen refleksjoner om musikk I skole og samfun', in Stolpe, S. and Nesheim, E. (eds), *Musik og Skole: Festskrift for Landslaget Musikk I Skolen.* Oslo: H. Aschehoug & Co., 1981

'Tradition and change in music education', in Dobbs, J. (ed.), *International Music Education,* ISME Yearbook IX, Mainz, B. Schott's Sőhne, 1982

'Personalities in world music education, no. 13—R. Murray Schafer', *International Journal of Music Education,* No. 18. Reading, ISME, 1991

'Il talento musicale: Come scoprilo, Come svilupparlo', in 'Mozart, non solo Mozart'. *La Discussione,* supplemento 17, May 1991, Rome

'Music and people: the import of structure and form', in Paynter, J. *et al.* (eds), *Companion to Contemporary Musical Thought,* Vol. 1. London and New York: Routledge, 1992

'Aufführen und Komponieren von Musik in den allgemeinbildenden Schulen Groß britanniens', in Kaiser, H. J. (ed.), *Musikalische Erfahrung: Wahrnehmen, Erkennen, Aneignen.* Essen: Die Blaue Eule Verlag, 1992

'The composer as educator: things that matter', in Heister, H.-W., Heister-Grech, K., and Scheit, G. (eds), *Zwischen Aufklärung & Kulturindustrie/Festschrift für Georg Knepler zum 85 Geburtstag,* III. Hamburg: von Bockel Verlag, 1993

'Keeping music musical: a British perspective', in Comte, M. (ed.), *Music Education: International Viewpoints/A Symposium in Honour of Emeritus Professor Sir Frank Callaway.* Nedlands, Western Australia: Australian Society for Music Education, 1994

'Working on one's inner world', in Webb, E. (ed.), *Powers of Being: David Holbrook and His Work.* London and New Jersey: Associated University Presses, 1995

'Renewal and revelation: Wilfrid Mellers at York'. *Popular Music,* **13,** 2. Cambridge: Cambridge University Press, May 1994

'Progetto di ricerca sull' educazione musicale creative,' *beQuadro,* 55/56. Fiesole, Centro di Ricerca e di Sperimentazione per la Didattica Musicale, 1994

'The form of finality: a context for musical education', *British Journal of Music Education,* **14,** 1. Cambridge: Cambridge University Press, March 1997

'Making progress with composing', *British Journal of Music Education,* **17,** 1. Cambridge: Cambridge University Press, March 2000

'Music in the school curriculum: why bother?', *British Journal of Music Education,* **19,** 3. Cambridge: Cambridge University Press, November 2002

Index